More Praise for **THE NEW TOURIST**

"With infectious curiosity and clear-eyed prose, McClanahan provides everything you expect from the best of travel—fascinating scenery to gawk at, rich history to imbibe, and eccentric characters to meet. *The New Tourist* fulfills the true transformative promise of travel, giving us not just new ideas, but new ways of seeing ourselves."

—Benjamin Lorr, author of *The Secret Life of Groceries*

"In this lively and rewarding book, Paige McClanahan wrestles with the complexities of twenty-first century tourism, deftly exploring the joys and the real-world consequences of world travel. I highly recommend *The New Tourist*."

—Elizabeth Becker, author of *Overbooked:*
The Exploding Business of Travel and Tourism

"A remarkable read—neither travel guide nor social history but a thoughtful and deeply researched amalgam covering the symbiosis of traveler and destination and their effect on each other's souls."

—Catherine Watson, author of *Roads Less Traveled:*
Dispatches from the Ends of the Earth

"An essential reconsideration of the impacts of tourism in our increasingly connected times. McClanahan delivers her mind-expanding philosophy of the world's largest industry inside her own vivid travel stories and adventures. It's about time that someone wrote this book, but only McClanahan would have made it so damn entertaining."

—Thomas Kohnstamm, novelist and author of
Do Travel Writers Go to Hell?

"A thought-provoking, fascinating, and very readable book for anyone who travels, wants to travel more mindfully, works in the tourism industry, or is interested in countries and destinations around the world—so, pretty much everyone."

—Eliza Reid, first lady of Iceland,
former UN ambassador for tourism

"Travel has changed radically over a generation while its impact on the world has grown. If you want a fresh and nuanced take on what it all means, buy this book. McClanahan is an embodiment of the New Tourist herself—thoughtfully traveling the world with curiosity and an open heart. I'd follow her anywhere."

—Ethan Watters, author of *Crazy Like Us:
The Globalization of the American Psyche*

"Groundbreaking. *The New Tourist* will enable you to have much better travel experiences. McClanahan understands that what we make of tourism has to do with the ways we interact and behave when we holiday in other peoples' homes. The choices we make about how, when, and where we travel make a real difference in whether we have positive or negative impacts."

—Harold Goodwin, professor emeritus at
Manchester Metropolitan University and director
of the Responsible Tourism Partnership

THE NEW TOURIST

TOURIST

Waking Up to the Power and Perils of Travel

Paige McClanahan

SCRIBNER

New York London Toronto Sydney New Delhi

Scribner

An Imprint of Simon & Schuster, LLC

1230 Avenue of the Americas

New York, NY 10020

First Scribner hardcover edition June 2024

SCRIBNER and design are trademarks of Simon & Schuster, LLC

Simon & Schuster: Celebrating 100 Years of Publishing in 2024

For information about special discounts for bulk purchases,
please contact Simon & Schuster Special Sales at 1-866-506-1949
or business@simonandschuster.com.

The Simon & Schuster Speakers Bureau can bring authors to
your live event. For more information or to book an event,
contact the Simon & Schuster Speakers Bureau at 1-866-248-3049
or visit our website at www.simonspeakers.com.

Interior design by Kyle Kabel

Manufactured in the United States of America

1   3   5   7   9   10   8   6   4   2

Library of Congress Cataloging-in-Publication Data has been applied for.

ISBN 978-1-6680-1177-5
ISBN 978-1-6680-1179-9 (ebook)

For Oli, Alice, and Nora

Contents

Author's Note

I've had two passions for as long as I can remember: writing and exploring the world around me. I pursued both of these passions in an earnest if somewhat scattershot fashion until my mid-twenties, when they began to merge. It was then that, in various ways, I started to write about the people, places, and events that I encountered as I moved through the world. About five years ago, my focus sharpened, and I started reporting on the people who facilitate humanity's movement around the planet for pleasure, as well as the systems and infrastructure that have been built to accommodate them. Which is to say that I started to write about tourism.

Over the past five years, by my estimate, I've interviewed somewhere around two thousand people in the world of tourism. (If you're one of them, thank you again for your time and your trust.) As I spoke to these people and, in many cases, as I saw where they worked, lived, and traveled, I learned a lot about the world, and I learned a lot about myself. And I kept being surprised by tourism's profound power to transform the communities, environments, economies, cultures, as well as the individuals that it touches—in ways that are good, bad, and always complicated. The more I learned, the more I became fascinated by the nuances of tourism, and the more I realized that the stakes of this phenomenon are much, much bigger than I had imagined.

In creating this book, my first task, as I understood it, was to listen and learn—then to think, write, and, finally, give the whole thing right back to the world. So here you have it: my own personal examination of the perils and power of tourism, an activity in which so many of us are lucky enough to participate, but which so rarely gets the attention or scrutiny it deserves. The book combines recorded interviews with my own fallible recollections. It is neither unbiased nor comprehensive. That said, I want to state up front that I accepted no freebies or discounts in reporting this book; I owe no favors to anyone represented in the pages that follow.

The individuals and scenes that I have chosen to convey represent a fraction of the myriad experiences I had in reporting this book. Those experiences are, in turn, microscopic slices of the whole truth of what's happening in the places I visited, to the extent that a "whole truth" even exists. You may disagree with some of the views or voices that you encounter here, or otherwise feel challenged by them. They certainly challenged me. But all the individuals who appear in this book have a perspective or a story that I felt needed telling. I've done my best to honor the trust of my interviewees, and to honor the places I visited, which we so often think of as "destinations," but which are always, and in the first place, someone's home.

So, whether you find yourself nodding in agreement, scratching your head, or grimacing in disgust, I urge you to keep reading. Because tourism is important, at a societal level as well as a deeply personal one. And this is a conversation we need to have.

Introduction

About nine hundred years ago, a group of monks built a stone abbey along the banks of a cold, clear river in a steep-sided valley high in the Alps. The religious men took up residence among the locals—people who spent their days tending cows and sheep, churning butter, weeding onions and turnips, scouring the forests for mushrooms, and chiseling sculptures from the local limestone. Centuries passed, and the abbey went through the typical cycles of decline and renewal, fire and renovation, until 1792, when an invading army (the French) claimed the monks' worldly possessions as their own—and kicked them out. Stripped of its holy residents, the abbey took on a new life as the headquarters of a company that mined the local iron ore, which was destined for the infrastructure of a rapidly industrializing Europe. Later, as wealthy Europeans began to seek out the restorative powers of alpine air, the abbey went through another reinvention: it became a hotel.

In the summer of 2018, my family and I moved to a house that sits a few miles from that abbey, whose tidy lawn now hosts a popular outdoor concert series every summer. The abbey's hotel closed in the nineties—a casualty of the rise in the popularity of chalet rentals over hotel rooms—but tourism in the valley is going strong. So much so that the people who live along the banks of the valley's cold, clear river now spend their days driving tourists to and from the airport; serving them espressos and blueberry tarts; cleaning their bathrooms and changing their sheets; and leading them along hiking trails, up rock-climbing routes, and down wide slopes of fresh, untracked snow. For the past fifty years, tourism has been the cornerstone of the local economy. It's also the main reason why the local village hasn't gone the way of so many villages across Western Europe since the end of the Second World War—and disappeared entirely.

My boyfriend and I first visited the valley as tourists, back in 2007. We were weekenders coming up with friends from Geneva, where we lived and worked. We fell in love with that cold, clear river and the high, jagged peaks, spliced with waterfalls, that soared above it. We returned to the valley eleven years later—now married and with two small children and having lived in three other countries in Africa and Europe. We moved into our house, applied for our residence permits and driver's licenses, and enrolled our children in the local school. We had spent most of our lives as visitors to tourist destinations. Now we were residents.

As we settled into life in the valley, we learned to adapt to the comings and goings of the tourists, a seasonal migration as predictable as the public holidays and school vacation schedules that dictate their movements. I came to love how tourists brought energy and life—as well as jobs and income—into our beautiful, sleepy corner of the world. I happily shared the local hiking trails and ski slopes with tourists, and enjoyed eating at our many local restaurants, most of which wouldn't survive without tourists' patronage.

But it wasn't all fun and games, as I discovered the first time I showed up at the local supermarket on a Saturday afternoon in August. Or the time my children were late for school because our usual parking lot was overflowing at 8:00 a.m. on a weekday. Or the times when I sat in bumper-to-bumper traffic on our rural, two-lane road—which leads both to our house and to a nature reserve that attracts a few hundred thousand visitors every year. Within weeks of moving to the valley, I began to appreciate—for the first time in my life—the depth, nuance, and significance of a phenomenon in which I had always, and usually unwittingly, played a part.

*　　*　　*

Tourism shapes our world—by which I mean it alters our economies and cultures, as well as our physical environments—in profound and surprising ways. The numbers are astonishing: in 2019, travel and tourism generated more than 10 percent of global economic output, which makes it more than double the size of the global agriculture industry. It also accounted for about one in ten jobs around the world, and one in *five* jobs created in the previous five years. In 2019, international visitors spent $1.9 trillion while traveling, which was well over double U.S. federal defense spending the same year.[1] And the numbers are only getting bigger: the global economic value of travel and tourism is expected to rise by an average of 5.8 percent per year until 2032, compared to a 2.7 percent predicted growth rate for the global economy overall.[2]

But the impacts of tourism go far beyond jobs and GDP. In many places, tourism is a significant source of funding for wildlife conservation;[3] tourism also generates about 8 percent of our greenhouse gas emissions.[4] And with roughly a billion international tourist arrivals every year,[5] tourism has become humanity's most important means of conversation across cultures. You don't even have to cross a border to feel the impact. If you've ever seen a hula girl on the dashboard of a taxi and thought of Hawai'i, you've felt tourism's influence. The same is probably true if an image of a flamenco dancer makes you think of Spain, or if you can name the capital of Iceland without consulting your phone.

Tourism shapes national narratives, creates national symbols, and frames our perceptions of other societies. It also intensifies the commodification of our cultures, even as it sometimes helps to sustain them. Tourism provides a powerful economic incentive to protect the world's natural wonders; it can also threaten their very existence. Tourism transforms villages like our own into vibrant places that are, for the most part, agreeable and welcoming to visitors and residents alike. But tourism can also destroy places' souls, hollowing out city centers and leaving empty urban shells whose most striking feature is sheer commercialism.

Governments, particularly local governments, have an enormous influence over whether the net impact of tourism in a place is positive or negative, though many governments have only recently woken up to this fact. Tourism businesses also affect the vitality of the places that underwrite their profits, and these profit-seeking ventures vary widely in terms of their self-awareness and willingness to ensure that their operations do more good than harm. But tourists play a role, too. Those of us who are privileged enough to fall into this category wield significant power, individually and collectively, in determining tourism's impact—both on the places we visit, and on ourselves.

*   *   *

Before we go any further, I should take a moment to define my terms here. Because while dictionary definitions of "tourism" tend to focus on the business side of accommodating people when they go on vacation, I have a broader understanding of the word. The UN World Tourism Organization tells us that tourism is "a social, cultural, and economic phenomenon which entails the movement of people to countries or places outside their usual environment for personal or business/professional purposes."[6] My understanding of tourism aligns with that one, although I would add a temporal component: tourist movements are for finite periods; we're not talking about immigration here.

A lot of people are uncomfortable with the word "tourist," at least when it's aimed in their direction. I'm hoping this book will help shake loose some of that stigma, because I don't think it's helpful. It irks me that some people insist on a distinction between "travelers" and "tourists," where the former are explorer types who are unsatisfied with anything short of an "authentic" experience, while the latter are philistines who are content with clichéd, mass-market experiences. In practice, I find that the biggest difference between the terms is that we use "traveler" when referring to ourselves and people close to us, while "tourist" is reserved for everyone else. I don't deny that people travel for a huge range of reasons, some higher-minded than others. So sure, call yourself a traveler, but never forget that you're a tourist, too. Our redemption as tourists lies not in wallowing in a sense of superiority over the people standing in line ahead of us as we wait to get into the Louvre. It lies in elevating our understanding of what tourists are, and the important role that they—that we—play in the world.

So how do we do that? Where do we begin? I find it helpful to imagine two tourist archetypes that lie at either end of a spectrum. On one side, we have *the new tourist*, who is a tourist in her most evolved state, her highest manifestation. This is in contrast to what we find at the other end of the spectrum—*the old tourist*, who represents an approach to tourism that we would all do well to leave behind. We might like to think of an old tourist as a loud-talking, gum-smacking, sneakers-wearing American who seeks out Starbucks abroad like a heat-seeking missile. But I have a somewhat more nuanced definition. The old tourist, in my view, is a pure consumer who sees the people and places he encounters when he travels as nothing more than a means to some self-serving end: an item crossed off a bucket list, a fun shot for his Instagram grid, one more thing to brag about to his peers. The old tourist confines his destination and its inhabitants to a preconceived story, which makes it impossible for him to consider the people or places he visits in any depth or with any real empathy. He projects his fantasies onto his destination of choice, and he reacts with disappointment or even outrage when the reality fails to match his notion of the ideal.

But I believe there's such a thing as a new tourist, too, which is the whole reason I wrote this book—and chose the title I did. In my view, it's entirely possible that the new tourist is an American who talks loudly, chews gum, wears sneakers, and sometimes likes to get a coffee at Starbucks when she's overseas. Those kinds of details don't matter much in the end. Here's what *does*: Even if, like all of us, she sometimes takes comfort in the familiar, the new tourist is humbled by her travels, which open her eyes to her smallness in the great stretch of history and the vast sea of humanity. The new tourist embraces the chance to encounter people whose backgrounds are very different from her own, and to learn from cultures or religions that she might otherwise fear or regard with contempt. The new tourist returns from her travels with a degree of skepticism for her native land that may not have occurred to her had she never left home. Because of her travels, the new tourist is inoculated against anyone who might try to convince her to hate or look down on people who look different from her, who speak a language other than her own, who pray to a different god, or who happen to live on the other side of a border. Because of her travels, the new tourist is a more open and generous human being.

All of us who travel fall somewhere between the old and new tourist archetypes, and we probably find ourselves sliding along the spectrum at different points in our travels. Rest assured, I'm somewhere in the middle with you. But if we understand what the new tourist looks like, we can at least aspire to reach her heights. I've been trying to find my way to the land of the new tourist for a while now. This book, as I see it, is my best and biggest effort to finally get there myself.

*   *   *

Travel presents us with a dizzying array of choices: where to go, when to go, how to go, what to do while we're there. Many books have been written about how to travel "sustainably," "responsibly," or "mindfully." I see this book as a sort of prequel to those. My goal here isn't to give you a list of dos and don'ts for your next vacation, because there's no way that I could provide an answer for every situation you might encounter. Only you can make those choices— in the moment, and within whatever constraints you happen to find yourself. Instead of prescribing, my aim here is twofold: to provide you with a framework that will help you come up with your own questions, and to inspire you to ask those questions—of yourself, of the companies you patronize, of your governments, and of the symbols and narratives that you encounter when you travel. Because that is the way of the new tourist.

My goal here is to tell the whole truth, messy as it may be, and to show how we tourists help to shape the phenomenon of tourism itself. Each chapter explores a complex question about tourism and its players, its impacts, its levers of power, and its stakes. How did a handful of young baby boomers transform the way millions of Westerners view the world? Is social media changing the way we see ourselves in relation to other cultures and landscapes? How does tourism influence a nation's image—and influence—on the world stage? When does tourism destroy the soul of a city, and when does it offer a place a new lease on life? Is "last-chance tourism" prompting a powerful change in perspective, or obliterating places we cherish? Is it possible to strike a balance between tourist fantasies of a place and the realities of everyday local life? Given all the negative headlines about tourists these days, would it be better for all of us just to stay at home?

To wake up to the consequences of our travels might sound like a lot of work, but doing so can bring deep and lasting rewards—for us as individuals, as well as for our societies. Some people are happy to roam the world as old tourists, pure consumers who remain willfully blind to the impacts of their wanderings. But I know that many of you are ready to join me in striving for a new, and better, way of doing things. I hope this book helps us get there together. Because to be a tourist is a privilege and, for many of us, it's one of life's great pleasures. With the right approach, which begins with a deep understanding of what's at stake, tourism can also be a powerful force for good.

THE NEW TOURIST

Chapter One

A Groove on the Map

O n July 4, 1972, a pair of young newlyweds named Tony and
Maureen backed out of the driveway of a family home in
the south of England. They were driving a used blue minivan that
they had bought for the princely sum of £65, and their goal was to
get to India. Or somewhere. They had a trunk full of food, cooking equipment, some spare parts for the car, a stack of traveler's
checks, some sleeping bags, and an old tent. As he eased the car
out of his parents' driveway, Tony called out to his mum and dad
that they'd be back in a year. Fate had other plans.[1]

So begins the story of Lonely Planet, the most powerful travel
brand of the twentieth century—a company that would influence
the movements and experiences of tens of millions of travelers,
while also shaping the fate of countless businesses and, in some
cases, entire communities. But the five-and-a-half-month overland
journey that led to the company's founding was hardly unprecedented. In many ways, those newlyweds—Tony and Maureen
Wheeler—were typical young baby boomers: they were eager to

see the world, and they wanted to do so in a way that had been both unthinkable and, in many cases, physically impossible for their parents. As they set off on their trip, Tony and Maureen were following in the footsteps of thousands of young travelers who'd already blazed the "Hippie Trail" across Asia. But these young newlyweds were also exceptional, which is why we're still talking about them today: Tony and Maureen's trip to India and beyond went on to inspire a business that would tap into the restless power of their generation, serving the millions of young Westerners who shared their drive to escape the confines of the comfortable postwar societies in which they'd been raised. The couple's business, which they would found in Australia at the other end of that now-fabled 1972 journey across Asia, would fundamentally change the way tourists experience the world. And it would change the world, too.

But back in the summer of 1972, the Wheelers were just a couple of kids. Maureen, who was born in Belfast in 1950, had quit her job as an office assistant in London a few weeks earlier. Tony, age twenty-five and fresh out of business school, had just been offered a job at Ford Motor Company's office in Essex; he declined, but asked if they would hold the position for him while he traveled for a year, and they agreed. And so they set off, fully believing that their jaunt across Asia would be nothing more than a little adventure before they settled down to a steady, middle-class life in England.

The Wheelers could have chosen to travel with one of the several Hippie Trail tour operators that were selling seats on buses that would make the whole trip across Asia in two or three months. But tagging along with a group wasn't their style. Also, they couldn't afford it. So they figured it out themselves, and it turned out to be just the kind of adventure these two young people craved: they got caught in a snowstorm in the Italian Alps; slept on the beach on the Greek island of Lesbos; bumped into the shah's motorcade in Iran; then sold their car and hung out with the hippies in Kabul. ("If you can remember it clearly then clearly you weren't there," Tony recalls of Afghanistan in the early seventies.)[2] From there, it was a bus to Pakistan, then on to India, Nepal, back to India, then a short flight to Bangkok because it was impossible to cross Burma by land. The couple hitchhiked south across Thailand and on through Malaysia and Singapore, where the immigration officer suggested that Tony cut his hair if he planned to stay for more than twenty-four hours. A fifty-pound loan from Tony's parents was enough to get them on a ship to Jakarta and then a bus to Bali, where they set out on the final leg of the trip: a one-week stint as crew on a yacht bound for the white sand coast of Western Australia. But the winds died, the engine broke, and one of their water tanks sprung a leak. By day eight on the yacht, they were eating the last of their food stores and severely rationing their water.

But they made it. A fellow crew member snapped a photo of the grinning couple on an empty Australian beach, thirty seconds after they'd set foot on land, their meager belongings scattered on the sand below them. They'd run out of gas multiple times in Europe; had their belongings stolen in Italy; been briefly held at gunpoint while camping on the coast of the Black Sea; and gotten the shits in just about every country since Afghanistan. (Already slim when they started out, Tony and Maureen each lost more than ten pounds in the five and a half months it took them to get from England to Australia.) They'd covered over ten thousand miles, and by the time they made it to Sydney they had precisely twenty-seven cents left to sustain them.

*   *   *

What did the young Wheelers have to guide them in all of this? The bookshops they could have visited back in England in 1972 would have had precious little to offer in the way of practical advice for their route. Travel guidebooks had been popular in Europe for well over a century, but those that existed in the early seventies didn't cater to the likes of Tony and Maureen. Series like the Blue Guides and Baedeker Guides that were so beloved by the Victorians were still going strong, but these would have been of little interest to them. For one thing, the guides were mostly devoid of information on things like cafés and restaurants, let alone nightlife; any aspect of a nation's culture that was more recent than about the eighteenth century was usually considered unworthy of description.

There were some books to consult that had a more up-to-date feel, but the range of the places they covered was still limited, and the audience they served was very different from the restless young baby boomer crowd. Arthur Frommer and Eugene Fodor were both producing popular travel guides at that point, and their books marked the beginning of an important shift in the genre. Frommer, born in Missouri in 1929, started publishing travel tips for his fellow GIs when he was serving in the military in Europe in the 1950s. He published *Europe on $5 a Day* for civilians after he got home, proving to his increasingly affluent American audience that they could indeed afford to travel on the Continent. Eugene Fodor, born in what's now Slovakia in 1905, was already a few steps ahead of him, having published his first guidebook in 1936, a 1,200-page guide to Europe that he researched and wrote entirely by himself. Two years later, the updated edition hit the *New York Times* bestseller list.*

Fodor and Frommer were groundbreaking in that they were among the first to respond to the practical needs of travelers, and to treat travel as an exploration rather than a dull but character-building accumulation of historic sites and masterpieces. They both offered practical tips on how to get around, as well as information on modern society and culture. And Frommer in particular proved that seeing the sights of Europe was very much within the budget of most middle-class Americans. Unlike their Victorian precedents, these new midcentury guides also pushed readers to look for human connections when they traveled. In fact, Fodor's motivation for his first book came in part from the lack of a "human element" in the guidebooks he could find in the thirties. And so he encouraged his readers to go beyond the sights of a place, and spend time with people "whose customs, habits and general outlook are different from your own."[3]

---

* Fodor paused his work to join the U.S. military during World War II, but he picked up where he left off in 1949, producing his first dedicated country guide to Greece. More would soon follow. But the expansion of Fodor's guides—which by the mid-1970s had sold close to 10 million copies—wasn't purely in response to market forces. In 1974, the *New York Times* revealed classified testimony from disgraced former CIA director E. Howard Hunt in which he described how the CIA had "funded, to a large extent, the activities of Fodor's Travel Guide." Hunt also testified that Eugene Fodor had been on the CIA payroll, and that CIA support for the company had continued for twelve to fifteen years. Fodor couldn't be reached for comment at the time, but he later admitted to providing cover for CIA agents working in Europe. "I told them to make sure to send me real writers, not civil engineers," Fodor told a journalist six months after the Hunt testimony was published. "I wanted to get some writing out of them, and I did too." (Seymour Hersch, "Hunt Tells of Early Work for a C.I.A. Domestic Unit," *New York Times*, December 31, 1974; 4 Roy Bongartz, "Where Tourists Go, Fodor's Been," *New York Times*, June 15, 1975.)

This was all very much in line with Tony and Maureen's way of thinking. But these savvy young boomers didn't necessarily need help navigating their way around Europe, where Frommer and Fodor continued to focus (although Fodor, with the help of the CIA, would branch out significantly in the 1970s). Nor were they interested in the moderate to upscale hotels that the Fodor's guides would list, or the major cities of Europe, which were the bread and butter of the Frommer's guide. That wasn't what the young Wheelers were about. They wanted to know where they could pitch their tent in Tehran, how to ask for marijuana in Kabul, and when the monsoon season would hit Malaysia. To find that kind of information, they were going to have to be a little more creative.

Only one helpful source would have been reliably available to Tony and Maureen in London at the time, and that was *Overland to India and Australia*. Published by BIT, an alternative information and exchange service based in London, BIT guides were a sort of hard-copy, baby boomer version of Craigslist. Much of the Asia overland guide was crowdsourced, and misinformation was rife—"You know some people were eight miles high when they wrote this stuff,"[4] Tony later recalled—but it was the single best resource they had. The edition that was published in April 1972, a few months before the Wheelers set off, could be obtained for a "minimum donation" of fifty pence and consisted of a grand total of twenty stapled pages. Still, it was better than nothing.

Had the Wheelers wanted to make a similar trip from, say, London to South Africa, they would have been equally hard-pressed to find detailed information on how to navigate their route. BIT also published a guide to overlanding in Africa, but it was a mere scattershot collection of travelers' stories, nothing like a comprehensive guide to the continent. And what if the Wheelers had wanted to chart their adventure along the "gringo trail" that was beginning to emerge between Mexico and the southern tip of Patagonia? The sole reliable resource they could have found in Britain would have been *The South American Handbook*, whose England-based editors updated the guide using information sent in from travelers. In 1972, with precious few exceptions, dedicated and well-researched English-language travel guides to individual countries in Africa, South America, and Asia simply didn't exist— for travelers of any budget.

But that's not to say that Tony and Maureen had *nothing* to guide them. As they would discover soon after setting off, their single best source of information was the other Western boomers whom they'd encounter on the road, often at hippie magnets like the Pudding Shop in Istanbul, Chicken Street in Kabul, or Freak Street in Kathmandu. Whenever they'd bump into fellow travelers, Tony and Maureen would pump them for information—and share information in return. Before long, they'd accumulated quite a bit of advice to share. On each day of the trip, Tony, always an assiduous notetaker, would jot down things like how far they'd traveled, how much they'd paid for their meals, what the roads were like, how they'd obtained their visas, as well as things he picked up about the local culture, religion, and history. These notes would later prove to be a very valuable resource indeed.

* * *

While the Wheelers were driving and thumbing their way across Asia, the world around them was opening up. The same year they set off on their adventure, U.S. president Richard Nixon made his famous eight-day visit to China, ending twenty-five years of frozen relations between the powers that would dominate geopolitics over the next half century. Six years after that widely televised trip—which Nixon called "the week that changed the world"—China would open its borders to international tourists for the first time since 1949. Closer to home for Tony and Maureen, the Iron Curtain remained drawn across Europe, but tourism was making that barrier increasingly porous. By the mid-1960s, more than a million Westerners were vacationing in the USSR every year, and tourist industry connections were deepening across the Cold War divide.[5]

But international travel remained highly exclusive: in the United States, the percentage of people who carried a passport would remain in the single digits well into the 1990s,[6] and for all but the most adventurous tourists, travel agents remained indispensable—and often expensive—gatekeepers to traveling overseas. Jet travel, which had begun to spread in the 1960s, remained unaffordable for many in the early seventies. But among a certain stratum of restless and relatively affluent young baby boomers, international travel was growing very quickly indeed.

In the United States, the Peace Corps—which John F. Kennedy launched in 1961 to allow Americans the opportunity to contribute to "the great common cause of world development"[7]—was sending thousands of young boomers to other countries every year. The arrival of the Beatles in India in 1968 riveted a generation, spotlighting a part of the world that had long been unknown to many in the West and generating ever more interest in the Hippie Trail, which had been attracting a trickle of travelers since the mid-fifties. Paul Theroux's travelogue *The Great Railway Bazaar*, which describes his travels along the Hippie Trail to India and beyond, became an international bestseller after it was published in 1975, adding ever more fuel to the fire.[8] By the time the Iranian Revolution and the Soviet invasion of Afghanistan brought the Hippie Trail to an abrupt end in 1979, tens of thousands of young travelers had made the trek.

But even with the closure of the Hippie Trail, by the dawn of the 1980s it was clear that, for a growing number of people, the world was shrinking very quickly indeed. In her travel memoir published in 1978, the journalist and author Martha Gellhorn observed that "perhaps the greatest social change since the Second World War is the way citizens of the free nations travel as never before in history." Gellhorn described the new class of global wanderers as both "a vast floating population and an industry" that was "essential to many national economies." ("Not that we are therefore treated with loving gratitude," she went on, "more as if we were gold-bearing locusts.")[9] In 1960, when Tony and Maureen were still schoolchildren, 69 million tourists crossed an international border. By the time the Hippie Trail closed in 1979, the figure had more than quadrupled, to 283 million. And many of those budding global travelers needed help finding their way.

*   *   *

"The Asian overland trip has become so popular in the past five years that there's almost a groove worn in the face of the map."[10]

So begins *Across Asia on the Cheap*, the slim, hand-stapled book that the Wheelers published within a year of arriving in Australia.

They hadn't set out to write a guidebook, but soon after they made it to Sydney, they found there was a huge interest in the notes and anecdotes they'd gathered along their route. Others wanted to follow in their footsteps. Demand was so great that the young Wheelers, who were still trying to earn money to buy their flights home to England, started to wonder if they could find a way to charge people for the information they were sharing. One day, Tony suggested they write a guidebook. "But how would we find a publisher?" Maureen asked. "We don't need a publisher," Tony replied. "We can publish it ourselves."[11]

And so they did. They wrote out the pages by hand in the evenings, after coming home from the office jobs they'd landed in Sydney. They wrote up their notes on how to score a fake student ID for discounts on flights and train tickets; which maps might get people in trouble at the Pakistani border; how "chicks" could "pick up easy money" working for the "quite respectable" escort services in Singapore; what they really thought of travel agents ("never fully believe them"); and how easy it was to obtain "dope" along the route ("If that's what you want then you are going to the right places!"). They included information on local history, culture, religion, and climate. They also offered some details on organized overland tours that travelers could join, but they urged people to embrace the adventure and go it alone: "If you don't mind roughing it a little you can join the thousands of people who really have dropped out of the nine to five rat race," Tony wrote.

Maureen typed up the handwritten pages on a typewriter she borrowed from her office, while Tony drew the maps and illustrations by hand. They found a small counterculture printer, Tomato Press, that typeset the book, and a friend of a friend with a printing press in his basement churned out the pages. They stapled together the sixteen-page "signatures" they received from the printer, then sheared the books' edges straight with a borrowed guillotine. The book was emblazoned with the name and logo of their fledgling publishing house, which appeared in a string of bubbly lowercase letters, backed by a thin circle, that Tony had sketched himself: lonely planet.

The Wheelers' first guide (which carried only Tony's name on the cover) was just under a hundred pages and sold for $1.80, in Australian dollars. Their first print run of 1,500 copies sold out within ten days of their first review in the Sydney *Sun-Herald*. They printed 3,500 more, and Tony took a suitcase of books to Melbourne to sell copies to booksellers there. Soon they ordered a second print run of 3,500, and they decided to delay their planned return to London.

They thought they might go traveling again, this time around Southeast Asia, where the Vietnam War was finally starting to die down. Most people in the West still thought of Southeast Asia as a war zone, but Tony and Maureen had seen for themselves that countries like Thailand, Malaysia, Indonesia, and Singapore held huge potential for tourism. Tony would later remember the region as "almost a terra incognita" in the early seventies.[12] They decided they'd try to write another guide.

Tony and Maureen had no way of knowing it at the time, but they were at the forefront of a small group of restless young adults who would collectively help to open up whole swathes of the planet to adventure-seeking, budget-minded Western travelers who wanted to avoid the traditional tourist infrastructure. The same year the Wheelers published *Across Asia on the Cheap*, a young man named Bill Dalton turned up at a festival in New South Wales with eight hundred mimeographed copies of the notes he'd taken while traveling in Indonesia, which he sold for fifty cents a pop. When he made $150 on his first day, he figured he was onto something good. And so Dalton launched a fledgling publishing house, which he dubbed Moon Publications.[13]

Also in 1973, a different pair of adventurous newlyweds set off to explore a continent. But in this case, it was South America. Like the Wheelers in Asia, Hilary Bradt, a Brit, and her American husband, George, had very little to guide them as they made their way on foot through the Andes—and they soon found themselves looking for a means of sharing the notes they'd collected along the way. In 1974, the Bradts published *Backpacking Along Ancient Ways in Peru and Bolivia*, which included the very first English-language descriptions of the Inca Trail. Bradt Guides to Mexico, Venezuela, Colombia, and Ecuador would soon follow—each one the first of its kind. Like the Wheelers' early publications, the Bradts' first books weren't especially eye-catching: the text was typed on a typewriter, the maps were hand-drawn, and there weren't any pretty pictures. But it didn't matter to the Bradts—or to their readers: the books contained information that would enable other travelers to follow in their footsteps.[14]

The travel scene was changing in Europe as well. As the eighties dawned, a recent university graduate named Mark Ellingham—another British baby boomer, though he was at the younger end of his generation—set out to write a new kind of travel guide to a centuries-old destination for British tourists: Greece. The Frommer's and Fodor's guides were too formal for Ellingham, who was born in 1959; they stuck to the high art and architecture, while skimping on the soccer, food, and festivals that interested him and his friends. Ellingham wanted a journalistic guide to Greece as a living country—the kind of guide that would introduce people to the country's beaches, bars, and modern politics, as well as its historic sites. He found a publisher in Britain who agreed to publish the book, but they wanted him to produce half a dozen guides, which they could sell as a series. They would call it the Rough Guides.

So Ellingham set off to Greece in 1981, and hired friends to help him with the other countries. It was an exciting time to be in the business. Because many of these places had little to no tourism—let alone guidebooks—Ellingham felt like he was doing frontline journalism, opening corners of the world that otherwise would have remained off the radar of most of his peers. Within five years, he and the friends he'd hired had produced about a dozen guides, to places like Spain, Portugal, Poland, Morocco, Tunisia, and Kenya. And people were eating it up: Ellingham was soon receiving hundreds of letters a week as readers wrote in with their suggestions and updates for the books. Sales were soon going so well that Ellingham was able to buy himself out from the publisher, and the Rough Guides came to be produced independently.[15]

Many young Americans were hungry for this kind of travel, too. In 1959, some enterprising Harvard undergrads led by Oliver Koppell, Class of '62 (and future New York attorney general), started sharing their notes on how to travel cheaply around Europe.[16] What started as a mimeographed pamphlet soon turned into a full-fledged guide to the Continent, which a fresh pack of wandering Harvard students would update every summer. In the 1980s, Let's Go began producing country guides to Britain,

France, and Italy; by 2005, the brand was publishing fifty titles, covering destinations on six continents.[17]

Beginning in the late seventies, on the other side of the country, a young man named Rick Steves started giving lectures about how to travel cheaply and efficiently across Europe, which he'd been doing since he was a teenager. His talks attracted so many people that Steves eventually typed up his lecture notes and turned them into a book: *Europe Through the Back Door*, his guide to traveling on the cheap and outside the mainstream tourism infrastructure. Like Arthur Frommer before him, Steves was helping to democratize an activity that many considered elitist. But Steves was writing for the new generation—for *his* generation: people who liked to get off the beaten track, and who weren't afraid to travel with a backpack.[18]

Between 1960 and 1990, the world went from a dearth of travel guides to an explosion of them—particularly from the perspective of relatively affluent young Anglophone Westerners who wanted to travel on the cheap, or to any destination off the well-worn tourist trails of Europe. The guidebook boom was both a response to the burgeoning demand for international, affordable travel and a catalyst for its further growth. As baby boomers went from schoolchildren to the edge of middle age, international tourist arrivals rose from 69 million to 435 million; the word "backpacker" went from niche to mainstream; and the development and spread of the Boeing 747 and other wide-body aircraft meant that the skies were fuller than ever of people traveling immense distances in mere hours. (With the 1978 deregulation of the airlines in the United States, the companies became free to set their own fares and routes: the newly competitive market drove prices down, making flying accessible to many who couldn't have afforded it before.)[19] International travel was still the domain of the very privileged, but the years between 1960 and 1990 saw the beginning of a true democratization of travel, a trend that would accelerate as the millennium drew to a close. And all those newly minted world travelers now had their choice of guidebooks to show them the way.

*　　*　　*

Tony and Maureen never made it back to England in the end, though they did move from Sydney to Melbourne, where they'd remain for more than thirty years. Their second guidebook, *South-East Asia on a Shoestring*, had sold well, just like their first. (Tony had chosen a different layout for the book. He liked the handy size and two-column format of *Reader's Digest* and thought it would work well for a travel guidebook, too. The format would remain pretty much unchanged for nearly fifty years.) The couple followed up the Southeast Asia book with a guide to trekking in the Himalayas, quickly followed by a travel guide to Nepal, a country that had been largely closed to foreign tourists until the 1950s. By 1977, Tony and Maureen were publishing (and doing their best to update) eight different guidebooks, and they were struggling mightily to manage all the work. Expenses were high and their cash flow was tight. For a couple of years, they weren't sure if they could hold things together.

The company's breakthrough came in 1981, when they published their first guide to India, a book that, according to Tony, "immediately kicked Lonely Planet into a higher and more stable orbit." Other guides to the country had been written, but Tony felt they weren't aimed at the new breed of travelers—the same people who were eating up Lonely Planet's other titles. He and Maureen spent five months trekking around central India; they hired two experienced friends—the British travel writer Geoff Crowther and the author Prakash Raj, based in Nepal—to cover the north and south. Tony's hunch was right. *India: A Travel Survival Kit* "lit up their sales charts" when it appeared, and within weeks they ordered the first of many reprints. The book's commercial success kick-started a period of rapid growth for the company, whose catalog would quadruple by the mid-eighties.

Around the time the Wheelers were preparing the India guide, a letter arrived out of the blue from a young American named Joe Cummings. Cummings had been a Peace Corps volunteer in Thailand, and he would soon head back to the country to do fieldwork for his master's thesis. Cummings had come across a few Lonely Planet guides when he was traveling, and he had an idea to write a dedicated country guide to Thailand while he was back. Tony had seen the potential for tourism in Thailand, and he thought a country guide was a great idea.[20]

Thailand in the early 1980s was just on the brink of its fame as a travel destination. International tourism in the country had been humming along at a fairly low level since 1947, when Pan Am added a stop in Bangkok to its first round-the-world flight (which also stopped in Delhi, Beirut, Istanbul, Frankfurt, and London as it made its way to New York). In the 1960s, the Vietnam War brought an influx of tens of thousands of American GIs, who were either assigned to bases in Thailand or who'd visit the country on their R&R—propping up the country's hotels and restaurants and feeding its sex tourism industry.

When Cummings first arrived in Thailand in 1977, very little in the way of travel information had been written for Western visitors, apart from the Thailand chapter of Tony and Maureen's guide to the region, which Cummings used himself. At the time, the only English-language guide devoted to Thailand—the *Guide to Bangkok with Notes on Siam*, published by the Royal State Railways of Siam—was already half a century old. So Cummings relied mainly on word of mouth on the rare and exciting occasions in which he'd bump into other Western travelers. "You'd run up to them, exchange information as much as you could—where they were coming from, where you were coming from," Cummings told me in a 2022 Zoom interview from Thailand, which he still calls home.

"You'd socialize with them, too. You'd be practically hugging them, you know, 'Let's have a drink! Let's have a drink!'" But that feeling wouldn't last. Before long, whenever Cummings would come across other Westerners in Thailand, he'd turn and walk the other way.

The guidebook that Cummings would write for Lonely Planet, as well as the many subsequent editions that he would prepare, would, even if inadvertently, play a part in feeding the Western tourism boom in Thailand, but exactly how big of a part is difficult to say. Tourism's potential in the country was already apparent when the first edition of Lonely Planet's Thailand guide appeared in 1982, which was the same year that tourism surpassed rice exports as the country's biggest foreign currency earner. At that point, the growth in visitors to the country was largely thanks to Thai government efforts to market the country to potential tourists, a job that was the express responsibility of the Tourism

Authority of Thailand, or TAT, established in 1960. It was a big operation. TAT opened its first overseas office in New York in 1965; within two decades, it would have a staff of five hundred, with eleven offices abroad and six in Thailand, all working hard to drum up interest in the country.

Other forces were at work, too. In 1979, Thailand's flagship carrier, Thai Airways, acquired its first fleet of jumbo jets; nonstop flights from Bangkok to cities like Los Angeles, Seattle, Stockholm, Madrid, and Auckland would soon follow. At the same time, popular media was helping to awaken Westerners to the country's many attractions. The 1974 James Bond movie, *The Man with the Golden Gun*, starring Roger Moore, featured scenes filmed in Bangkok and on the stunning beaches in Phuket. An October 1988 issue of *Time* magazine ran a story about Thailand, written by the travel writer and essayist Pico Iyer, still in his early thirties.[21] The piece, titled "The Smiling Lures of Thailand," described the country as "a freshly discovered starlet" that offered "first-class services at Third World prices" and "exoticism crossed with elegance." A photo of a bikini-clad Thai woman accompanied the headline in the issue's table of contents. The same year that *Time* piece appeared, the winner of the Miss Universe Pageant hailed from Thailand, adding to the country's growing sex appeal on the world stage. And the 1988 *Sports Illustrated* swimsuit issue put Thailand on display, right alongside the supermodels the editors hired for the shoot. The cover featured Elle Macpherson on the beach at Phang Nga Bay, alongside the headline "Thailand Fling."[22]

International tourist arrivals in Thailand went from only 81,000 in 1960 to 1.1 million in 1975, to more than 5 million in 1990.[23] By the end of that stretch, many of those foreign tourists were wandering around the country with a two-columned guide-book whose cover bore a spare, lowercase logo, as well as—in those early days—the author's name in the lower right-hand corner.

By the early 1990s, Joe Cummings had become something of a celebrity among Thailand's burgeoning backpacker crowd, who saw him as the ultimate source of need-to-know information on the country. Cummings had by then produced a few editions of Lonely Planet's Thailand guide, as well as a Thai phrase book, which first appeared in 1984. As sales of the books grew, Cummings began to attract the attention of business owners who wanted in on the Lonely Planet game. Restaurant owners, hoteliers, guesthouse managers, and the like would either reach out to him at home or track him down on the road. For this reason, Cummings would always do his best to remain anonymous as he ventured into new areas to take notes. This was both to guarantee that he'd receive the same treatment as any tourist, and to save himself the hassle and attention he'd attract if word got out about what he was up to. (The same was true of guidebook writers in many other destinations—but not all. Longtime Lonely Planet writer Kevin Raub told me that the owner of a hostel in Brazil once chased him down at the airport, begging for his listing to be maintained in the next edition.)[24] But when Cummings was spotted, despite his stealth, business owners would offer him bribes in the form of meals and hotel rooms, but also prostitutes, opium, and other drugs. Despite the temptations, Cummings told me he tried to stay true to the Lonely Planet credo, which was that the company's writers "don't take freebies in exchange for positive coverage."[25]

The wording of that credo—which in those days was included in a note inside each book—left some important wiggle room.

For instance, imagine a situation in which a writer already knew he was going to include a hotel in the next edition of the guide because it was a place he knew and liked from previous visits. Would it violate the credo for him to accept a free room? Strictly speaking, in that case, the room wouldn't be "in exchange for" a listing in the guidebook. The writer might see the offer as a reasonable way to offset some of the hefty expenses incurred in the weeks and months he would spend doing his research. Like other guidebook publishers, Lonely Planet didn't cover travel expenses, which writers were supposed to manage themselves using the overall fee they were paid for their work. Would accepting that free hotel room distort the views of the writer or lead to biased coverage in the book?

Whatever your opinion on this question, it's worth noting that travel writing has long been rife with freebies: sponsored trips, discounted hotel stays, free flights in exchange for a splashy feature in a magazine. With a handful of important exceptions, many of the travel features you read in newspapers or magazines are the result of a trip that's been paid for by a tour operator, hotel, airline, or tourism marketing agency. The sponsored nature of the coverage is sometimes—but not always—noted at the bottom of the piece. (You can see examples of this type of content in the *Guardian*, the *Financial Times*, CNN, and *Travel + Leisure*, among many other media outlets.) This approach certainly helps to finance a lot of travel writing that publications might not otherwise be able to afford, but the obvious pitfall is that readers may struggle to distinguish a piece of journalism from, effectively, a thousand-word advertisement right alongside the day's news. But there are some important editorial holdouts, including the Travel desk at the *New*

York Times, which forbids its staff and contributors from taking discounts or freebies. So the spectrum of pay-to-play travel writing is pretty wide; perhaps Lonely Planet falls somewhere in the middle.

But whether it was in Thailand, Brazil, or otherwise, it's easy to see why the owner of a hotel or restaurant might try to buy their way into the guidebook in the 1980s and '90s. As Lonely Planet's sales grew, so, too, did the brand's influence. Already beloved by young Australian backpackers, the company soon developed a faithful following among their counterparts in the United States, where Lonely Planet sold some 100,000 copies of its guides and phrase books in 1985, the year after it opened its first distribution center in California. Within a decade, the United States became Lonely Planet's biggest market. Among the company's many early devotees was a well-traveled American business reporter named Nicholas D. Kristof.

"The Lonely Planet guidebooks are, quite simply, like no others," Kristof, still in his mid-twenties, wrote in a story for the Travel section of the *New York Times* in February 1986, after opening the piece with an account of a restless night he spent on the slow train to Ouagadougou, the capital of Burkina Faso.[26] While most guidebooks stuck to the typical listings of hotels and tour operators, Kristof noted, Lonely Planet would tell its readers "how to hop a free ride on a boat on Nicaragua's Caribbean coast, where to find families to stay with in Timbuktu and where to find penicillin in Bangkok." He went on to describe a small hotel in India that bore a sign saying "Tony Wheeler slept here," alongside the page from the hotel register that Tony had signed years before. "Travelers gaze at it wistfully," Kristof wrote; "the hotel has been touched by the gods."

It's true that Tony himself (and Maureen, to a lesser extent) had become celebrities among adventure travelers, and their fame would soon spread. In 1996, a year in which Lonely Planet published 216 titles in eleven languages, the *New York Times Magazine* profiled the Wheelers, with a focus on Tony, whom the piece described as the "trailblazing patron saint of the world's backpackers and adventure travelers" and "a man whose name makes hostel owners and budget restaurateurs tremble from Polynesia to the Pampas."[27]

By the time that profile appeared, Lonely Planet had come a long way from its scrappy beginnings, and so had Tony and Maureen. While many of their competitors—including the Rough Guides series as well as the Frommer's and Fodor's guides—had been scooped up by major publishing houses, the Wheelers had transformed Lonely Planet into the largest independent travel book company in the Anglophone world. Their formula had been to corner the growing market for travel guides to Asia, Africa, and Latin America—and they'd largely succeeded. By 1996, Lonely Planet was churning through $15 million in revenue every year, and according to the *New York Times Magazine*, their guides had become "the gospel of adventure travel" for "tens of millions of globetrotting readers."[28]

As their guidebooks gained traction, the Wheelers grew up alongside their company. They continued to travel and research their books, especially Tony. But by the mid-nineties, they had two teenage children at home and were well into middle age. The Wheelers were still in Melbourne, although instead of occupying a nondescript apartment near the city center, they now lived in a home with its own Balinese water garden. And Tony had a lipstick-red Ferrari parked in the garage.

*   *   *

A degree of pushback was probably inevitable. Travel guidebooks—and the people who carry them—have long made easy targets. In *A Room with a View*, E. M. Forster's 1908 novel that's partially set in Florence, the characters who like to consider themselves sophisticated seem to enjoy looking down on their fellow tourists who cling to their Baedekers, that classic Victorian travel guide. ("Tut, tut! Miss Lucy! I hope we shall soon emancipate you from Baedeker," an extravagant character named Miss Lavish tells our young protagonist. "He does but touch the surface of things. As to the true Italy—he does not even dream of it.") Half a century later, Arthur Frommer would be criticized for guiding too many American tourists to the particular restaurants he favored in the great cities of Europe, where the menu items he recommended were quick to sell out. Half a century later still, in his book *The Tao of Travel*, Paul Theroux summed up a common disparagement of guidebooks in sharing a quote from the celebrated travel writer Dervla Murphy: "Choose your country, use guidebooks to identify the areas most frequented by foreigners," she said, "and then go in the opposite direction."

Perhaps no guidebooks have attracted more scrutiny than those published by Lonely Planet, and it's easy to see why: the company sold more than 120 million guidebooks in its first four decades, and in many parts of the world it had few strong competitors.[29] This was certainly true in Thailand, where Joe Cummings was still writing for Lonely Planet in the mid-nineties. At that point, he told me, Thailand was backpacker central—a very hip place to be. But by the turn of the millennium, that cool-kid, rave-on-the-beach vibe would give way to a rising tide of mass tourism. Whether justified or not, those who bemoaned this shift sometimes pointed a finger at the guides that Cummings was writing for Lonely Planet.

In 1996, the same year that the Wheelers were profiled in the *New York Times Magazine*, a twenty-something Brit named Alex Garland published his first novel, a dystopian backpacker satire set in Thailand. ("Here goes the latest ill-fated invasion of Southeast Asia," quipped one of the book's reviewers.)[30] *The Beach* tells the story of an international group of wandering young Gen Xers who try to maintain their own slice of untrammeled paradise in an illegal commune-cum-beach resort inside a nature reserve that's officially off-limits to tourists. Tired of chasing the next hot destination, Garland's fictional pot-smoking nomads have sworn themselves to secrecy to prevent their commune from succumbing to the inevitable slide into the tourist mainstream that they've seen play out on all the beaches they used to consider worthy of their time. "There's no way you can keep it out of the Lonely Planet," one character sighs, explaining why they could never maintain their paradise on an island already known to tourists. "And once that happens it's countdown to doomsday."[31]

Garland's novel gained a cult following among the backpacking crowd and was soon made into a film of the same name, starring Leonardo DiCaprio, still in his mid-twenties and riding high on the fame of his turn as Jack in *Titanic*. In a delicious piece of irony, the movie version of the novel that mocked Lonely Planet ended up having a much more significant influence on a single, stunning Thai beach than a mere guidebook listing could ever have managed. After the movie's release, the site chosen for the filming—Maya Bay, on the Thai island of Phi Phi—became so inundated with visitors and their trash that Thai authorities eventually shut off access to the beach entirely to allow the ecosystem to recover. After nearly four years of closure, Maya Bay reopened in 2022, but under strict protocols: swimming is allowed only in designated areas, tourist numbers are capped, and visitors are limited to the time slots they reserve in advance. If you want to get all the details on the new rules, you can find everything you need to know on the Lonely Planet website.[32]

Fairly or not, by the time Lonely Planet celebrated its fortieth birthday in 2013, a new term had established itself in the travelers' lexicon. "We are both very conscious of the 'Lonely Planet Effect' and hence we are withholding locational information to ensure small private businesses . . . are not swamped with visitors," the authors of a niche travel blog wrote in 2006.[33] The following year, a Reuters story described how "the Lonely Planet effect" had inspired frenzied competition among the rival owners of food stalls in a particular corner of Jodhpur, India. ("I think people are overdependent on it," one tourist said of the Lonely Planet guide as he chowed down on a sandwich from a food stall recommended in the book.)[34] A 2011 entry in a popular travel blog described "the Lonely Planet effect" as the price inflation that can follow a hotel or restaurant's listing in the travel bible. In that sense, the author opined, Lonely Planet was "the greatest gentrification device of the travel world."[35]

"We're regularly asked if we feel guilty for what we've done to—choose your destination—anywhere from Bali to Thailand, Nepal, Cambodia or Vietnam," Tony wrote in *Unlikely Destinations*, the business memoir that he and Maureen coauthored in 2005. "Somehow our little guidebook-publishing company has expanded the airport, bought the aircraft, increased the flight frequencies, sold the package tours, built the hotels and restaurants, equipped the rent-a-car fleets and convinced all the visitors to go there. Of course, we haven't done that." Elsewhere, Tony has stressed that, when there's a problem with tourism in a place, some degree of government mismanagement—a lack of infrastructure, regulation, or planning—is often at the root of the strain. And he believes the approach to travel that Lonely Planet champions—as opposed to, say, package tours or all-inclusive resorts—tends to support small businesses, generate local employment, and encourage interactions between visitors and locals.[36]

Back in Thailand, Cummings was never convinced that a listing in Lonely Planet had much influence on visitors' movements. As evidence of this, he told me that, throughout the twenty-five years he was writing about Thailand for Lonely Planet, he was always trying to promote the northeastern corner of the country—a less visited area that he found fascinating and beautiful, with excellent food and sights for visitors. But despite Cummings's efforts to attract attention to the place, visitor numbers to northeastern Thailand remained stubbornly low throughout his tenure as a guidebook writer. He also saw that travelers neglected some of the restaurants that he touted as his favorites in the guidebook—probably, he thinks, because their menus were only in Thai. Rather than go out of their way, most tourists seemed to choose restaurants with English menus that happened to be close to wherever they were staying. They might sit there with their Lonely Planet guide perched on the table next to them, like a security blanket, Cummings told me; that didn't mean they were using it.

But Lonely Planet did have an outsized impact by directing its readers to particular restaurants or hotels within a destination, an effect that Tony has acknowledged. This phenomenon was most pronounced in places where tourism was a relatively new phenomenon, and where the company had few strong competitors. Lonely Planet writers I spoke to said they could see this effect on the ground. "When you update, you go to the places that were there in the last edition, and you walk in and everyone is sitting there with a guidebook," Kevin Raub told me, adding that this is "a huge problem" in places like Thailand and India. Raub shared the story of when the owner of a beautiful wildlife sanctuary in Colombia begged him not to list her establishment in Lonely Planet because she wasn't equipped to handle the influx of visitors that would ensue. "At the time, I'm like, 'Listen, I don't answer to you. I answer to my editors and my readers,'" Raub said. "And if I don't put this in, then they're going to be like, 'What the fuck? He missed this amazing place.' So that's the struggle that you have."

Thomas Kohnstamm, an American who contributed to more than a dozen Lonely Planet guides and phrase books in Latin America and the Caribbean between 1998 and 2006, also saw that a single guidebook mention could have a big impact on a place.[37] He remembers that it was often the European or American business owners in Latin America who were the savviest about positioning themselves for a listing—a fact that only further entrenched the "gringo trail," to the detriment of many locally owned businesses. Kohnstamm, who has a master's degree in Latin American Studies from Stanford, told me that his background in development theory strongly influenced his understanding of what he was doing on the ground as a guidebook writer. He saw the early 2000s as the beginning of a shift away from the model of the "parachute artist"—in which a Westerner (almost always white, usually male) drops into a foreign place and leaves behind a trail of breadcrumbs for his peers to follow—to the more dispersed, organic, and chaotic sourcing of travel information from the internet.

In addition to writing for Lonely Planet, Kohnstamm worked as an editor for Rough Guides and freelanced for Bill Dalton's Moon Guides as well as a variety of national travel magazines and newspapers. But his career in the guidebook world came to a crashing end in 2008 with the publication of his memoir—*Do Travel Writers Go to Hell?*—in which he recounts some of his experiences working as "a full-time mercenary travel hack."[38] In the book, Kohnstamm details his issues with guidebooks and their model of production, even as he acknowledges his own role in fueling the machine. You get the sense that the whole experience leaves Kohnstamm feeling disillusioned: guidebooks may give travelers a sense of independence, he writes, but "they are often little more than a paper arrow pointing you down an overhyped tourist route." And because writers' pay is so low (Kohnstamm admits in the book that he resorted to selling ecstasy—or at least *trying* to sell ecstasy—to cover his costs), they are obliged to stick to the path that earlier guidebook writers have already beaten, which "only contributes to the further entrenchment of a narrow Lonely Planet trail."

Ahead of his book's publication, Kohnstamm gave an interview to an Australian newspaper. Among many other topics covered in the conversation, the journalist asked Kohnstamm if he could substantiate a rumor that Lonely Planet writers didn't always travel to the locations they covered. He responded that it was standard practice for writers not to travel if they're working on the sections of Lonely Planet's guide to a country that can be researched elsewhere, namely the history, culture, or environment sections, and he added that he hadn't actually traveled to Colombia when he was updating those parts of the country's guide. Instead, Kohnstamm—who'd been to Colombia several times previously—told the journalist he'd gotten the background information from the Colombian consulate in San Francisco, where a former girlfriend worked.

The journalist took that piece of the conversation and ran with it, quoting Kohnstamm as saying he got his information "from a chick I was dating—an intern at the Colombian consulate," in a story that framed him as a lazy guidebook writer who did all his work remotely.[39] The story got picked up by the *Guardian*, the *Times* of London, Reuters, and beyond. Kohnstamm remembers that he even made it onto the crawl on CNN. Just after BRITNEY SPEARS IN MINOR ACCIDENT ON LA FREEWAY and OBAMA TALKS GUNS, GOD, was TRAVEL WRITER TELLS NEWSPAPER HE PLAGIARIZED, DEALT DRUGS.

"I was like, 'Holy shit!'" Kohnstamm told me.[40] The blowback was so intense that at one point his email inbox was full of death threats, and he informed the police. Remember this was 2008, a moment when the Lonely Planet brand was at or near the peak of its global influence. At that point, Lonely Planet held such sway over our collective imagination, so much cachet as the bible of travel guides, that the idea of a Lonely Planet writer who shirked his duties or gamed the system seemed to cause many people deep and personal offense. Perhaps the severity of the pushback against Kohnstamm's revelations proved the worthiness of his goal in writing a memoir in the first place: "Maybe if people see what arbitrary bullshit goes into the making of a guidebook," he wrote in the book's introduction, "they will realize that it is just a loose tool to give basic information and is not the singular or necessarily the correct way to approach a destination."[41]

*   *   *

As Lonely Planet's size and influence grew over the years, so too did the global population of international travelers. In 2007, the year in which the Wheelers would initiate the sale of Lonely Planet to the BBC, 913 million tourists crossed an international border, well over four times the figure from 1973, the year they published their first guidebook. Was some of that global rise in international travel driven by guidebooks themselves? It's possible there was a degree of influence, but two much bigger forces were driving the rising travel trend over the next decade: the growth of the global middle class and the increasing ease of making travel bookings online.

And, of course, the power of Lonely Planet wasn't to last: the digital world was coming, and it was coming fast. "Print Travel Books Are Dead, and There's No Good Replacement," ran a *Time* magazine headline in March 2013.[42] A month later, a journalist writing for the *Atlantic* wondered aloud whether the days of wandering around Europe with a guidebook in hand were long gone. Her conclusion: "It certainly looks that way."[43]

It's easy to see where these observers were coming from: in 2012, the publisher John Wiley & Sons, which was then managing the publication of the Frommer's travel guides, sold the brand to Google for an undisclosed amount. Also that year, Penguin, which was then the publisher of the Rough Guides, announced that the company was evaluating whether future editions of the guides would be digital only. A few years later, Penguin Random House sold the Fodor's travel guide series to a company with the beguiling name of Internet Brands, which also owns Medscape and WebMD.

Tony and Maureen were changing, too. They began to shift their approach in the early 2000s, aiming to keep sales high by making their books appeal to a broader audience. The backpackers who bought their books in the eighties now had children and mortgages and limited vacation time—and they needed travel information that suited their needs. It didn't take long for this to come through in the editorial direction for guidebook writers. When he was updating Lonely Planet's Brazil guide in 2003, Kohnstamm was told to dedicate 60 percent of his coverage to midrange listings, 20 percent to high-end, and only 20 percent to budget—a big change from the previous edition, in which 70 percent of the hotel and restaurant listings fell into the "budget" category. Around the same time, the company was also moving longtime writers like Joe Cummings off royalties, instead offering them one-off payments for their work, which is now the dominant model across the industry. This move allowed Lonely Planet to rein in costs; it also helped to streamline the company for its eventual sale.

Which is exactly where they were headed. Tony and Maureen were always quick to admit that the digital world was alien to them. Plus, by the mid-2000s they were empty nesters who were pushing sixty, and ready to move on to other things. So in 2007, after several months of negotiations, the Wheelers sold 75 percent of their shares in Lonely Planet to the BBC, in a deal that valued the company at about £100 million, roughly $200 million at the going exchange rate. At that point, Lonely Planet was publishing five hundred titles—including country and region guides, activity guides, shoestring guides, and phrase books—while also producing web content and developing programming for broadcasters. They had a staff of five hundred, in addition to three hundred writers who were working for them as hired guns.[44] Three and a half years after that initial sale, the Wheelers sold their remaining 25 percent stake, completely severing their ties to the company. Maureen—who'd been pushing the sale more than Tony—later remembered the day of the sale as one of the saddest of her life.[45]

The investment didn't turn out so well for the BBC. Just two years after the Wheelers sold the last of their shares, the broadcaster turned around and sold the brand to the American tobacco billionaire Brad Kelley ("the most price-elastic buyer it could find," opined the travel media guru Rafat Ali, who broke the news),[46] at a loss of roughly £80 million. Kelley hired twenty-four-year-old Daniel Houghton—a former wedding photographer—to serve as CEO. Massive layoffs soon followed, but it wasn't enough to put the company back on a solid footing. In 2020, Kelley sold Lonely Planet to a company called Red Ventures, which also owns CreditCards .com and Reviews.com, among other digital-first businesses. The sum was undisclosed, but it was rumored to be around $50 million, which, given inflation, is less than a quarter of what the company was valued at thirteen years earlier. But probably to the relief of many Lonely Planet diehards, the new owner of the brand said at the time that it remained "committed to publishing the guidebooks." How many people would buy them was another question.

*   *   *

Others had laid the foundations for them, but it was a cadre of baby boomers (or nearly)—Rick Steves, Hilary Bradt, Mark Ellingham, Bill Dalton, Oliver Koppell, and Tony and Maureen Wheeler—who transformed the way millions of English-speaking Westerners thought about and explored the world. These boomers also grew up alongside their market: penniless young explorers turned into scrappy entrepreneurs, who eventually became comfortable in their success—and either cashed out or kept working. Their arc through adulthood coincided with a rapid rise in affluence around the world, the opening up of borders, and the swift development of jet flight and other technologies that would make international travel more accessible to many. The guidebooks that these boomers wrote along the way were both a narration of the fantastic growth in international travel that their generation witnessed and a blueprint for its further expansion. In some cases, their guidebooks probably did further deepen the "grooves on the map" of international tourism. But compared to the enormous influence that these publications wielded in the eighties, nineties, and early 2000s, their power today is clearly on the wane—though it hasn't disappeared completely.

In fact, you might be surprised to learn that guidebook sales aren't doing that badly. In 2013, just six months after his former publisher sold his brand to Google, an eighty-something Arthur Frommer and his daughter, Pauline, bought the whole thing back from the tech giant, bringing Frommer's Travel Guides into the family again for the first time since the late 1970s, when Frommer first licensed his books to a major publisher. The Frommers have been managing the publication of their books ever since, Pauline Frommer told me, and sales are climbing.[47] Their strategy is essentially to stick to what they've always done, with maybe a few tweaks: providing readers with concrete, unbiased, and easy-to-use information, supplemented by some helpful maps and suggested itineraries.

Rick Steves told me essentially the same thing. Over the years, Steves has quietly built an empire, and he now publishes some of the bestselling travel guides in the United States. Steves still gets out on the road every summer to chip in on revising the hotel and restaurant listings, and he insists that this kind of ground-truthed information is precisely what readers are still willing to pay for. Like Pauline Frommer, Steves is sticking to a tried-and-true formula, and it seems to be working: he told me that he now sells about a million books a year. In the UK, Hilary Bradt, now in her eighties (and long divorced from George), still runs Bradt Travel Guides from the company's offices outside of London. She also told me that sales are good these days, particularly for their guides to various parts of Britain, titles that sold well even at the height of the pandemic. (She's researched and written several of these herself.) Things have been going so well that, in 2019, Bradt was able to buy one of its competitors.

Others may be getting back to basics, but Lonely Planet is betting on a new model. The brand's die-hard fans are getting older, and it needs to find a way to appeal to today's young people, who in at least one important way are the polar opposite of Tony and Maureen: they're digital natives.[48] In 2022, Lonely Planet, still under the ownership of Red Ventures, announced it was launching a new series of "anti-guidebook" experience guides that are "designed for a new generation of savvy travelers looking for a more interactive way to explore." These (anti-) guides feature short articles, often written by a local expert, about different things that travelers can do: wine tastings, road trips, whale-watching tours, and the like. Many of the maps and hotel and restaurant listings have disappeared from the books—everyone finds those things online these days anyway. Instead of providing a Yellow Pages–style list of practical information, the new guides focus on *curation*, Nitya Chambers, Lonely Planet's senior vice president of content and executive editor, told me. The new guides also drop the *Reader's Digest*-inspired layout that Tony improvised half a century ago, opting instead for a design that embraces photographs, image cutouts, and infographics.

"It's much more visual than the blue-spine guidebooks have been," Chambers said. "It brings in that sense of visual immersion that you get from social media."

Chapter Two

Under the Influence

We have to wait a good fifteen minutes for the opening in the crowds that Bobby tells me we need. I'm not sure what he has in mind here, but we've already spent half a day together, so by now I'm used to the drill: Bobby tells me to hand over my unlocked phone and shows me exactly where to stand. Then he steps back and starts shouting detailed instructions as he takes a stream of photos of me, all while directing me like a photographer in a fashion shoot.

"Okay, point your shoulders toward the temple, now turn back and look at me. Verrrrry niiiiiiice! Now turn toward me and raise your arms over your head. All the way up! Yesssss. Gorgeous. I got it!"

But the moment for our photo shoot has yet to arrive here in the Tomb Raider Temple, which isn't the official name of this place, but Bobby tells me that's what everyone calls it. There are just too many people around to get any photos that can convey an appropriate level of wild and alluring isolation. So Bobby* and I loiter around for a little while in the heavy tropical heat, watching a stream of my fellow tourists pick their way through the crumbling stone towers and lichen-covered archways that have occupied this patch of jungle for more than eight centuries.

I've never seen the Angelina Jolie blockbuster that made this temple so famous, but I can certainly see why the place would make a good filming location. Spiderlike strangler figs and majestic silk-cotton trees grow in, around, and over the ancient stone structures, prying apart the ruins, while also shading them and their tourist inhabitants from the fierce midday sun. The crumbling temple is intricate and beautifully carved, but it seems clear to me that Mother Nature has the starring role here. Moss colonizes the towering piles of stone bricks that the tropical monsoons and ever-spreading tree roots have strewn throughout the scene. The sharp cries of unseen tropical birds cut through the polylingual tourist thrum, while the fresh odor of forest and decaying leaves overwhelms the scent of sweating human bodies. I have the feeling that if humanity were to abandon the temple completely, it would take only a few years for the jungle to consume the place whole, like a python swallowing a mouse.

But on this weekday at the beginning of the tourist high season, there's certainly no sign that humans will abandon the site anytime soon. Of the temples that Bobby and I have seen so far today, Ta Prohm—which is how this site is marked on my official map of the Angkor complex—is by far the busiest. (When I remark on

---

* This isn't his real name, by the way; he wasn't authorized to be quoted by a journalist.

the number of people wandering around, Bobby tells me I should have seen the place before the pandemic.) It's a pretty typical international crowd: I spy a pair of athleisure-clad young women with matching blond French braids laughing as they make faces for photos being taken by their blond-braided compatriot. There's a South Asian family posing under a suspended tree root that's as thick as my torso, and a tour group of maybe a dozen retirees wandering around with matching badges and audio guides strung around their necks. I notice a few of Bobby's fellow official tour guides—all in the same uniform of smart trousers and a yellow button-down shirt with a colorful badge sewn on the shoulder. But most of the tourists appear to be exploring the temple unaccompanied.

A promising gap in the crowds begins to emerge, when a deeply tanned woman in late middle age stops to pose for a photo immediately in front of us. The woman is adorned in heavy gold jewelry and she's wearing red hot pants and a skimpy white tank top that struggles to contain her enormous breasts, which she thrusts forward as she raises a knee and places one hand on her hip. Shaking his head, Bobby walks over and interrupts the moment.

"You need to cover yourself," he tells her. "You're in a temple. Be respectful."

The woman looks annoyed, but she digs a gauzy red scarf out of her bag and drapes it over herself. As she resumes her stance, the scarf slides off the side of her bare shoulder. Her friend snaps the picture. Bobby looks at me and shakes his head again.

But then—finally—the crowd parts and it's my turn to play model. Bobby hurries to give me my instructions: I'm supposed to stand on point X while I gaze up at the jungly canopy behind me.

Then I walk in through one door of a small stone building and out the opposite side, at which point I turn to gaze back at Bobby and my phone, which he will be using to document my progression. Instructions relayed, Bobby takes up his position, calls action, and I do my best to execute the sequence with a semblance of the grace that I imagine he's hoping for. The whole thing feels more awkward than anything else, but at least I manage not to trip— and I'm happy to see that Bobby seems pleased with the result: a panoramic shot in which I magically appear in two places at once. There's Paige, wearing a long patterned dress, on the left side of the ancient building, gazing up at the forest. And there's Paige again on the right side of the building, looking straight into the camera. No other human appears in the scene. The image makes me look like some kind of ethereal explorer, or maybe a temple witch who's inspecting her lair. "You see what I did?" Bobby asks, grinning. I do. I'm fascinated. I'm also a little creeped out.

Several hours earlier, when I hired Bobby as my tour guide for the day, I wasn't expecting to get a personal photographer as part of the deal, but as you can see that's kind of how things worked out. By the end of the day, I had photos of myself on the top of stair-cases, under archways, with the sun rising behind me, and even with my arms raised to the sky in the middle of a two-lane road— Bobby snapped that one very quickly, between passing tuk tuks. But I don't mean to imply that Bobby's focus on photography got in the way of his guiding. On that front, he was excellent: Bobby was full of information about the ancient and modern history of the temples; the religious symbolism of the various sculptures and engravings; and the structural integrity of the temples and the many physical pressures they face. He knew his stuff, spoke fluent English, and demonstrated remarkable physical stamina for wandering around ruins in ninety-degree heat for several hours on end. When I asked him why he put such an emphasis on photos, he shrugged. It's what his clients are always asking for, he told me—and he's eager to give them what they want.

Sure enough, a couple of days after I get home from the trip, I use several of Bobby's photos in a short, fast-moving reel that I post to Instagram. Layered over a dreamy tune that I find in the app under "suggested audio," I stitch together a classic shot of Angkor Wat at sunrise (with all the other tourists cropped out); a snippet from a video I took riding through the jungle on the back of Bobby's motorbike; a photo of me appearing to kiss the mouth of a temple deity; and a shot of me seated between two fat stone pillars, the triple towers of Angkor Wat rising in the background.

"Come tour Angkor with me," I write in the caption, followed by a short string of emojis: a golden sparkle, the Cambodian flag, a pair of praying hands in my own pale shade of Caucasian. I add some hashtags, hit post, and off it flies into the yawning maw of the algorithm.

*　　*　　*

Writing in 1981, the British travel writer Jonathan Raban described travel writing as "a notoriously raffish open house" that welcomes "with indiscriminate hospitality" forms as varied as "the private diary, the essay, the short story, the prose poem, the rough note and polished table talk."[1] I'm inclined to agree with his assessment, but Raban's list could use a major twenty-first-century update. These days, I believe, the open house of travel writing is also home to travel-related posts shared on Instagram, TikTok, Facebook, and YouTube. Purists may disagree, but I'm hardly the first to argue that social media posts should be considered a form of travel writing. Some academics have even claimed that the travel selfie alone—especially when accompanied by a caption and hashtags—can be considered a visual mode of the genre.[2]

That travel writing has jumped from the page to the screen is a natural extension of the deep transformation in tourism that has its roots in the 1990s, when the industry joined just about everything else in our lives in the gradual but inexorable shift from analog to online.[3] It's easy to forget, but until the mid-nineties, most people couldn't make travel reservations without walking into an office, sending a fax, or at least speaking to someone on the phone. But that started to change in early 1996, when two travel companies came together to launch a consumer-facing version of the kind of flight booking system that travel agents had long been using. They called the site Travelocity, and it registered 1.2 million views in its first three months—this at a moment when less than a quarter of Americans went online from home, work, or school.

A flurry of start-ups and new ventures would soon follow. Microsoft joined the party with the launch of Expedia in October 1996, marking the first foray of a major tech company into the world of online travel services. "Being able to tap into and book the latest, lowest airfares right from your PC with Expedia is very compelling," Microsoft chairman and CEO Bill Gates said in the press release that announced the launch. "We think it will reshape the way consumers plan and purchase their travel." The following month, on the other side of the Atlantic, a young Dutch entrepreneur named

Geert-Jan Bruinsma founded Bookings.nl, a service that allowed people who were visiting or traveling within the Netherlands to reserve a hotel room online. Bruinsma raised about $50,000 to fund the website launch, with much of the investment coming from friends and family. In 2005, he sold the company—which had since become Booking.com—for $133 million.

Other early movers experienced similarly explosive growth. In April 1998, Priceline launched its service offering travelers the chance to make last-minute bids for empty plane seats and hotel rooms that would otherwise go unused. Demand was so high that the company's two servers crashed on the opening day. When Priceline went public the following year, founder Jay Walker became an instant billionaire. Tripadvisor debuted in 2000, starting off as an aggregator of professional reviews of hotels and other travel operators. One year in, they added a little button for people to leave their own reviews—and the company took off. By the time a fledgling company called Airbed & Breakfast changed its name to Airbnb in 2009, people were so used to booking their accommodations online that the idea of paying to stay in a stranger's home struck many of us as a perfectly reasonable thing to do. The launch of Google Flights two years later further deepened travel's entrenchment in the digital space, offering people new search options that made it easier than ever to find a flight they wanted to buy. Google would later create its own travel app—Google Trips, which later merged with the website Google Travel, a one-stop shop for anyone looking to plan and book a trip anywhere in the world. By 2017, Google's travel business was worth around $100 billion, or roughly 15 percent of Google's total stock value.

Between the mid-nineties and the eve of the pandemic, travel operators executed a profound shift from analog to digital, further fueling the rising trend in international travel, which had been growing steadily since the 1960s alongside the steady uptick in global income. But now that people could book their own travel in just a few clicks, growth in international travel was supercharged. Between the launch of Travelocity and Expedia in 1996 and the debut of Google Flights fifteen years later, the number of tourists who crossed an international border every year shot up from 563 million to just over a billion. And the pace of growth would get faster still.

Just as the old analog world of travel was falling away, the analog world of travel *writing* was experiencing its own moment of reckoning. This was in part because international travel wasn't nearly as exclusive as it had been in the past. People who enjoyed the travelogues of Mark Twain, Freya Stark, Lawrence of Arabia, and even Bruce Chatwin, writing in the 1970s and '80s, probably did so because there was little chance they themselves would ever be able to travel to Hawai'i, Patagonia, or the deserts and high mountain passes of the Middle East. In another era, travel writing was an irreplaceable window to another world. These days, the very idea of "another world" seems quaint: unless you're seriously put off by war zones, human travelers have been (and *can go*, if they have the money) just about everywhere, including the darkest depths of the ocean and the inner fringes of outer space.

In 2010, the journalist Graeme Wood declared in the pages of *Foreign Policy* that travel writing was officially dead.[4] He decried Elizabeth Gilbert's runaway bestseller, *Eat, Pray, Love*, as "the nail in the coffin" of the genre, which he said had devolved into a self-indulgent form in which the writer narrates "a tedious inner crisis" while traveling, but fails to leave the reader with any insights about the places she visits. "The simplest reason for this catastrophic turn," Wood opined, "is that it is easier than ever to travel, and not at all easier to write well." Think what you will of Gilbert's hit—which I happen to love—but on that last point, at least, Wood wasn't wrong. His obituary for travel writing was published on October 5, 2010. The very next day, Instagram made its global debut in Apple's App Store; twenty-five thousand people downloaded the app on launch day.[5]

As social media gained momentum in the travel world, others joined Wood in declaring the death of travel writing, or at least in publicly debating whether the genre still had a pulse. In 2017, Malcolm Jones wrote in the *Daily Beast* that, while travel books "still have something to tell us," "their subject matter"—the unexplored and undescribed corners of the world—"is literally running out."[6] The same year, an entire issue of *Granta*—a British literary quarterly that's known in part for its highbrow travel writing—was devoted to this very question, with entries from some of the most celebrated travel writers of the moment: Pico Iyer, Colin Thubron, Geoff Dyer, and Robert Macfarlane among them.[7] The conclusions were mixed, with most deciding that the genre was alive but perhaps not well, and definitely undergoing a major shift. Thubron declared travel writing an "infinitely resilient and varied" genre whose "continuance over the centuries belies its death sentence." Iyer opined that the modern travel writers would need to travel "further inward, into the realm of silence and nuance and personal enquiry" if they wanted to successfully compete with the likes of YouTube. (I can almost hear Graeme Wood clucking at him now.) Ian Jack, the editor of the magazine at the time, rightly noted that travel writing "has the history of colonialism perched on its shoulder" and looked forward to reading first-person accounts of a visitor from Asia, for instance, describing what it felt like to travel through the West—perhaps giving Westerners a taste of their own condescending medicine. "Travel writing isn't dead," Jack concluded. "It just isn't what it was."

But none of those commentators anticipated the dizzying extent to which the genre was shifting under their feet. In 2021, Houghton Mifflin Harcourt announced they were discontinuing *The Best American Travel Writing*, an annual series that had been running for more than two decades. Jason Wilson, the editor of the series, later explained the series' ending in an interview with Jeremy Bassetti on the *Travel Writing World* podcast. It wasn't that there was a dearth of high-quality travel writing to choose from, he said; there just weren't enough people interested in buying the book. And that was true even during the first year of the pandemic, when all of us were stuck at home. Sales of the book had been declining steadily ever since the series launched twenty-one years earlier.[8]

But over the same stretch, sales of some popular travel guidebook series actually rose, as we saw in the last chapter—as did the number of people with Instagram accounts. We were still willing to spend money on books about travel, but not so that we could relive the adventures of a lofty author-narrator. We wanted travel books that would instruct us on how to plan our own adventures. And we wanted to tell our own stories, too.

But can a seven-second video posted to Instagram—something like, say, my little reel from Angkor—really be considered a form of

46

travel writing? Let's pick this apart. Tim Youngs, in *The Cambridge Introduction to Travel Writing*, defines travel writing as "predominantly factual, first-person prose accounts of travels that have been undertaken by the author-narrator." The caption for my Angkor Instagram reel technically comprised five words of prose—which is more than nothing. And the string of videos and images that I used were certainly a factual, first-person account of my travels. So I think my reel qualifies. But would it fit Graeme Wood's derisive definition of the twenty-first-century version of travel writing? I didn't narrate a tedious inner crisis in my seven seconds of temple content. But then again, I didn't offer any insights into the history, symbolism, or current challenges facing the temples or the people who live in their vicinity. No, on reflection, my little reel was nothing more than ego-fueled, escapist travel content. But perhaps an even more embarrassing indictment, at least for someone who likes to call herself a writer, is that my seven seconds of narcissistic wallowing didn't even include a scrap of narrative tension.

My Instagram following is middling—as are my reels-making skills, let's be honest—so my reel didn't make its way in front of too many eyeballs. But in the hands of someone gifted at social media, a seven-second video about the temples of Angkor could easily reach tens of thousands, if not tens of millions, of Instagram users. According to an analysis from the company Backlinko, in 2023 the app had 170 million users in the United States alone, over half the national population. Worldwide, over a billion people are active on the app every month. Those of us who are on Instagram spend an average of twenty-nine minutes consuming its content daily, which is nearly as much time as the average American spent socializing every day in 2022.[9] And Instagram isn't even the most popular form of social media: Facebook and YouTube—two other popular modes of sharing travel content—both have higher user numbers than Instagram, while Facebook tends to hold our attention for even longer.[10]

So that seven-second reel could easily, and almost instantaneously, reach an audience of millions—who could consume it for free and with zero effort, perhaps while sitting on the toilet, riding the train to work, or waiting in line at the supermarket. Compare that to the reach of a 250-page travelogue for which you might have to pay $25 at your local bookstore—or even a thousand-word literary essay that lives behind a paywall. In the modern age of tourism, social media isn't only a legitimate form of travel writing; it's also, by far, the most important. Or I could even say *influential*.

*   *   *

Forty-something years ago, "the raffish open house" of travel writing that Jonathan Raban described was indeed home to many narrative forms. Travel writers themselves, however, tended to hail from a very narrow slice of humanity. There are some important exceptions, but the typical anglophone "travel writer" of the past hundred years has been white, male, middle- to upper-class, and has hailed almost exclusively from Britain or the United States. Of the twelve writers listed in a 2011 article in *Newsweek* claiming to identify "The Best Travel Writers of All Time," all but one hailed from Europe or the U.S.; all but one was Caucasian; and nine of the twelve listed were male (not counting Jan Morris, a trans woman who transitioned in midlife).[11] Salon's "Top Ten Travel Books" of the twentieth century included only two books by women (including one by Morris), and only one by a non-Caucasian.[12]

From this perspective, the rise of social media as the world's newest form of travel writing could be seen as a form of liberation for both the producers and consumers of the genre. No longer are budding travel writers limited by the slow-to-shift strictures and often discriminatory barriers to entry of the modern newspaper, magazine, or publishing industries. And no longer are those of us who enjoy travel writing forced to choose from such a narrow range of perspectives. Where we used to draw our travel inspiration from articles in *National Geographic*, the local newspaper, or the travel section at our favorite bookstore—the classic hangouts of the twentieth-century travel writer—we now have access to millions of potential sources of information and inspiration. Are you a Nigerian woman wondering what it will feel like to take your first trip to Europe? A lesbian who wants to know if you'll feel at ease in Singapore? A wheelchair user who's unsure about long-haul flying? A lover of street art, #vanlife, or hot-air ballooning? In all these cases, I know of at least one Instagram account for you to follow.

"What the online world did was democratize the whole process of travel writing," Shivya Nath, an Indian travel writer, told me, adding that this process has changed the entire understanding of what it means to be a travel writer in the first place. "You don't have gatekeepers like guidebook editors and publication editors anymore—these people who say whether or not you're the right person to write a story. You could have five thousand followers on Instagram and be writing great stories and inspiring people to make certain choices."[14]

Nath, who has more than 110,000 followers on Instagram (you can find her @shivya), started a blog on a whim back in 2009. At first, she wrote general updates about her life, but in 2011 she quit her marketing job and started traveling, and that soon became both the focus of her writing and the source of her income. For seven years, Nath traveled the world, living out of two bags and making original content for her blog, Twitter, and Facebook. An Indian woman traveling alone, Nath was writing about solo female travel at a moment when that type of content was still relatively rare—and she quickly found a following of women, young and old, who turned to her for inspiration. A couple of years after she started traveling full-time, she got an email from a woman who thanked Nath for inspiring her to travel by herself for the first time. "She said that she had spent her entire life just shuffling between these roles that women are supposed to have—daughter, wife, mother, grandmother," Nath remembered. "But she'd been reading my blog for a while and, at the age of sixty-three, she decided that she was going to do something for herself."

These days, we're not looking for our travel writers to paint evocative, detailed scenes of distant lands that we will never reach. These days, we want to feel a sense of connection with our travel writers—we want to feel like we know them—and we want them to inspire us. The immediacy of the internet means that such an intimate relationship is eminently possible: whereas the analog travel writer was forever barricaded behind the high walls of the publishing industry, today's travel writer is right here, right now—a virtual friend who checks in on us every day.

In a typical post, the American travel content creator Gabby Beckford (you can find her @packslight) might share how she takes care of her mental health while traveling, offer tips for solo women travelers, encourage young people to take a gap year, or offer a list of travel grants available to creative types. Her content clearly strikes a chord: Beckford has more than 150,000 followers on Instagram and double that number on TikTok; over 20,000 people subscribe to her email list.[14]

"I think people follow me for the inspiration, mostly in terms of mindset and confidence," Beckford told me. "They want to be doing what I'm doing, not necessarily because they want to stay at the exact hotels that I'm staying at or because they want to do exactly what I'm doing. They're just like, 'Oh, how did this girl make it happen? And how can I, by following her, be in proximity to this and make it happen for myself?'" And the identity thing is big, says Beckford, who, as a Black woman, also cofounded the Black Travel Alliance because she hopes to "create a more equitable travel industry for Black creators—and as a result all Black people in tourism and travel."[15]

Beckford, who was born in 1995, jumped straight into the world of Instagram and TikTok when she started earning money as an influencer in 2019, although she's kept up a blog as well. Nath, who is several years older, was slower to join the shift to Instagram, but when she did, her community followed her there, too. Today, Nath's focus is sustainable tourism, and—in addition to creating content—she also advises travel businesses on how to measure and manage their social and environmental impact. This ethos translates to her Instagram feed, which, as of 2023, Nath was updating at least a couple of times a week. Typical posts on Instagram include a reel that explores the links between travel and climate change, another that offers a rundown of "conscious stays" in Kashmir, and even a reel—posted in May 2022 but pinned to the top of her Instagram profile at the time of this writing—that opens with a provocative line of text: "How Instagram is ruining travel."

"Its algorithm prioritizes pretty landscapes, trending audio and unrealistic fashion over discussions on responsible travel, overtourism, and climate change," we read in text that appears over beautiful landscape scenes as some eerie-sounding choral music plays in the background. Nath added more thoughts in the caption: "I've tried not to spend much time on the app in the past few months, but every time I do, I just cringe," she wrote. "IRL and on the 'gram, people seem to be 'traveling' only to get the perfect photos or videos—hardly ever delving deeper into what a place or its people are about, or questioning the impact of our travels and Instagram posts on them."

"Are you and I part of the problem?" a line of text asks us at the end of the reel, followed by a nudge to "read and discuss," with an arrow emoji pointing to the comments section below. At the moment I wrote this in 2023, the reel had been viewed more than 400,000 times. Nearly 15,000 people had tapped the little heart icon to show their approval, and over 400 had left a comment. The vast majority of commenters chimed in to thank Nath for the thoughtful post, or to declare their agreement with her criticisms. But there were some detractors, too.

"Influencers like you are equally responsible for the mass destruction of places," wrote one viewer of the reel, in a comment that attracted several likes from fellow users. "Don't think that your mindfulness now will absolve you from all of this."

*   *   *

Fanney Gunnarsdóttir has a neat line of bangs and two tidy braids, barely streaked with gray, that reach past her shoulders. Something about the hairstyle—or maybe it's her no-nonsense demeanor—makes me think of Laura Ingalls from *Little House on the Prairie*, all grown up. But instead of a calico dress and sunbonnet, Gunnarsdóttir is wearing high-wicking performance wear and thick rubber clogs, which are essential for all the mud she has to deal with in her job with the Environment Agency of Iceland. And instead of an American twang, she speaks with the soft tones and *r*-rolling lilts so common in her native corner of the North Atlantic.

I'm standing with Gunnarsdóttir on the edge of a small but overflowing gravel parking lot a couple of miles off the two-lane highway that rims Iceland's rugged southern coastline. The landscape here is stark and open: we're surrounded by low hills covered in grass, moss, and rock; a river sparkles in the distance. The sky above us is wide and clear and full of wind that whips Gunnarsdóttir's braids over her face and sometimes steals her voice right out of her mouth. She has agreed to indulge me in an impromptu interview here on the edge of the parking lot, but she's still on the job, so she can't afford to give me her full attention. Every couple of minutes, she interrupts herself midsentence to help the driver of an SUV edge into a tight parking spot, or to speak to another group of approaching visitors, who often look a bit lost. In the forty-five minutes we spend together, she repeats the following lines at least a dozen times, always speaking with the same cheerful force.

"Hi! Welcome! The path is one kilometer long, with three sighting places. It's the same way up and down. Always stay on the path and never cross any limits. Enjoy yourselves!"[16]

Gunnarsdóttir is a government ranger at one of the most popular canyons in Iceland, and this is the mantra that she has been repeating for much of the last seven years that she has been working here. Today, however, Gunnarsdóttir has added additional lines to her normal script. It's mid-April and the small block of restrooms that has been built next to the parking lot is still closed for the winter season. So in addition to telling the tourists where to walk, she also tells them where they can—and can't—pee.

"Do like the Icelanders," she instructs a man carrying a massive camera who has been so bold as to ask whether she might be able to open the bathrooms for him. "We always go to the shops and go to the toilet, have something to drink and things like that—*before* we go out to the nature. Because we do not expect toilets everywhere we go."

Noted.

Things haven't always been so busy in this remote corner of the Icelandic countryside. Twenty years ago, the place where we're now standing was pretty much empty. The same family that owned and farmed the land for decades had moved to Reykjavík, three and a half hours away. A few visitors occasionally stumbled upon the area, which—in addition to being an excellent pasture for grazing sheep—is also home to a narrow, steep-sided canyon that looks like it could be straight out of *Lord of the Rings*. And then some-time around 2013, a few intrepid travelers started posting photos of the canyon on social media—sometimes with a geolocation tag attached. Suddenly, anyone with an internet connection could navigate their way to this stunning, out-of-the-way location. As you can imagine, the crowds quickly started to grow.

And then, in 2015, the other shoe dropped: Justin Bieber showed up with a film crew. They were there to make the music video for Bieber's song "I'll Show You," and they shot in several spots along Iceland's south coast: at a glacial lagoon, where they filmed Bieber diving into the freezing water in his tighty-whities; at the site of a crashed airplane on the beach, over whose rusting fuselage Bieber rode his skateboard; and on top of a cliff overlooking the ocean, where they filmed Bieber gazing wistfully into the distance. But the opening shot of the video came from the very canyon where Gunnarsdóttir now works.

As the video fades in, we see Bieber in jeans and an oversized hoodie, walking in his sneakers along a cliff edge, which I now know lies less than a five-minute walk from a small gravel parking lot. "My life is a movie / And everyone's watchin'," we hear Bieber sing from the canyon rim. Since the video was posted on YouTube in November 2015, it's been viewed more than half a billion times.[17]

The effects of the video showed up quickly, Gunnarsdóttir tells me. Within a few years, the number of people visiting the canyon went from around 3,000 per year to 300,000. But for the first few years, there wasn't even a real parking lot for visitors, let alone any bathrooms, walkways, or interpretive signs to guide the crowds. Without any infrastructure to protect it, the landscape quickly turned into a mud pit—and the owners of the canyon barely knew what hit them. "They didn't expect that their land would suddenly become a mass tourist place," Gunnarsdóttir says. "It was a bit of a shock."

Gunnarsdóttir wants to help me understand the scale of the impact of this tourist influx, so she walks to her silver pickup truck and comes back holding a laminated piece of paper that bears two contrasting photos of the landscape. In the earlier photo, taken in 2017, we see a field that looks like it has just hosted a weeklong music festival in the driving rain: it's a riot of mud, with barely any grass in sight. Gunnarsdóttir recalls that soon after that photo was taken, the authorities closed off the site to give the fragile landscape some time to recover. They closed it again the following year, this time for a full five months. During the closures, the authorities built a walking path and toilets, and they added ropes and signs instructing visitors where they should and shouldn't go. The second photo, taken from the same vantage point in 2021, shows a field of short golden grass with a tidy roped path cutting across it.

The scene looks very much like the view we have today, but the land still hasn't fully healed. Gunnarsdóttir leads me a few steps up the path and squats down to show me how the new grass along the edge of the trail remains thin. Given Iceland's short growing season, she says, it will take fifty to a hundred years for the landscape's natural carpet of grass and moss to recover its full thickness. The landscape here in Iceland, she says, is a lot more vulnerable than people realize.

"The problem was how he disrespected nature," she tells me of Bieber's music video. "He was rolling in the moss. He was on the cliff edges. He was in the glacial lagoon in his underwear—which is not safe, with all the currents streaming out and in. Other people want to copy what famous people do and they follow in his footsteps, and that's a problem."

But Gunnarsdóttir doesn't lay all the blame on Bieber—he didn't make the canyon popular, she says; he just accelerated a trend that was already in motion. In her opinion, the more fundamental problem is the way that social media has shaped our attitudes toward travel. She sees hundreds of visitors come and go every day: they park, walk up the path, take a few photos, then return to their cars and carry on. She doesn't see as many selfie sticks as she did before the pandemic, but the vibe hasn't changed: visitors rarely ask any questions or express any sort of curiosity about the place. It's like they're just there to take a picture and tick a box. Social media, she thinks, has fueled this kind of mentality and changed the way people travel—and not only in Iceland.

"It seems like people have more longing to travel and have photos of themselves in all of those places, kind of to show off," she says, adding that this makes it easier for people to ignore the impacts of their presence on the people or places they're visiting. I ask her what a better situation might look like here in the canyon, and she answers without hesitation: she wants people to come, but she wants them to linger and learn—to try to have a more meaningful interaction with the place.

"Most people are traveling to see *landscapes*," she says. "In the future, I hope they will get more interested in nature—and *learn* about nature."

*   *   *

The Justin Bieber canyon isn't the only tourist destination in Iceland that was "created on social media," as Skarphedinn Berg Steinarsson, the former director general of the Icelandic Tourist Board, once put it to me.[18] But the story here is much more complicated than it might first appear. In Iceland, at least, social media's powerful influence on tourist behavior also helped pull the country out of a recession.

Flashback to 2008, when the global financial crisis triggered a near total collapse of the Icelandic economy. The situation was so severe that the Icelandic government was forced to borrow more than $10 billion—or roughly $33,000 per resident—just to get back on its feet.[19] With its financial sector in a shambles, the country turned its attention to tourism, a small but growing industry that offered a lot of promise and that, by definition, couldn't be outsourced. Tourist numbers, which had been climbing steadily for several years, continued to edge up. But then another disaster struck: the eruption of a volcano on the country's southern coast shut down large swathes of airspace across the North Atlantic, and Iceland was once again attracting negative international attention. This was the biggest shutdown of European air traffic since the Second World War; more than a hundred thousand commercial flights were canceled.[20] As the headlines piled up about the extent of the ash cloud, the World Health Organization issued a public warning about the dangers of ash inhalation—and Iceland suddenly seemed like a very dangerous place indeed. Tourism leaders in the country saw an immediate impact: a flash survey showed that consumer sentiment toward Iceland plummeted in the days after the eruption, forcing officials to revise downward their forecasts for the busy summer season.[21]

Tourism leaders in Iceland wanted to move fast to change the narrative, but a media campaign that came straight from the government would smell too much like propaganda. So they took another approach, one that would harness two potent forces: Icelanders' fierce pride in their home country and social media. The campaign, which was designed and led by a New York ad agency, went like this: on June 3, 2010, the prime minister of Iceland made a live television address to launch "Iceland Hour," sixty minutes in which people across the country were meant to stop what they were doing and share a story about Iceland online. Instagram was still a few months away from launch, but the ad agency "created an army of fans" to get the message out on Facebook, Twitter, and Vimeo. They set up webcams at scenic locations around the country so people around the world could livestream the beautiful, ash-free Icelandic landscape straight into their living rooms. And they created the Inspired by Iceland website, where they collected stories and videos from across the country.

The campaign was a success: Before the end of the first day, 1.5 million people had downloaded videos from the site. Within the first six weeks, more than half of the Icelandic population had joined in to share their stories—and the narrative about the country began to shift. Iceland's visitor numbers that summer ended up surging past the downgraded forecasts, and it didn't even cost them that much money. The government spent about $3 million to set up and deploy the Inspired by Iceland campaign, but it generated over $200 million for the country's economy. The campaign was so effective—and so innovative, at the time—that it won a major advertising award the following year. One of the keys to the campaign's success, as one of the ad agency's staff members later wrote in a brief, was its focus on "activating people as media."

This was a new concept in 2010, back when tourism marketers were still doing what they'd been doing for decades: buying ads in magazines and newspapers and putting their commercials on TV. But the idea that social media users themselves could be the bearers of marketing messages quickly caught on—especially in the world of tourism, where all of us suddenly seemed to be finding our voices as the narrators of our own adventures.

In 2011, amid the chaos of headlines triggered by the Arab Spring, the government of Jordan launched a campaign to assure potential visitors that their country was still a safe place to visit. But instead of following Iceland's lead and tapping into the voices of everyday Jordanians, they paid sixteen travel bloggers—people with proven travel-writing skills, who already had big audiences—to visit Jordan and write about it. "Twitter, Facebook, and blogs are quickly becoming the go-to source of information," Nayef Al-Fayez, the managing director of Jordan's tourism board, said in an interview in the spring of 2011. "So often traditional news outlets sensationalize actual events, and so we relied on the genuine approach of firsthand experience."[22]

At the end of the year, one of those travel bloggers, a former investment banker named Keith Jenkins, came up with the idea of organizing a one-week social media blitz to share all the Jordan travel content that the bloggers had made over the year. The bloggers would be paid and publicly thanked for their work, and Jordan would enjoy a seven-day warm bath of publicity. Jenkins pitched the idea to some people from Jordan's tourism board over lunch one day, and they took him up on it. Jenkins had never seen that kind of campaign before, let alone run one—but it just seemed to make sense.[23]

"It was a huge success," Jenkins said over a video call from his office in Amsterdam, twelve years later, adding that the weeklong campaign was covered by Lonely Planet and other media outlets. It also led him to found his company, iambassador, a digital marketing agency that is still designing and running social media campaigns for national tourist boards and tourism brands around the world.

"I remember going to trade shows at the end of the year and people were saying, 'Oh, you're such a disruptor,'" Jenkins told me. "I'm like, 'I'm a disruptor? That's awesome.'"

The type of campaign that was pioneered in Iceland and Jordan spread quickly through the world of tourism. And before long, the travel bloggers of the late 2000s and early 2010s transformed into our newest iteration of the modern travel writer: the travel influencer. And much like Herodotus of ancient Greece, Marco Polo of thirteenth-century Venice, and Mark Twain of the nineteenth-century United States, this latest breed of travel writer has the power to inspire a lot of people—and move a lot of money.

In 2023, the influencer industry, in the travel world and otherwise, was estimated to be worth over $21 billion, more than double the value from just three years earlier.[24] It's hard to parse how much of that money was spent in the travel world, but influencers' power in tourism is plain to see, particularly when it comes to the choice of travel destination. In a 2019 survey of consumers in the United States, Britain, and Australia, nearly half of respondents said that social media content from an influencer or celebrity had inspired them to travel to a specific destination. Among members of Gen Z, the figure rose to 66 percent.[25] A 2018 Expedia survey found an even stronger impact: 84 percent of Gen Z travelers said they looked to social media for travel inspiration.[26] Today's top travel influencers are adept at capitalizing on their ability to shape their followers' decisions. Gabby Beckford earned $170,000 as a full-time content creator in 2021, her first full year on the job. In 2023, she grossed more than $100,000—in the first quarter alone.

It might seem like the world's easiest job—get paid to go to beautiful places and promote them—but to make it as a travel influencer these days, you have to be business savvy and fluent in a variety of media and professional contexts. In a single week, you might write a blog post, develop a marketing campaign, direct and star in a couple of ten-second videos, and address a crowd of hundreds at a travel conference. It's a real job that requires hard skills and that delivers tangible—and highly marketable—value to a whole lot of people. But the term "travel influencer" has come to carry a lot of baggage (ahem), to the extent that some people who might be labeled as such would rather be called something else entirely.

Shivya Nath is one of those people. She told me she would rather be described as a travel writer, sustainable tourism consultant, the founder of a tourism consulting agency—anything but "influencer." When I asked her what bothers her about the term, she didn't hesitate: to her, an influencer is someone who uses the place or its inhabitants as a colorful backdrop for their own ego, or who otherwise presents a destination in a shallow or ego-serving way. For example, she said, an influencer might post "a pretty video of a place that might be going through a lot of complex issues, or that might have an ancient culture—but all you see is this glorification." Inserting oneself into the story "has always been an intrinsic part of travel writing," she said. "But with Instagram, that story has become so shallow. You are your story—again and again and again."

Justin Bieber's video could certainly fit Nath's definition of typical "influencer" content, as does (let's be honest) my own little Angkor reel, which I made and posted several months before I interviewed her. It's easy to see the negative impacts of a video from a mega-celebrity like Bieber. But what about when it comes from a little social media nobody like me—is it really all that bad? It turns out that those of us with low follower counts have a lot more influence than I would have thought: the same 2019 survey where nearly half of respondents looked to influencers for travel inspiration revealed that a full *86 percent* chose their travel destinations based on social media content posted by a friend, family member, or peer. Among Gen Z, the latter figure rose to 92 percent. It turns out that people really are interested in our vacation photos, at least when they pop up in their social media feed. And this can turn into a self-perpetuating cycle.

"The things that get Instagrammed the most and shared online the most, and that also have a hundred years of being talked about in the media—your minds just go right there," Donald Leadbetter, the tourism program manager at the U.S. National Park Service, told me.[27] He's seen the concentrating effect of social media in national parks across the United States—but not all of them. While overall visitor numbers to the parks have been going up over the last several years, with a real surge during the pandemic, the effect is lopsided: "Visitation increases are really concentrated at some of your marquee, most famous parks," Leadbetter said. "It's a self-reinforcing cycle where the places that are most well known and most visited get repeatedly displayed on advertising and social media. And they just get this rolling momentum that's unstoppable." At the same time, he added, there's a "long tail" of parks in which visitor numbers have been stagnant or falling over the last few decades. "Once you get an idea in your mind about what you want to do and where you want to go, it's really difficult to change that decision path," he said. "We can't process all the information coming at us these days, so we use all of our unconscious biases and all the shortcuts we have in our minds to make really quick decisions."

Popular media helps to keep this cycle moving. We see stories like *Elle* magazine's "Thirty Places to Instagram in 2023," which includes a rundown of the resorts, restaurants, and nature spots "that deserve a coveted spot on your grid—and maybe even cross-promotion on TikTok."[28] A quick online search reveals dozens of articles that encourage us to follow the selfie-taking herd: the "72 Most Instagrammable Places in Paris," the "50 Most Instagrammable Countries," the "11 most Instagrammable Spots in Europe." And young people are lapping it up: a 2017 survey of British adults aged eighteen to thirty-three found that 40 percent of respondents cited "how 'Instagrammable'" a travel destination would be as their *most important* motivator when deciding where to go on vacation.[29] A follow-up survey of Gen Z travelers found that "how many TikTok views and likes their holiday videos will likely generate" was the single most influential factor in their destination decisions, coming in at number one for 43 percent of respondents.[30] And if you look at a ranking of the world's most Instagrammed locations, tourist destinations fill the list. Disney-land, the Eiffel Tower, Big Ben, Niagara Falls, Machu Picchu, and Waikīkī all made a recent top twenty.[31]

The idea of seeing a travel destination primarily as a place to lay claim to on our Instagram profiles reminds me of the most important criticism that travel writing has faced over the years: that the genre perpetuates colonial tropes—or worse, that it creates new ones. Because even as social media has exploded the number and diversity of travel writers around the world, it has also prompted many of us to roam the globe looking for people and landscapes that we can exploit for our own personal gain.

The academic Sean Smith of Tilburg University is making a career out of studying this very phenomenon. It's important to understand these dynamics, he says, because Instagram isn't just fun and games: the images that are shared on the app offer us a blueprint of the ideologies that underlie modern tourism. In his work, Smith has documented how many of our Instagram posts perpetuate colonial stereotypes, and he cites a few specific, recurring examples: "the tropical exotic" (for example, Paige standing alone in a Cambodian ruin); "the promontory gaze" (Bieber pondering the Icelandic landscape from the edge of a cliff); and, finally, "fantasized assimilation" (a tourist dons a sari and poses with a group of Indian women to get a shot to show off to her friends).[32] Smith argues that these kinds of recurring visual motifs, full of colonial echoes, portray tourist destinations "as available for possession and consumption." And the making and sharing of these kinds of images—again, and again, and again—perpetuates the sense that wealthy tourists have the right to "consume" a destination in this kind of way. Smith says that, while many of us have become sensitive to the colonial overtones of travel writing from the twentieth century and earlier, we now need to bring the same scrutiny to what we see—and what we produce—on social media. "As a new multimodal form of travel writing," Smith writes, "Instagram offers a largely uncritical space for antiquated notions of travel."

So what's a new tourist to do here? Quit social media—or at least quit posting? Tempting, but I don't think so—at least not necessarily. We can start by questioning the value of what we see on social media, and by being sensitive to meanings and implications that lie below the surface of the images. And when we create a post, we can put something or someone other than ourselves at the center. We can share something that represents the kind of perspective or story that we hope someone else might share about us, or about our own hometown. And we can remind ourselves that we hold a lot of power as "influencers" over the people who follow us, even if they're just our old high school acquaintances and second cousins. Because people are watching what we're doing—and it's shaping how they see the world.

Looking back on my Angkor reel, I can't say I'm proud of it. On reflection, I'm not sure what I was thinking when I posted it. During my trip to Cambodia, I spent hours talking to Bobby—asking him about his family, his childhood memories of his country's war, the training he's been through to become a tour guide, and the challenges he now faces, both at home and on the job. But when I sat down to post about the trip on social media, it didn't even occur to me to try to add any of that depth or nuance to my little seven-second reel. I just wanted to do something quick and fun that would attract plenty of views, and maybe a follower or two. At least at the moment I hit post, that felt like enough.

Chapter Three

Tourism Comes to Power

In March 2004, the journalist and author Thomas Friedman took a Southwest Airlines flight from Baltimore, Maryland, to Hartford, Connecticut, where he was going to visit his college-age daughter. But when Friedman arrived at the airport a full ninety-five minutes before his flight, he was incensed to discover that he'd been put in the "B" boarding group, instead of the coveted "A"—a privilege that he thought his relatively early (remember: this was 2004) arrival time would have guaranteed him. How could so many people have checked in before him? Friedman wondered. But as the plane started to board, he looked around and saw the answer: many of his fellow passengers were clutching crumpled boarding passes that they had downloaded and printed at home—long before they arrived at the airport. Friedman recounted the story in his bestselling book *The World Is Flat*, which was published the following year:

"'Friedman,' I said to myself, looking at this scene, 'you are so twentieth-century.' . . . In Globalization 2.0 the e-ticket machine replaced the ticket agent. In Globalization 3.0 *you* are your own ticket agent."[1]

Friedman used the anecdote, among many others, to illustrate the power and reach of the forces that he saw "flattening the world" at the dawn of the twenty-first century: the end of the Cold War and the domination of free-market capitalism; the creation of a single global market; the spread of internet browsing, workflow software, open-sourcing, outsourcing, and offshoring; the rise of global supply-chaining and logistics management; and the power of services offered by Google, Skype, and—yes—Napster (remember: this was twenty years ago) to transform people's everyday lives.

The analog-to-digital jump and nascent boom of global tourism was both a driver and a consequence of the "flattening" phenomenon of globalization, broadly speaking, that Friedman described in his book, though at that point the real impacts of the shift were only starting to make themselves apparent. But thanks to the flattening forces that Friedman identified, travel in 2004 was cheaper, more accessible, and more autonomous (as he saw himself) than ever before. And because the logistics of travel had become so streamlined, tourism was taking off—enabling a level of personal contact and exchange across cultures and borders that was unprecedented in the history of humanity. At both the individual and societal levels, tourism was flattening our experiences of the world. But in the early years of the new millennium, most serious observers, Friedman included, didn't appear to spend much time considering the global relevance of tourism—his airport anecdote aside. In the original edition of Friedman's nearly five-hundred-page book about what he considered the most important forces shaping the world, the word "tourism" appeared only twice.

The same year that Friedman flew from Baltimore to Hartford, Joseph S. Nye Jr., a former dean of the Kennedy School of Government at Harvard and a former assistant secretary of defense, published a book called *Soft Power: The Means to Success in World Politics*. The book expounded on an idea that Nye had introduced more than a decade earlier—an idea that, at that point, was increasingly being thrown around by politicians and commentators. Soft power, as Nye defined it, described a country's ability to attract and persuade, and was a type of power that he thought should be considered alongside traditional hard power, as exemplified by military force and economic sanctions. "A country may be able to get the outcomes it wants in world politics," Nye explained, "because other countries—admiring its values, emulating its example, aspiring to its level of prosperity and openness—want to follow it."[2]

Under the right conditions, Nye argued, soft power emerges from three sources: a country's culture, its political values, and its foreign policies. In describing the cultural component, Nye talked about the potential significance of university exchanges, traveling theater productions, the music and film industries, and—given his focus on the United States—sports leagues like the NBA and the NFL. "Much of American soft power has been produced by Hollywood, Harvard, Microsoft, and Michael Jordan," he wrote. "But the fact that civil society is the origin of much soft power does not disprove its existence."[3] Nye acknowledged that a nation's culture could be transmitted through "personal contacts" and "visits," but he appeared to give little weight to tourism as a source, let alone a tool, of a nation's power.

But over the course of the next decade—as international tourist arrivals inched up to and beyond the 1 billion mark—tourism as an economic, political, and social force became increasingly difficult to ignore. In her investigation of the world's tourism industry, *Overbooked: The Exploding Business of Travel and Tourism*, published in 2013, the *New York Times* economic journalist Elizabeth Becker offered the first major mainstream work to give global tourism the scrutiny it deserved. But still, she was fighting an uphill battle. Most people "don't think of travel as one of the world's biggest businesses, an often cutthroat, high-risk and high-profit industry," Becker acknowledged in the book's introduction. "Few foreign policy experts, economists or international policy gurus discuss the subject, much less ask whether tourism is enhancing or undermining a distinct regional culture, a fragile environment, an impoverished country," she wrote. But already in 2013, Becker could see that a failure to take tourism seriously could lead to devastating consequences. In a chapter titled "Getting It Wrong," she described how tourism in Cambodia had fueled corruption, land grabbing, child prostitution, and the creation of moneymaking "orphanages" where Western tourists would hang out with children whose relatives had been paid to give them up. But elsewhere in the book, Becker described examples of places where tourism had inspired and funded new urban regeneration projects and national parks. "Like any industry, tourism has winners and losers," Becker wrote, "and keeping it out of the critical discussions about the direction of the economy or international debates about the environment is short-sighted.

"The best and worst of tourism," she concluded, "have governments at the center."[4]

*   *   *

It's a balmy Tuesday evening in June 2023, and the Pier Head in Liverpool is a delightful place for a stroll. The lowering sun is illuminating the gleaming white facades of a pair of stately limestone-clad buildings that face out over the River Mersey. To my right, and toward the water, the bright, modern angles of the Museum of Liverpool strike a sharp contrast to the other buildings' staid baroque fronts. Gulls cry and a warm breeze gusts across the wide, clean plaza, where a street musician is packing up after a long day of playing Beatles covers to passing tourists, who come to snap photos of the life-sized statues of John, Paul, George, and Ringo that forever grace the waterfront. But at this point late in the day, the area around me is full of people who look very much like residents: a couple lounges in the grass, enjoying the shade thrown by a towering statue of King Edward VII; a couple of teenagers practice tricks on their skateboards on the plaza's smooth flagstones; small groups of friends cluster here and there, enjoying little picnics on the eve of the summer solstice.

A voice to my left interrupts my daydreamy people-watching. It's a man's voice and it sounds friendly, but the accent is so different from what I'm used to that at first I struggle to decipher the meaning of the words. I turn to discover a man pointing up at one of the buildings in front of us. He looks roughly retirement age, and he's bald apart from a few short wisps of white hair that cling to his temples. He's telling me the history of one of the buildings, going into some depth on the symbolism of the two towering bird sculptures that stand atop the building's twin clocktowers—mythical Liver Birds that represent the soul of the city, he says.

I listen to his explanation, then thank him and introduce myself. When the man hears my American accent, his eyes light up—which is not a reaction that I've come to expect in this part of the world. My husband and I lived in England for two years about a decade ago, much farther south. I can't remember a single instance from that period of a stranger approaching me on the street to begin a conversation, and I found that my American accent sometimes—though certainly not always—elicited a frosty reception. I've been in Liverpool for under twenty-four hours when this man, who tells me his name is John, offers me a Liverpudlian history lesson that feels equal parts impromptu and heartfelt. This, I think, is a very different type of English city.

John finishes his bit about the building, but I get the sense that he has a whole lot more to tell me—and he looks game for an outing. He wears cargo shorts, Nikes, wraparound sunglasses, and a T-shirt that declares "Liverpool: One Magnificent City"—a souvenir from a culture festival a few years back. He walks with a hint of a limp, but he has the shoulders and forearms of a man with many years of hard labor under his belt. His smile is bright, his eyes mischievous, and his accent strong and Liverpudlian. I tell John it's my first time in Liverpool, and that I'm a journalist who's come to try to understand how tourism has changed the city. John tells me that Liverpool has been home his entire life. "Come on," he says, gesturing for me to walk with him. "I'll tell you anything you need to know."

To a much younger version of John Fitzpatrick, who was born on Valentine's Day in 1959, the scene before us on this warm summer evening would have been unthinkable. When he was growing up, John tells me, all the buildings were jet-black from pollution. The city's docks were still full of ships back then; he learned to swim among them, sometimes climbing up their slick sides or hitching an unofficial ride on the ferry for a day out on the beach. He lived with his parents, seven sisters, and three brothers one road up from the docks, the same shipyards that in the nineteenth century had thrust Liverpool onto the global stage, transforming it into the "second city" of the sprawling British Empire.

But that prestige was long gone by the time John came into the world. The slow demise of the docks that began in the early twentieth century was exacerbated by the intense bombing the city endured during the Second World War, which devastated Liverpool's infrastructure and left more than seventy thousand people homeless. The decades that followed were a bleak period for the city. By the time John was a young man, in the 1980s, many of the factories and docks had closed, and jobs were hard to come by. If young people could leave, they did, he tells me—but many were stuck. John was fortunate enough to find work on an oil rig, and the work suited him, but not everyone was so lucky. In 1981, riots broke out in Liverpool, as anger over unemployment, unfair policing, and racial discrimination came to a violent head, leading to what one British academic has described as "some of the worst scenes of urban disorder in the history of the United Kingdom."[5] John remembers this as a time of intense confusion and anger: a moment of reckoning following decades of poverty and deprivation. An influx of heroin in the mid-eighties earned Liverpool the nickname "Smack City." In 1993, the European Union recognized Liverpool's county of Merseyside as one of the poorest urban areas in Europe.[6]

Back in those days, people from other parts of Britain were too scared to come to Liverpool, John tells me, because they thought they would be robbed or stabbed. So intense was the city's reputation for violence and lawlessness that whenever he traveled outside his home city, people would sneer at his accent and feign fear that he would snatch their bags. When John was a young man, the few tourists who dared to venture to Liverpool were either Beatles fanatics or supporters of one of the area's two Premier League soccer teams. What else was there to attract anyone?

But over the course of the nineties and early 2000s, Liverpool went through a profound transformation. The real changes began with the government-backed Merseyside Development Corporation, which was established in the wake of the riots and which reclaimed nearly a thousand acres of derelict land with the aim of revitalizing them through "mixed use" development. In the MDC's original strategy, 55 percent of the reclaimed land would be set aside for industrial activity, while the rest would be set aside for a mix of residential, commercial, and recreational purposes, or for the use of the port itself.

But new industrial activity failed to materialize in the abandoned docks, and it quickly became clear that the most lucrative types of development were not linked to industry at all, at least not in a traditional understanding of the word—but to tourism.[7] Within a few years of its founding, the MDC launched an international garden festival as well as a tall ships race, which together attracted more than 3 million visitors to the city. A few years later, following the redevelopment of the abandoned Royal Albert Dock, the city saw the opening of the Tate Liverpool, a world-class modern art museum to rival its counterpart on the banks of the Thames in London. In May 1988, a thirty-nine-year-old Prince Charles attended the grand opening of both the renovated Albert Dock and the new museum, for an event that was broadcast live on national television.[8] An in-depth write-up in the *New York Times* noted that visitors to Liverpool's new waterfront museum could admire works by Dalí, Picasso, Miró, and Rothko.[9]

More transformation was still to come, but already, in less than a decade, the Liverpool waterfront had gone from a site of industrial decline to a premier destination for cultural heritage—and the momentum grew from there. A Beatles museum opened in 1990, also on the Albert Dock, followed by a host of new hotels, restaurants, and shops as visitor numbers began to grow. In 2004, the city won a successful campaign to be inscribed on the UNESCO World Heritage List, with the United Nations agency describing the city's historic waterfront as "the supreme example of a commercial port at the time of Britain's greatest global influence."[10]

But perhaps the biggest win for the city came a year earlier, when it was announced that Liverpool had beaten out half a dozen other British cities to be named one of two European Capitals of Culture for 2008. (The BBC noted Liverpool's "unexpected success" in securing the bid.)[11] The designation, announced five years in advance, attracted a lot of media attention—as well as plenty of funding. In anticipation of the event, private investors pooled £1 billion to build Liverpool ONE, an ambitious forty-two-acre pedestrianized urban shopping zone that revitalized the city center, just a short walk from the water. Liverpool ONE opened to the public in 2008—the same year the Capital of Culture events attracted 9.7 million visitors to the city. Beyoncé, Kanye West, and Katy Perry were among the big names who performed in Liverpool that year, alongside local celebrities Paul McCartney and Ringo Starr. The Klimt exhibition at the Tate Liverpool that summer drew 200,000 people in just four months. Another tall ships race saw dozens of vessels from around the world compete in the River Mersey, in full view of the city's revamped waterfront.[12]

All told, the European Capital of Culture ended up generating £750 million for the Liverpool economy; it also gave the city a boost in both local morale and international reputation. A subsequent survey of residents found that 85 percent agreed that the events had made the city a better place to live. Media coverage of Liverpool's cultural attractions doubled in 2008, and for the first time in decades, positive news stories outweighed the negative ones.

Liverpool's fortunes had turned, and tourism was becoming an increasingly important driver of the city's economic engine. Between 2009 and 2017, the value of Liverpool's "visitor economy" rose from £2.7 billion to £4.5 billion, an average growth of more than 6 percent per year. The city's visitor numbers climbed steadily over the same stretch, reaching 38 million on the eve of the pandemic. So cemented was the city's image as a tourist destination that, in 2021, when UNESCO stripped Liverpool of its status as a World Heritage site—on the grounds that urban development had resulted in the "serious deterioration and irreversible loss" of the "outstanding universal value" that had merited the city's inscription—the city's potential future guests didn't even seem to notice.[13] Visitor numbers in 2022 were up 32 percent from the year before as tourism in the city bounced back from the pandemic; the city's economic gains from tourism jumped even higher, up 46 percent from 2021.[14] Liverpool was forging ahead; UNESCO was in the rearview mirror.

And in May 2023, one month before my visit to Liverpool, the city played host to the Eurovision Song Contest, a multiday extravaganza of over-the-top music and partying that attracted half a million people to the city—five times the number of visitors that city leaders had forecast—as well as a global television audience of some 180 million. Liverpool had beaten out nineteen other British cities in vying to host the event, and the editors of the *Guardian*, at least, believed the city was the right choice. "It is true that the city has suffered its share of civic problems over the decades," the editors opined in the run-up to the competition final, but they believed the place had changed for the better. Liverpool is "a vivacious and opinionated city that lives by its own rules," the editors concluded, "but can put on a great show when it wants to."[15]

The world was taking note. The same year John's hometown hosted Eurovision, a global survey of fifteen thousand people placed Liverpool thirty-fourth among one hundred global cities in terms of the strength of its "city brand"—putting the once-infamous "Smack City" ahead of the likes of Dublin, Montreal, Hong Kong, and Oslo in terms of its global reputation. (London, New York, and Paris topped the list.)[16] In the span of John's adult life, tourism in Liverpool had transformed the city's image on the world stage. It had also transformed the city itself.

"You can't stand in the way of change and progress," John says when I ask him how he feels about Liverpool's renaissance. "Tourism has brought really good things to Liverpool. And people here love outsiders."

The same welcoming attitude toward tourists crops up in half a dozen other interviews I do during my visit to Liverpool—with academics, city officials, a social activist, as well as with people who work in tourism locally. This kind of broad-based support for tourism is something I've encountered only occasionally in my work as a journalist, but in Liverpool, it seems widespread.

In John's case, he likes the energy that tourists bring to the city; they also support his income. Because these days, in addition to working as a union leader, he also owns and rents out properties to tourists, and he occasionally works as a tour guide. When he tells me that last detail, it doesn't surprise me at all.

But Liverpool's journey to tourism success wasn't all sunshine and roses. Some residents and leaders were upset over the UNESCO delisting, and there have been many legitimate complaints that the city's development has proceeded either too quickly or with too little oversight. Allegations of corruption and misgovernance—often connected to development contracts—have plagued the city council. In 2020, former mayor Joe Anderson was arrested on suspicion of conspiracy to commit bribery and witness intimidation, and the allegations were linked to building deals in the city. Anderson has denied wrongdoing; as of late 2023, the investigation was ongoing.[17]

And even John isn't a fan of the 52,000-seat soccer stadium that's being built about a mile and a half upriver from the Pier Head, and which was one of the main sources of concern among the UNESCO officials. He doesn't mind the idea of a new stadium, but he says the logistics are impractical—and he doubts whether it will bring the economic uplift that city leaders have promised. But that doesn't change John's opinion that, overall, building in the city with an eye to attracting visitors has done Liverpool a whole lot of good.

Did tourism in Liverpool increase the city's "soft power" in any real sense? Because, sure, a better reputation on the world stage is certainly a nice thing to have—but does that translate into any real change in a city's ability to achieve its objectives, to pursue its interests? In Liverpool's case, the answer is yes. The success of tourism in the city brought the funding as well as the broad-based national and international support that the city needed to develop on its own terms and in line with its own values: of freedom, innovation, and open-mindedness, mixed with a healthy dose of contrarianism. In that sense, tourism both revived Liverpool and empowered the city to rally its allies behind its very own—and very Liverpudlian—vision of the future.

Other cities have experienced similar tourism-induced transformations over the past few decades, though some of these shifts have gone more smoothly than others: Dubai, Doha, Dubrovnik, Reykjavík, Seville, Barcelona (more on that in a moment), and Medellín, Colombia, to name a handful. Two other European Capitals of Culture—Porto, Portugal, and Vilnius, Lithuania—saw similar tourism-induced transformations in the first two decades of this century, although the latter also got a major boost from a titillating, and award-winning, tourism marketing campaign that declared the Lithuanian capital the G-spot of Europe. ("Nobody knows where it is," ran the tagline, "but when you find it—it's amazing.")[18]

But a city is one thing, and a country—the traditional holder of power, both hard and soft—is quite another. Can tourism transform the political fortunes and future of a nation? In one case, at least, it's clear that it has.

*   *   *

In August 2003, a twenty-seven-year-old woman named Eliza Reid, who was born and raised in rural Ontario, moved to Reykjavík with an Icelandic man whom she'd met in graduate school in England. The two had recently become engaged (she proposed), and they were planning to set up a home together in the Icelandic capital so that her fiancé, Guðni, could be close to his young daughter from his first marriage. Eliza was excited for the move, but when she told friends, family, or acquaintances about the country that would be her new home, she found she was often met with puzzled expressions. People would ask if she meant Ireland instead of Iceland. Or they would just draw a blank.

It's easy to see why. Iceland in 2003 hardly registered a blip on the international radar screen. The country's population was under 300,000, meaning the nation was home to about as many people as the American cities of Anchorage, Alaska, or Saint Paul, Minnesota. Iceland had never attacked a foreign country; it didn't (and doesn't) have a standing army. Reykjavík's famous Cold War chess match three decades earlier had long since faded from the public imagination, while the country's GDP in 2003 was less than half the size of the economy of the state of Vermont.[19] Iceland's three largest banks had been deregulated only two years before, so the country's role in the financial world remained small. And tourism was still very much in its early stages, with only a few hundred thousand international visitors that year—a fraction of what the country would attract two decades later.[20] So to an outsider in 2003, it was all too easy to think of Iceland (to the extent that anyone thought of the country at all) as a frozen flyover zone floating somewhere in the North Atlantic. In terms of power on the world stage, whether hard or soft, Iceland in 2003 carried virtually no weight whatsoever.

But that changed with the events recounted in the previous chapter: the collapse of the banks, the eruption of the volcano, the heroic grassroots tourism marketing campaign, the sharp rise in visitor numbers. Eliza Reid, who married Guðni the year after they moved to Reykjavík, was there to witness it all. She watched the growth in tourism first from the sidelines, then increasingly as an active player in the boom. After a stint at a software start-up, she began to work as a freelance writer, pitching articles to Iceland's English-language news outlets and magazines. She was soon hired to edit the in-flight magazine of Icelandair, a job that had her writing and commissioning articles about what visitors could do and experience during their visit to that wild and only semi-frozen corner of the Far North. As the years passed, Eliza got to know her adopted country and became fluent in Icelandic. She and Guðni, who landed a tenure-track job at the University of Iceland, had four children together. Their life was busy, happy, and fairly quiet—until the day in 2016 when Guðni was elected the nation's president.*

By that point, tourism had become a powerful force in Iceland. Nearly 1.8 million foreign visitors came to the country in 2016, a year in which tourism accounted for 8.4 percent of Iceland's GDP and more than a third of its foreign exchange earnings. Tourism also employed about twenty-five thousand people in the country that year, or roughly 14 percent of the Icelandic workforce. By the time Eliza's husband took office, Iceland had already managed to pay off—ahead of schedule—the $2.1 billion loan that the

---

* Eliza Reid recounts her life in Iceland, as well as the stories of many other notable Icelandic women, in her highly readable book, *Secrets of the Sprakkar: Iceland's Extraordinary Women and How They Are Changing the World*, published in 2022. My writing in this section draws from that account, as well as my personal interview with Reid, conducted in April 2023.

International Monetary Fund had given the country at the peak of its economic crisis in 2008. Iceland's ability to repay its enormous debt, as Eliza would later write, was "aided in no small part" by the country's "dramatic increase in tourism."[21]

And so, within a few months of her fortieth birthday, Eliza quit her job managing the in-flight magazine of Icelandair and became the first lady of her adopted country, at a moment when it appeared that tourism was coming to the nation's rescue.

I interviewed Eliza, or perhaps I should now call her Ms. Reid, on the same trip to Iceland that brought me to the Justin Bieber canyon. I sat down with her inside the presidential residence, a stark-white building that sits on a bare, blustery point overlooking the water, a short drive from Reykjavík. The building's somber exterior befits the harsh natural beauty of its surroundings, but the interior of the residence is warm and wood-lined. In the hour or so we had together in a cozy corner of a library, Reid and I talked about the growth in tourism and how it has shaped the country. She told me a story of how, a year after her husband was elected, they walked together down a busy Reykjavík street and the country's president went virtually unrecognized—because almost everyone around them was a tourist. She told me about fun things for visitors to do in Iceland, and about how she has embodied the status that tourism has given her adopted country on the world stage.

In 2017, Reid was named a United Nations special ambassador for tourism and the sustainable development goals, a role that had her both representing her nation and promoting tourism as a force for good in venues around the world. In accepting the honor, she stressed tourism's links to the political sphere, noting her "belief in the power of sustainable tourism to help reduce inequality and increase tolerance" as well as the "strong, positive correlation" between tourism and peace.[22] And two years later, she took on a role with a public-private organization whose purpose was to promote Iceland as a welcome place for foreign investment—including through tourism. "I will be a kind of spokesperson, you could say, for Iceland generally, but for tourism, innovation, and equal rights in the country, as well," she said at the time.[23]

Officially speaking, my interview with Iceland's first lady was both for this book and for the *New York Times*, where my editors on the Travel desk were interested in publishing a Q&A with her. When I filed the piece to my editors, I hoped the paper's readers would be as interested as I was in learning about the experiences of the spouse of the head of state of a small and remote Nordic country. But I'll admit that I worried the piece might not find an audience. As a journalist, I've come to expect some of my stories to sink like a stone, barely making a ripple on the water surface, while others will get caught up in some sort of an invisible tsunami and travel around the world and back to me, with the wave arriving in my inbox in the form of a flood of reader emails (some more polite than others). I've found that I'm lousy at predicting which articles will sink and which will soar. But my fears in the case of the Icelandic first lady were very much misplaced. Within a few days of the article going online—under the headline "Iceland Is a Magnet for Tourists. Its First Lady Has Some Advice for Them"—the story climbed to the top of the *New York Times*'s most-emailed list. More than four hundred people added their comments to the piece. And my inbox was very full indeed. [24]

Would an interview with the first lady of another Nordic country—say Finland or Sweden—have garnered as much interest?

I doubt it. Nearly half a million Americans visited Iceland in 2022, the year before that Q&A was published, making the United States the single biggest source of the country's overseas visitors. Many of the readers of the *New York Times* had heard of Iceland; more than that, they were probably fascinated by it—and maybe even planning a visit themselves. A level of interest that emerged from the country's status as a tourist destination fed readers' appetites for a conversation with one of Iceland's most important political figureheads. If that's not soft power, then I don't know what is. Reid confirmed this when I asked her how tourism had shaped her country's image overseas. "The biggest answer is that the outside world sees Iceland," she said. "In our case, it was less that we had a negative image that had to become more positive; we just *created an image.*"

Egill Bjarnason, an Icelandic journalist and author of *How Iceland Changed the World*, told me he has experienced a similar phenomenon.[25] In 2016, when he moved back to Iceland after a stint in the United States, there had never really been a foreign correspondent based in his home country—but he found a strong appetite for stories about Iceland among editors at outlets like the Associated Press, Al Jazeera, and (again) the *New York Times*.

"I found that editors and readers were interested in stories about innovative policy work in Iceland," he said—which surprised him. He wrote a story for the *New York Times* about how the country was managing an invasive plant; another story about the country's policies on gender equity in pay. "In some cases, Iceland was not the inventor of these policies, but they were pushing for it and it was progressive. And it really fit the image of Iceland," he said, adding that ten years earlier, no editor would have considered commissioning a policy-focused story from his native country. But tourism—and to some extent the country's remarkable comeback from its banking crisis—were essential to fueling interest in those kinds of pieces, Bjarnason added. "Those things combined have given us an authority that Iceland has never enjoyed in the past," he said.

Iceland's goals in the international arena, Bjarnason told me, relate to persuading other countries to adopt Iceland's values—of acceptance, equality, and environmental sustainability. He also said that Icelanders, who like to say they suffer from "small nation complex," might be gratified by the attention itself. To the extent that tourism has drawn people to the country—whether by compelling them to board a plane, or just to click on a link to an article about an Icelandic social policy—it has magnified the country's influence and attractiveness on the world stage, creating a degree of soft power where none used to exist.

Iceland still has no military. Its economy, though fully recovered from its crisis, remains smaller than the economy of Vermont. But in September 2019, Mike Pence became the first sitting U.S. vice president to visit Iceland since George H. W. Bush stopped by in 1983. (Bjarnason reported for the Associated Press that Pence's heavily armed security detail "set eyes popping" in the country, where Eliza's husband, Guðni, the nation's president, "travels unaccompanied on private errands and is often spotted in a geothermal bath popular with locals.")[26] And in 2023, just a month after I sat down with Reid, the country hosted dozens of European heads of state and government at a summit of the Council of Europe, where the leaders came to rally political and legal support for Ukraine. The meeting marked the council's first summit in eighteen years, and only the fourth such summit since the organization's founding in 1949. And it happened right there in Reykjavík.

As in Liverpool, tourism in Iceland transformed the fortunes of the place, offering it a financial lifeline at a moment of economic desperation. But instead of transforming the country's image, as tourism has done to Liverpool, tourism in Iceland created an image from scratch—aided in large part by the Inspired by Iceland campaign described in chapter 2. Had tourism not come along to throw a positive spotlight on the country, it probably would have faded back into the nether regions of global consciousness as soon as the banking headlines had died down and the volcanic ash cleared. But the country's success in tourism demanded otherwise.

*　　　*　　　*

The idea that tourism can transform a national image and revive a national economy isn't a new one, although the global rise in tourism over the past few decades has certainly provided more fuel for that particular fire. But as far back as the 1950s, the Spanish dictator Francisco Franco turned to tourism to bolster the flagging national economy and improve Spain's image overseas—and by most accounts, his attempt was a success. Its traces can still be seen today in the centrality of flamenco dancing to Spanish tourism. Because it was Franco who promoted flamenco as the image of Spain overseas, even as his fascist regime suppressed other forms of dance within the country. "The Spanish government was now trying to establish itself as an ally to the United States," the academic Eva Moreda Rodríguez has written of Spain under

Franco in the 1950s. "Flamenco became the symbol of an exotic but appealing Spain, a country that still clung to the old ways in many respects ... but was at the same time not excessively threatening, willing to embrace some of the perks of Western modernity."[27] The Franco regime also used the dance to force a sense of collective identity across Spain: in promoting flamenco, they effectively obliterated regional differences in culture and music.[28]

We can see other examples of the links between tourism, national image, and economic growth in a nation like Costa Rica, whose global reputation as an environmental leader is closely tied to its fame as a destination for ecotourism. Countries like Rwanda, Croatia, and to some extent Colombia have successfully used tourism marketing to revitalize their economies in the wake of headline-grabbing violent conflict; their reputations on the world stage have also enjoyed a boost. In his analysis of India's multiyear "Incredible India" marketing campaign, the academic David Geary argues that the country's tourism marketing is a means of "relandscaping an image of the country as a rising world power." To that extent, India's tourism marketers are both "cultural brokers" and "political brokers who have a direct influence on the way India is positioned and imagined within the global economic and political system."[29]

The perceptions we gain as tourists, or even just as consumers of tourism marketing, help to determine where we're inclined to spend our tourist dollars in the future—as well as which cities or countries we're inclined to regard with empathy. Jose Torres, the founder of Bloom Consulting and one of the world's top experts on "nation branding," told me in an interview that it was in the early 2000s—right around when Thomas Friedman took his flight to Hartford—that governments started to pay more attention to their global reputations and how those reputations were linked to tourism.[30] So many more people were traveling at that point, Torres explained, thanks to the forces that Friedman described. And governments began to realize that they would need to be competitive if they wanted a piece of the fast-growing tourism pie. It was also becoming increasingly clear that, if you wanted someone to like your country, one of the most important things you could do was to encourage them to come and see it for themselves.

"The minute you put your feet on the ground, you land in the place, your perception starts changing for the better—in ninety percent of cases," Torres said. "You land in Riyadh, or you land in Islamabad—it doesn't matter. Your perception will improve immediately."

Image. Influence. Income. All of these are intricately linked to the power that can come with success in what many governments call "the visitor economy." When tourism really gets going in a place, its power reveals itself most obviously, and most immediately, in the form of the money it brings in. Who manages that power, and who imposes regulations on it (or fails to) has profound implications for the ultimate impacts that tourism will have on the place itself, not to mention its residents. There are any number of ways to do this. In France—which receives more foreign tourists than any other nation in the world—the power of tourism is baked into the structure of the state, with the decision-making power over tourism matching the government hierarchy (federal, departmental, municipal) that touches almost every other aspect of life in the country. And at each level, government employees are setting and enforcing the rules, and managing the budgets.

But in other places, the private sector has more sway. As tourism grows in size and influence, it can give powerful positions to people whose primary interest is not the public interest but their own bottom line.

*   *   *

The Hawai'i Convention Center is a glass-encased hulk of a building that occupies nearly half a city block in Honolulu, just over the canal from Waikīkī. A few minutes before nine thirty on a Thursday morning in July, I step into the building's airy atrium, then take an elevator up to Executive Boardroom A, a large, plush meeting space that sits above the offices of the Hawai'i Tourism Authority. The room is already full when I walk in: every one of its leather swivel chairs is occupied, and then some. I do a quick pass of the generous catering spread at the back of the room, then find a seat in one of the straight-backed chairs along the wall.

I catch the eye of John De Fries, who is sitting at the head of the varnished boardroom table. Nearly two years earlier, at the height of the pandemic, John made history when he became the first Native Hawaiian to be appointed to head the Hawai'i Tourism Authority, or HTA, the state's lead agency for tourism. I first met John in this very room a couple of weeks earlier, when we sat down for what turned out to be a nearly three-hour interview that covered his childhood in Waikīkī in the 1950s, his vision for tourism in the state, and his deeply spiritual beliefs about values like sustainability and community. John was the one who invited me to the meeting today, which is the HTA's monthly board meeting; now he's up at the head of the table, running the show.

I scan my briefing pack and note that there are a lot of big industry players in attendance. Among others seated at the table, we have the general manager of Disney's $800 million Aulani Resort, the president of the Hawai'i Chamber of Commerce, the former president of the largest hotel group in the state, and an executive from one of Hawai'i's major restaurant chains. Many of these are successful people who have made money, often big money, through Hawai'i's visitor economy. As members of the board of HTA, they are also in many ways the authorities to whom John, a high-ranking government employee, must answer at the end of the day. This setup strikes me as strange right off the bat, but I vow to keep my mind as open as possible as I listen in on their conversations. A few minutes after he opens the meeting, John introduces the visiting journalist sitting in the corner. A roomful of faces turns to me and smiles.

It's the summer of 2022, and Hawai'i's tourism industry is in a deep state of flux. Three years earlier, on the eve of the pandemic, a record-breaking 10.4 million tourists came to the state.[31] The same year, resident sentiment toward tourism hit a new low, with only 58 percent of respondents agreeing with the statement that tourism had "brought more benefits than problems," down from 80 percent in 2010.[32] Local support for tourism fell even further with the pandemic: instead of pining after the lost income from all those absent tourists, people in Hawai'i seemed to realize just how much they had been sacrificing for tourists for so long. When visitors returned in 2021, only 36 percent of respondents said that tourism was "mostly positive" for their families, down a full twenty percentage points from two decades before.[33]

While community support for tourism was down, there was also a quiet battle raging among the industry's leaders: since the very beginnings of Hawai'i's tourism industry—dating back to the turn of the twentieth century—an organization that's now known as the Hawai'i Visitors & Convention Bureau (HVCB) had been the government-sanctioned steward of Hawai'i's brand. But about a month before I arrived in Hawai'i, John's organization, HTA, made an about-face: instead of awarding HVCB the next multimillion-dollar contract to market Hawai'i to the world, it gave the contract to the Council for Native Hawaiian Advancement, a nonprofit group with little to no tourism marketing experience. Three weeks before I arrived, HVCB filed a protest, claiming that the contract—which is worth about $100 million over several years—had been unfairly awarded. As of my arrival, that protest was pending.[34]

It might seem like a boring procurement question, but that contract dispute gets to the heart of one of the trickiest questions in Hawai'i tourism today: Who is telling the story—more precisely, who is *selling* the story—of Hawai'i to tourists and potential tourists? Is it a hundred-year-old firm with a Caucasian man at its head, or an Indigenous nonprofit led by a charismatic young Native Hawaiian named after a Hawaiian prince? John declines to comment on the ongoing dispute, but it's clear he believes that tourism in Hawai'i is in a moment of deep transition—quite apart from the question of the contract. In our first conversation, he was eager to tell me about Hawai'i's new "Destination Management Action Plans," an approach that aims to give residents more say in how tourism is run. And he spent a long time talking about *huliau*, a Hawaiian word that means "deep change" or "transformation." For John, a recent sequence of extraordinary events—geological phenomena, astronomical sightings, geopolitical achievements, cultural breakthroughs—have all been pointing to the same thing:

"For about the last five years, I've been having this gut experience, this feeling that we are inside this phase of *huliau*, and this is even before the pandemic," John told me in that first interview. "I don't expect everybody to understand this, but for me, these things are connected. I'm sensing that we're inside this space. And so you've got to pay attention. You've got to be alert."

*   *   *

Born in Waikīkī in 1951, John spent his early childhood in a modest family home just a mile and a half from Executive Boardroom A. In the year John was born, about fifty-one thousand tourists came to Hawai'i, and Waikīkī had about a dozen hotels, none taller than the six-story, bubble-gum-pink Royal Hawaiian, which was built in the 1920s.[35] Hawaiian statehood, which came just a few weeks after John's eighth birthday, marked the beginning of Hawai'i's tourist boom: that year, Pan Am launched a regular jet service from the U.S. mainland, and other airlines soon followed suit. Momentum grew in the 1960s as flight prices plummeted and the government-backed Hawai'i Visitors Bureau sent Hawaiian entertainers and promoters around the world to lure tourists to the new state.[36] The hula girl—an exotic yet (now) American young woman who was at once sexualized and family friendly—became entrenched in Hawai'i's tourism iconography from the very beginning. In many ways she was essential to the state's pitch as a tourist destination: the image of a unique, attractive, and welcoming native people set Hawai'i apart from the tropical beaches with which the state was competing for tourists. There were things that you, the visitor, could see and do in Hawai'i—eat at a lū'au, watch a hula show, get a taste of the aloha spirit—that you could see and do nowhere else in the world, or so went the marketing pitch. Hawai'i's tourism operators have long been aware of the advantage that the state's native community affords them; they continue to exploit this asset as best they can.[37]

By the time John turned thirty, in 1981, Hawai'i's annual visitor numbers had mushroomed to nearly 4 million, and a parade of high-rise hotels had been built along the Waikīkī coast, including on John's old street, Cartwright Road, where a multistory Hyatt now towered over the place where his family used to roast meat in their traditional *imu*, or underground oven. By that point, tourism had already become the state's economic powerhouse, beating out Hawai'i's next three biggest industries: the military, sugar production, and pineapple production. By the time John hit his sixtieth birthday, Hawai'i was starting to show some of the classic signs of a "mature" tourist destination: the state was spending tens of millions of dollars every year to market itself to the world; visitor numbers had plateaued (though this ended up being temporary); and some measures of resident support for the industry had begun to decline. The record-breaking visitor numbers in 2019—followed by the pandemic-induced collapse in tourism the following year, and the rise in local antipathy to the visitor industry—marked the beginnings of a new, unknown phase for tourism in Hawai'i. John's appointment to head the HTA in September 2020, when the state's biggest industry was in free fall, seemed emblematic: in a moment of extreme crisis for tourism, a white-haired, sixty-nine-year-old Native Hawaiian was taking the reins.

There's a concept in tourism management called Butler's Tourism Area Life Cycle Model.[38] It's the brainchild of the Scottish academic Richard Butler, who first described the idea in a paper published in 1980. The idea is that tourist destinations follow a typical cycle over time, and it goes something like this: First, the place attracts only a small number of visitors and has no dedicated tourist infrastructure; in this "exploration" phase, residents barely register tourists' presence. Then, in the "involvement phase," visitor numbers rise and a tourist "season" emerges; residents take enough notice of tourists to start selling them goods and services. By the time a destination reaches the "development stage," local authorities and businesses are spending a significant amount of money to advertise the place to a well-defined tourist market. At the same time, tourism is leaving a visible trace on the destination, and the government is probably getting involved in managing things. Next comes the "consolidation stage," when visitor numbers may start to plateau. By now, tourism has become a major part of the place's economy, but residents—particularly those who don't work in tourism—are increasingly unhappy with the industry's impact. This leads the destination into the "stagnation stage," when the place "will have a well-established image but it will no longer be in fashion." At this point, the destination is at or over its carrying capacity on a number of fronts, and it suffers environmental, social, and economic problems as a result.

In Butler's model, it's the reaching of the limit set by these carrying capacities—for natural resources like land and water, as well for social goods like public transportation, accommodation, and community support—that ultimately drives the destination into one of two final stages. Either it goes into decline or the place pivots hard and experiences a complete rejuvenation (think: a nineteenth-century European spa town becomes a twenty-first-century hiking destination). From there, presumably, the cycle starts again.

Back in Executive Boardroom A, we're about an hour into what ends up being a more than four-hour meeting, when the mood turns somber. A tourism consultant is joining via Zoom, and he has some disquieting results to share: a recent statewide survey has revealed that Hawai'i is below the tourism industry average on every single one of the twelve indicators that the consulting company uses to measure a quality they call "destination alignment," which is meant to assess how well public, private, and civic interests align with the local tourism industry. Not only is Hawai'i below average on this front, but its scores on all nine of the indicators that were measured in 2019—which include things like workforce development, regional cooperation, and community group and resident support—have dropped by 2022. Among the nearly fifteen hundred people surveyed across Hawai'i, community leaders and young adults gave the tourism industry the lowest ratings. An hour or so later, HTA's director of tourism research presents the most recent visitor statistics, which have just been released that morning: during the previous month, June 2022, visitor numbers were down more than 4 percent compared to June 2019. Here on the island of O'ahu, home of Honolulu and Waikīkī, tourist numbers plummeted 22 percent from three years before. But the visitors who did come stayed longer and spent more money.

Watching the presentation from my corner of the room, I wonder if this might be a sign that Hawai'i has finally reached the beginning of Butler's stagnation phase. And this doesn't strike me as a bad thing. Fewer people spending more money: What's not to like? But that sentiment doesn't seem to be shared by everyone in the leather swivel chairs. After the presentation is finished, a hotelier member of the board switches on his long-stemmed mic to share some information he's been getting from his wholesalers. They're reporting that next year's bookings to Mexico and Europe—Hawai'i's competitors—are up well over 100 percent compared to 2019, while Hawai'i is down 20 to 25 percent over the same period.

"It's always a game of Chicken Little, right?" the board member says, referencing the fable in which an anxious fowl convinces her friends that the end of the world is nigh. "How do you complain when you have fewer visitors spending a heck of a lot more—but generally solid visitor levels? I would guess that the declines we're starting to see now are going to accelerate.... So I think this board is going to spend a lot of its time thinking about how you manage inbound visitors when, by next month or two months from now, I suspect all of the inbound metrics are going to be down and pointing further down as we go into 2023."

Another hotelier chimes in:

"Focusing on generating a lot of business from high-paying travelers is a nice goal. *We're kind of there.* But when you get high, you can just fall farther.... So, I share the concern that we've got a challenging year coming up. I think we're all doing quite well financially now, but we have to be concerned about where we're going as other destinations open up."

I look at John, who is following the conversation with an even gaze from the head of the table, and I remember an analogy he shared with me in our first interview.

"If you have a hundred-room hotel and it's full, when the hundred-and-first guest comes in, you don't say, 'Oh, you can sleep in my lobby,' right?" John told me. "My hotel has a carrying capacity that I have to obey. The industry has to understand that the natural world has a capacity. We've lost sight of that. More, more, more; consume, consume, consume. That way of thinking is what we have to change."

The meeting finishes, and I step back out into the airy atrium of the Hawai'i Convention Center. I'm due to have a phone interview, and I have to find a place to take the call. But I need a moment to collect my thoughts, because my head is aching after all I've heard. I see that John is working hard to put things right. But I see the push and pull that's going on around him—and above him—and I can sense the many layers behind it, not least the tension over Native Hawaiian control of the narrative.

But my phone interview is coming at the right moment. It's with Frank Haas, who's been around. Haas is a former vice president and marketing director of the HTA, and a former assistant dean of the University of Hawai'i School of Travel Industry Management. Haas was part of the team that developed Hawai'i's strategic plan for tourism from 2005 to 2015—which had ambitious aims to transform tourism for the better. But he tells me that plan was never fully implemented, and that a lot of the barriers were structural.

"The problem is that the Hawai'i Tourism Authority as an organization does not really have authority over things like the natural environment; that's a separate state department. Same with workforce training; that's the Department of Labor and Industrial Relations. Same with Hawaiian culture; that's the Office of Hawaiian Affairs. So even though there were very good intentions of that plan, it never really got fully implemented." Haas is offering me a condensed version of an argument he made alongside two colleagues in 2019, when he wrote that, two decades after its founding, the HTA "has neither been given the authority nor the resources" it needs to effectively manage the complexities of tourism in the state.[39]

But Haas adds that some positive changes have been made in the last few years, and he praises John De Fries, the new resident-led action plans he's promoting, and the way that HTA under his leadership is rallying other parts of the government in support of its cause. But many of those structural problems remain. "Honestly, HTA still doesn't have the authority to actually do a lot of this stuff," Haas says. "They really have to rely on their bully pulpit and coordinating with other agencies."

I tell Haas about the meeting I've just walked out of, and how I was struck by the different perspectives in the room—even on the fundamental question of whether Hawai'i can sustain as many tourists as it's had in the past.

"People can argue about the big number, but it's a fruitless argument," he tells me. "We have built the infrastructure to host a lot of tourists, and the people who own that infrastructure are going to fill those rooms."

Chapter Four

Tourists, Go Home

When Mar Santamaría Varas was growing up in Barcelona in the 1980s, she didn't spend sunny days at the local beach, because it didn't exist. The city's coastline was industrial: any views of the Mediterranean were blocked by a high concrete wall. But that, and so much else, changed when the city hosted the Olympics in the summer of 1992. As Barcelona prepared for the limelight, the city's leaders spent hundreds of millions of dollars cleaning up old neighborhoods and creating vibrant public spaces—a botanic garden, a center for contemporary art, and a two-mile-long beachfront made of sand shipped in from Egypt. They invited international hotel chains to set up shop in the city, despite the protests of local hotel owners; they built public transportation networks and constructed ring roads to reduce congestion; and they made major investments in the long-overlooked Montjuïc area on the city's outskirts, which they chose as the site of the city's new Olympic Stadium. All the changes went hand in hand with local leaders' desire to move the city away from industrial activity, which had dominated Barcelona's economy for two centuries, and toward a future in which services—and tourism—would reign.[1]

Mar was twelve years old in 1992, and what sticks out most in her memory of that time is a powerful sense of excitement and movement in her home city. The Olympics came and went, but Barcelona's changes were just beginning. The city's sixteen days in the global spotlight in the summer of 1992 fixed it firmly on Europe's tourist map, and city leaders did all they could to keep it there. The following year, they established Turisme de Barcelona, whose mandate was the "intense, efficient and professional" promotion of "Destination Barcelona." The new agency—which was financed by a mix of public and private funds, and whose board was chaired by the mayor—was the first of its kind in Spain, and it went about its work with surprising effectiveness. Officials at the agency grouped the region's attractions into discrete "tourism areas"—sea and sand, food and drink, inland landscapes, and the like—which they then packaged and marketed to different segments of potential future visitors in Europe and beyond.[2]

The city's tourism push aligned with a rapid rise in global mobility, and the effects were profound: visitor numbers to the city climbed steadily, as did tourism's share of Barcelona's economy. In 2019, a year in which the population of Barcelona's urban area checked in at roughly 5.5 million, the city saw nearly 30 million overnight stays in hotels, hostels, tourist apartments, and other visitor accommodations; that's a far cry from the 3.8 million overnight hotel stays the city registered in 1990. By the eve of the pandemic, tourism had come to account for 14 percent of the city's GDP and 9 percent of total employment.[3]

But as tourist numbers grew, so too did the sense among many in Barcelona that the city was nearing its capacity for visitors. The annoyances started to mount: drunken partying in the streets at all hours of the night; noisy strangers coming and going; heavy crowds for residents to navigate; rising rents; and the eruption of a plethora of low-quality tourist shops in the historic center, often at the expense of businesses that had long served residents. For many Barcelonans the city seemed to be slipping away. In the summer of 2014, anti-tourism protests erupted in the beachfront Barceloneta neighborhood, where locals were fed up with the noise and raucous behavior of visitors who'd come there to party. Anti-tourism graffiti sprouted up around the city, with tags like TOURISTS GO HOME and YOUR LUXURY TRIP/MY DAILY MISERY. In 2017, a group of masked, left-wing activists surrounded an open-top bus filled with tourists, slashed the tires, and spray-painted "Tourism kills neighborhoods" in Catalan across the windshield.[4]

For Mar, the turning point came in 2013, when she moved with her husband from the outskirts of Barcelona back into the center, where she'd lived as a girl. It felt nothing like the city she knew. Greengrocers, tailors, newsagents, and butchers had been replaced by cocktail bars, souvenir shops, and brunch places that advertised Bloody Marys and eggs Benedict on glossy menus written only in English. The squares and sidewalks were so full of people that she learned to avoid some places entirely at certain times of the year. But the worst part for Mar was that the city center had become financially out of reach for many of her peers. Old friends and former classmates had moved out of Barcelona to more affordable places in the distant suburbs. And plenty of people were forced from their homes: for a while before the pandemic, she said, the newspapers were full of stories about the latest wave of evictions.

"It's sad to say, 'My city is not providing what I need'—which is a house, and a good environment where I can go buy my groceries and just lead a normal life," Mar told me. "But at the same time that we were transforming parts of the city for the better, we were also pushing out the poorest people who were living there."

*　　*　　*

It's a clear and breezy early evening in mid-August, and Mar—a fine-boned woman wearing delicate gold jewelry and her dark hair loose around her shoulders—is standing in the shadow of a medieval cathedral and rolling her eyes at her six-year-old son, Max. The boy has just bolted across the square in front of us to join a crowd lingering outside a shop selling rows and rows of colorful dolls. "Children love these things," Mar says with a laugh and a shake of her head. Her husband, Pablo Martínez, jogs across the square to lure Max back.

Upon closer inspection, the objects of his fascination are not exactly dolls, but *caganers*, traditional figurines of a man popping a squat, with the resulting excrement piled in a tidy swirl on the ground beneath him. The classic version of the defecating figure, an everyman in a white shirt and a traditional Catalan red hat, has been an off-color feature of Nativity scenes in Barcelona's region of Catalonia for hundreds of years. But local retailers have riffed on the theme, and tourists snap up their offerings. The shop whose window Max is now admiring offers modern versions of the bare-bottomed figure (Donald Trump, the pope, Hermione

Granger) that would never appear in a classic manger scene. Mar calls it "a fake shop."

We're about twenty minutes into a walking tour that will take us through the heart of Barcelona—from the edge of the Parc de la Ciutadella through the trendy El Born neighborhood, the historic Ciutat Vella, the gritty Raval quarter, and finally to the up-and-coming Sant Antoni neighborhood. The distance is only about a mile and a half as the crow flies, but with all the twists and turns and different urban landscapes we encounter, it feels like we cover at least twice that distance. And Mar and her husband make for excellent guides: both are architects who have lived in the city nearly their entire lives; in 2014, they cofounded an urban planning agency that's bringing a powerful new tool to discussions about Barcelona's future: big data. Through hi-tech cartography, data visualization, and analysis, Mar and Pablo are diagnosing complex urban problems, and proposing solutions that are grounded in numbers. The couple has consulted in cities across Europe, but their passion lies in their home of Barcelona and its biggest challenge of the moment: making sure the city can once again be a good home to its residents.

From what Mar tells me, there aren't many residents to see here in the Plaça de Santa María, where Max is safely back with his parents. We stand and watch for a few minutes as dozens of people amble around the small square gazing up at the church steeple behind us, their backpacks strapped across their chests, their phone cameras aimed at the same Insta-worthy stonework on the church's exterior. I scan the businesses that are open and note two midrange-looking restaurants filled with diners browsing laminated English menus. I see a take-out coffee place (still rare in Spain, where locals tend to drink single-shot espressos in thimble-sized cups) advertising breakfast smoothies and iced banana lattes, and a hole-in-the-wall eatery offering a 15 percent discount on poke bowls. And, of course, there's the *caganers* shop.

"If you look at photos from ten years ago, this was a really nice street with well-curated shops, but now you can't even buy an apple," Mar says. "And I can guarantee you that none of those people are from Barcelona." She raises her dark eyebrows at the diners hunched over heaping plates of food at their tables in the middle of the square. It's about 6:30 p.m.—nowhere near mealtime for a local.

Our tour continues from here. Mar and Pablo are warm and enthusiastic, and they exude a kind of heartfelt devotion to their city that reminds me of a pair of adult children caring for a frail and aging parent. Every so often, on not-too-crowded streets, Mar pulls an iPad out of her canvas tote to show me the bright, detailed maps, charts, and graphs that she and Pablo have created to bring some visual order to the chaotic evolution that they've watched unfold. The images show that tourist accommodation used to be concentrated in just a handful of areas; now it's just about everywhere. They show that rents have risen in the areas with the highest concentrations of short-term tourist apartments. And they show those places in the city—along the Passeig de Gràcia, in the area around the Sagrada Família—where tourists and residents are most fiercely competing for the use of public space.

We move on from the Plaça de Santa María, and Mar and Pablo lead me down a narrow alleyway to a small, shady square that has a primary school at one end. There are no children there on this summer evening, but they tell me that during the school year, authorities had to set up barriers to prevent tourists from wandering into the children's playground.

"There are a lot of angry people," Mar says, and she describes complaints they've heard from residents about how their daily lives have been disrupted by the presence of tourists. Mar and Pablo sat in on one community association in which the leader said that it felt as though her city were being treated like an open bar.

We're still about a hundred yards away from La Rambla when they warn me to watch my bag. I tighten the straps, but Pablo says that's not enough. "Hold it tight, and on your front." I do as I'm told. Perhaps Barcelona's most famous street, La Rambla—a broad, shady boulevard on the edge of the Ciutat Vella—has long been at the top of many a tourist's bucket list. I know, because when I first came to Barcelona as a backpacking, Eurail-riding American eighteen-year-old, I made a beeline for what I believed was one of Europe's most iconic streets. I remember gawking at the fragrant and overflowing flower shops, taking photos of the kiosks selling exotic-looking birds, and encountering one of the first human statues I'd ever seen: a man who appeared to be encased entirely in gold. Now, twenty-one years later, I see that the street's tall, shade-giving trees have survived, but the shops below them have for the most part either disappeared or been transformed into bland-looking stalls selling postcards, magnets, key chains, phone cases, and other cheap tourist trinkets that you might find on any street corner anywhere in the world. There are a handful of flower sellers, but I see no creative performers, no brightly colored birds peering out of Victorian-era birdcages. There are just hordes of people walking up and down, walking nowhere, walking fast—and often jostling me as I trail behind Mar, who is gripping Max's hand. I hold my bag tight to my chest, and I wonder how a place can at once feel so crowded—and so vacant.

Our tour ends in the Sant Antoni neighborhood, a quiet, leafy quarter that lies apart from the city center, near the foot of Montjuïc. "This is one of the areas that worries us a lot," Mar says, and she points out the signs of gentrification that are creeping in: formerly "normal streets" are now filled with restaurants, large terraces, and broad pedestrian zones lined with enormous potted plants. The scene strikes me as pleasant and inviting, but there is a lot going on here that this outsider doesn't see. The neighborhood is home to a lot of older people, Mar tells me, including her aunt, who has lived in the same apartment for almost eighteen years. When those elderly tenants die, their apartments will sell for a very high price—and the fabric of the neighborhood will shift.

"All of this will bring the Airbnbs," Mar says of the recent changes, and her husband offers a little shrug of agreement. Perhaps by the time their young son is a teenager, this neighborhood that Mar has known her whole life will become yet another part of the city that she no longer recognizes.

*   *   *

If we think back to Butler's cycle, and the movement from tourism's beginnings in a place through the phases of growth, plateau, and decline, it's clear that governments exert important influence here, in a couple of ways. First, demand: What is the government doing, and how much is it spending, to increase the place's visitor numbers, and to shift its visitor profile from the adventuring type who tends to show up early in the cycle to the mass-market package tourists who dominate its later stages? In Barcelona, local leaders in the 1990s made explicit and sustained efforts to transform their overlooked city into an unmissable stop on any visitor's tour of Europe. There was no guarantee that their efforts would bear any fruit: plenty of governments pour money into tourism marketing campaigns and end up with little to show for it. But local leaders in Barcelona suffered no such fate. Their efforts were so successful that they ended up triggering a tsunami of popularity that ultimately attracted more tourists than local leaders probably had ever imagined. But the impetus began with them. From that perspective, it seems perverse to follow the lead of many media outlets in either overtly or implicitly blaming tourists for choosing to visit such a destination. Even as support for tourism among Barcelona residents began to ebb, the many tens of millions of tourists who visited the city between 1992 and the mid-2010s were all doing precisely what the local government was asking of them.

Butler's model also takes for granted the notion that, as a tourist destination becomes more popular, quality of life for residents will inevitably suffer. But that doesn't have to be the case: so much depends on the government's inclination and ability to set up the physical and institutional structures that are required to manage all the visitors that it's working so hard to attract. As a government spends its resources on promotion, it must also invest in building the infrastructure to manage the new influx of tourists; in creating regulatory frameworks to structure tourist activity; and in imposing taxes and financial incentives to make sure that most of the income from tourism ends up going back into the pockets of people who live in the local community.

This might seem like an obvious point, but too many governments seem to be caught behind the curve here, waking up late to the need to regulate. Justin Francis, the cofounder and CEO of a British tour company called Responsible Travel, and an advisor to the British government on sustainable business, captured it perfectly in an interview he gave to a journalist from the *Guardian* in the summer of 2018, at a moment when headlines on both sides of the Atlantic were full of stories of "overtourism."

"Broadly speaking, tourism globally has been unmanaged and never been taken seriously by government," Francis said. "It's fun, everybody's happy, right? But really, tourism is one of the biggest and in some cases most aggressive industries on Earth and it is taking governments a very long time to recognize that it needs managing."[5]

*   *   *

Almost a year to the day after my walking tour of Barcelona, I'm cruising down a wide canal in a low-slung motorboat called a shikara. I'm in Kerala, a state in south India that's known for its backwater lagoons, fiery cuisine, and tranquil, sandy beaches that stretch for miles. My tour guide, Sabu Mamparambil Purushothaman, is a fifty-something man with short-cropped hair and a thick black mustache. He stands watch at the front of the boat while Suresh Attuchira Sugunan, the soft-spoken driver, is quick to smile from his perch at the back. Both men wear polo shirts and lungi—cloth wraps that they have folded so they hit just above the knee. The three of us are heading toward a neighborhood called Aymanam, where I'm going to have a "Village Life Experience"—a tour for visitors that will take up most of the morning. But for now, I'm enjoying the view from the boat: the canal is lined with dense, jungly forest that occasionally breaks for a view of a Hindu temple or a modest family home. When we cruise past a cluster of radiant pink water lilies, Sabu picks one of the flowers and deftly weaves its long stem into a necklace that he places over my head.

At our first stop, Sabu helps me out of the boat, then leads me down a short dirt path to a single-story family home that's painted a deep shade of coral. This is the house of Suresh, our boat driver, and he beams as he introduces me to his wife, Ajitha Suresh, who has stepped out in the yard to greet us. A few healthy-looking chickens are pecking around in the dirt by our feet, looking for a bite to eat. All around us, the family garden is overflowing with flowering plants, shrubs, and trees that I don't recognize. Sabu starts to show me around, plucking leaves, crunching them in his fingers, then holding them up to my nose for a sniff: nutmeg, turmeric, lemongrass, tamarind, wild ginger. We go to the yard in front of the house, where Ajitha is sitting on the ground next to a burlap sack and a pile of rough brown fibers that Sabu tells me are from coconut husks. Ajitha shows me how she spins the rough material between her hands until it winds away from her as a thin, sturdy rope. Then she takes my hands between her own and helps me make some of the rope myself—which appears from between my palms like some sort of magic.

I don't speak Malayalam and Ajitha doesn't speak English, so we communicate through smiles and gestures. Sabu sometimes jumps in with a translation, but we seem to understand each other just fine. After showing me the ropemaking, Ajitha leads me inside the house, into the family's living room. She picks up one of her saris, a cream and burgundy one with sparkles of golden thread, and begins to wind the thick, rich fabric around my waist, then over one of my shoulders. She grins. Ajitha and her husband, Suresh, are sharing their home with me. I realize that it could be a show, but the warmth that I see in their faces as they show me around feels genuine. It feels more like I'm visiting a new neighbor than participating in a tour. And thanks to the government of Kerala, Ajitha, Suresh, and Sabu are also earning money by doing this.

In 2019, more than 19 million domestic and international tourists came to Kerala—that's more than *eight times* the number of visitors Iceland received the same year.[6] Kerala isn't very big—it's about half the size of South Carolina. But it has a population of roughly 34 million, just a shade under the population of California. And tourism in the state is big business: it employs nearly a quarter of Kerala's workforce and accounts for 10 percent of the state's GDP.[7] When I visited Kerala in August and September of 2022, tourism had broad community support: in the nine days or so that I spent exploring the state, I didn't find a single tuk tuk driver, waiter, food stall owner, or other community member who had anything but effusively positive things to say about local tourism. People's responses were probably influenced by the fact that a visitor was posing the questions. But I ask for people's opinions about their local tourism industry just about everywhere I go, including in my own village in the French Alps. And nowhere else in the world—apart from Liverpool, which I would visit the following year—have I ever had anything like such an overwhelmingly positive response.

But tourism in Kerala hasn't always been seen as such a good thing. Just fifteen years ago, residents were so unhappy with local tourism that they took to the streets to demonstrate. One of the leaders of those protests was a thoughtful, serious man named Rupesh Kumar, who sits down with me for an interview a few days after my experience in Aymanam. Rupesh is from the Keralan village of Maravanthuruthu, which lies along the jungly banks of the Muvattupuzha River, and he still lives in the area with his wife and teenage daughter. These days, Rupesh is excited about what tourism is bringing to his community. But that wasn't the case fifteen years ago.

Back then, Rupesh tells me, tourism in Kerala was an industry that operated in isolation from the people who lived there year-round. Hotels, resorts, and tourist-facing restaurants didn't hire local people, and they didn't purchase any of their supplies from local producers. Rupesh tells me that not a single vegetable or egg or even a drop of milk was sourced from the farmers of Kerala—everything was imported from other parts of India or abroad. At the same time, rice paddies were being filled in to create land on which ever more resorts and hotels could be built. And residents' beloved canals were strewn with litter left behind by visitors. So Rupesh, whose thick beard is now more white than black, started to organize his community members, eventually becoming, as he describes it, "one of the leading personalities" in the fight against the ills of tourism in Kerala.

Protests of the type that Rupesh was helping to organize in the early 2000s are hardly unique. But in Kerala, the demonstrations led to real change—and quickly, too. In 2008, the state hosted its first conference on Responsible Tourism, which itself attracted protests from anti-tourism demonstrators. The government, under the direction of the state's tourism secretary at the time, Dr. Venu

Vasudevan, invited tourism experts from abroad to help them think about how they could reshape their local industry. Dr. Harold Goodwin, who founded the International Center for Responsible Tourism in 2002, was one of those experts. In too many parts of the world, Dr. Goodwin told me, "community tourism" means rich tourists paying to ride on a bus through a village, but the residents aren't compensated, let alone consulted on how or whether they want to open up their communities to visitors. In those cases, "community tourism" can look a lot like exploitation. But from the very beginning of the discussions about this, leaders in Kerala committed to taking an entirely different approach: they would empower the communities themselves to dictate the terms of the tourism that happened (or didn't) within their borders.[8]

Coming out of that conference in 2008, Kerala's tourism leaders came up with a plan: they would launch pilot projects in four villages, and they would see which was most successful. The Village Life Experience—a version of which I got to sample in Aymanam—came out the winner. But they also had some other successes along the way: they brought together producers of furniture, as well as fruit, vegetables, and meat, and created producer groups that could provide hotels and resorts with the volume and quality of goods they required. And they reached out to Kerala's tour operators and travel agents, convincing 70 percent to promote the tours and activities of this new movement in tourism, which very quickly attracted the "responsible" label.

This approach—which insists that tourism should make destinations better places to live *and* better places to visit—is now in practice throughout Kerala, and beyond. At its core is Kerala's governance system, which draws its strength from the state's network of panchayats, or local councils. In each community, the panchayat is the authority that decides when and how the local area will receive its visitors.

This approach has worked: a 2015 survey found broad community support for the tourism industry.[9] Of the more than two thousand local families who were surveyed, only six reported that tourism had only a negative impact on their household. In 2017, the state government adopted Responsible Tourism as its official tourism policy, and they set up a Responsible Tourism office to manage that work across the state. They hired Rupesh to serve as its first director. He still holds the position today, and tourism in Kerala continues to grow: Rupesh says that visitor numbers bounced back quickly after COVID, and new projects are opening up, including in his hometown. The activities vary from crafting a musical instrument to visiting a spice plantation, going on an outing with a local fisherman, or cruising the canals in a shikara. But each is built around the idea of welcoming visitors under conditions that are dictated by community leaders, who ensure that the economic benefits flow directly to locals.

The history of tourism in Kerala, Rupesh tells me, is the story of "confrontation to cooperation." And he believes—he insists—that other tourist destinations can go through the same transformation that Kerala has experienced. Now Rupesh is working to help other state governments in India create their own versions of "Responsible Tourism." He hopes to one day advise governments overseas as well. With tweaks, Rupesh says, the model that Kerala has pioneered can be made to work anywhere in the world.

*   *   *

There's a scene in an episode of *The Brady Bunch* in which Mrs. Brady, her three daughters, and Alice, the goofy housekeeper, don fake grass skirts and take a group hula lesson. They're on vacation in Hawai'i, of course, and their lesson takes place on the lawn of a Waikīkī hotel, under a blue sky and with white-capped ocean waves breaking silently in the distance. The Brady crew wave their arms and twist awkwardly until Alice seems to get stuck in a muscle spasm that brings the lesson to a premature close. The hula teacher—a beautiful woman in a bikini top and thigh-skimming grass skirt, with wavy black hair that reaches past her waist—smiles, sways her hips, and remains mute for the entirety of the ninety-second clip.[10]

That scene was filmed just outside the Sheraton Waikiki, which was still brand-new when the episode aired in September 1972. Half a century later, I'm wandering through the same hotel grounds, which I don't quite recognize from the episode: I have a hunch that the hula lesson was filmed in the spot now occupied by the adults-only infinity pool. But no matter: I'm not here to have a *Brady Bunch* fangirl moment. I'm here to meet Native Hawaiians.

It's July 2022, and the Sheraton Waikiki is playing host to this year's annual convention of the Council for Native Hawaiian Advancement, the preeminent association of the community whose population probably numbered more than a million when Captain Cook became the first European to land in the Islands in 1778. The conference promises four days of cultural workshops, debates, and panel discussions. I've circled all the tourism-related events in my official program and brought along my voice recorder. I'm ready to solicit some opinions.

Things get interesting on the afternoon of the second day. Two panels on tourism have been scheduled back to back, and interest in the topic is so high that the organizers have to move both events to a bigger room, where I and about two hundred other people take our seats around round tables covered in starched white linens, from which a lunch service has just been cleared away.

The first session goes smoothly: John De Fries of the Hawai'i Tourism Authority is up there, giving a version of the *huliau* presentation that I have already heard in his office. His fellow panel members, some from the Native Hawaiian community, are similar graybeards in the state's tourism industry—people with decades of experience and impressive job titles to match. The tone of their talks tends toward the earnest and passionate: tourism is a powerful tool that must serve our community, not break it down; Native Hawaiian culture must shape tourism, not the other way around; if we get tourism right, we can extend the Hawaiian spirit of aloha across the globe—and raise the vibration of humanity.

The second session, whose panelists are somewhat less senior, begins with a similar vibe. But the tone of the discussion, and the feeling in the room, takes a sharp turn about an hour in.

"I'm going to say something that's not going to be popular here, but I believe it needs to be said while I still have the mic."

This is how the fourth speaker, whose name is given in the program as Kū'ike Kamakea-Ohelo, opens his talk. The speakers before him addressed the audience from their chairs. But Kū'ike, dressed in a T-shirt and board shorts and probably in his mid-thirties, stands to speak. And he projects.

"Tourism is the driving factor of how they colonized Hawai'i. Period. There are no analytics or data that you can show me today that will tell me that tourism has directly benefited the Native Hawaiian community."

Kūʻike describes himself as a native son of Waimānalo, a community that lies about forty minutes outside Honolulu, along Oʻahu's windward coast.

"You ask me: What has tourism contributed to our community? I will tell you: Trash. Rubbish. The city and county are inundated with rubbish. Is that what you want as Native Hawaiians?"

He waits. Two hundred people seem to hold a collective breath.

"How can tourism benefit Waimānalo? I will tell you how: Stop coming. Until such a time where we, as a Native Hawaiian community, can come up with a strategy and have autonomy over these resources; until such a time where we, as a community, develop the infrastructure to ensure that our *keiki** have something left for them—tourism will never be sustainable, and it will never be regenerative.

"*Mahalo* for coming to my TED Talk."

Kūʻike remains standing as the audience roars to life: a standing ovation.

One week later, a Toyota pickup truck with blacked-out windows and a camouflage paint job pulls into the baking-hot parking lot at Waimānalo Beach Park. With the truck's engine still running, Kūʻike emerges from behind the steering wheel, walks a few steps to meet me on the curb, and shakes my hand. He has invited me here, he says, so I can see "the reality."

Kūʻike parks his truck, then leads me to the main area of the park: a smooth lawn, punctuated here and there by spindly trees and

* The Hawaiian word for "children."

picnic tables, that slopes very gently down to a white sand beach, where azure waves lap at the gently sloping shore. A family of beach-goers lug their cooler and boogie board down the path toward the sand; a mother and kids wander out of the tidy-looking bathroom block; a group of teenagers clad in rash guards and board shorts chat and flirt in a shady corner of the parking lot. The place has the feel of a moderately busy state park, with one notable exception.

"So, you see right over here—tourists, visitors," Kūʻike says, motioning across the trim lawn and toward the ocean beyond. "And then right over there, you have locals and Indigenous people."

He turns now to a row of more than two dozen tents that line the far side of the lawn, just on the edge of the road. The tents look well established: several have clotheslines strung up; others have Hawaiian flags, bicycles, coolers, folding chairs, small dogs pulling at leashes attached to poles driven into the ground. Those tents are homes, Kūʻike says, for Native Hawaiians who can't afford houses.

He turns to me: "Now you can see the direct benefit of tourism to our community."

Kūʻike leads me to an empty picnic table, and we settle in across from each other. It's late afternoon, the wind is picking up, and the broad features on Kūʻike's face are thrown into relief by the light of the lowering sun. He has a thin mustache and a wispy beard that reaches to his chest, where it nestles just above a fat jade pendant. He speaks with conviction and at times in great detail about the policy issues, laws, and hypocrisies that he wants me to understand. He occasionally slows his pace and glances with meaning at my notebook: he wants to make sure that I get all of this down.

Kūʻike is a state land use commissioner who also serves as president of the board of two nonprofits, both of which work to support the Native Hawaiian community. He trained as a farmer, working the land, but he says that he hasn't been able to make a living in agriculture; 90 percent of the work he does now is voluntary. Kūʻike is thirty-six years old, the father of six children, and at that moment, he tells me about an hour into our conversation, he has no more than a hundred dollars to his name.

"Why are our Indigenous people, our Native Hawaiians, still on the beach here when our tourism industry brings in more than seventeen billion dollars every year?"

This is the question that Kūʻike just can't square. He explains that the land we're sitting on belongs to the Department of Hawaiian Home Lands, a state agency tasked with managing lands that have been set aside for members of the Native Hawaiian community. But DHHL leases Waimānalo's beachfront park to the county for $1 a year. In return, the county mows the lawn, cleans the bathrooms, and turns a blind eye to the few dozen Native Hawaiians who camp in the park permanently and without a permit.

From Kūʻike's perspective, this is anything but a fair trade. His community is giving up land that belongs to them—prime real estate that could house any number of Hawaiians—just so visitors, people who have no rightful claim to the land, can have yet another place to play on the beach. Moreover, tourism is the whole reason that so many Native Hawaiians can no longer afford to buy homes in Waimānalo: the current median home price in the community is $1.4 million. Kūʻike tells me this is due to all the visitors who have bought or built expensive second homes along the coast. But even bigger than the housing issue, he says, is the disenfranchisement of his people. Kūʻike is convinced that a colonial mindset has seeped into local psychology, of both Hawaiians and *haoles* (a Hawaiian word for "white people," or foreigners in general). "The perpetual machine of tourism," as Kūʻike calls it, is part of that status quo, and it has only driven Hawaiians further into poverty.

In a perfect world, Kūʻike says, the tourism industry would be forced to shut down, at least for a while. Before his community can welcome tourists, they first have to determine which resources they, as Native Hawaiians, have the responsibility to manage. Only then can they decide whether and how they might want to welcome visitors back. And any new form of tourism that might emerge would operate exclusively on Hawaiians' own terms.

"We're not saying that we want a seat at the table," Kūʻike says. "In this circumstance, we own the table."

As tourism skyrocketed in Hawaiʻi in the 1960s and '70s, Kūʻike's hometown developed a reputation as a place where tourists were likely to have their bags stolen, car windows smashed, or purses snatched while they were enjoying a dip in those warm and inviting waves. I'd heard this much about Waimānalo before, but I'd never been to the community until I went to meet Kūʻike. He brings up the subject himself when talking about his childhood in the 1990s, when he says there were times when the only food at home was a rusting can of kidney beans. He remembers his cousins and other kids in the neighborhood ripping off tourists on the beach, then selling the loot. I ask him if he ever took part; he shakes his head and says he doesn't have the heart for that kind of thing. I'm inclined to believe him.

At this point in the conversation, I'm sitting in the passenger seat of Kūʻike's camo-colored pickup truck, the AC blasting full force in my face. Kūʻike is driving us northwest along Waimānalo's two-lane Kalaniana'ole Highway, the ocean on our right. After more than an hour at the picnic table, Kū'ike asked if he could show me something down the road. "I've got water bottles there, just help yourself," he said as I hauled myself into the truck. "Sorry, they're not chilled."

He wants to take me to a place that has been known for a long time as the Sherwoods, but which was recently given back its original name, Hūnānāniho, which means, roughly, to hide something sacred or personal. Before Europeans arrived, this was a Hawaiian burial ground. Today, it's an extension of the Waimānalo Beach Park—another tract of land set aside for Hawaiians, but managed by the county.

Kū'ike takes us down a narrow road that leads to a parking lot, nearly empty, that's shaded by a thick grove of needle-bearing ironwoods. A white sand beach glimmers in the distance, beyond the trees. As we make a quick pass of the parking lot, Kū'ike explains that this place was called the Sherwoods for so long because it's where locals would abscond with the goods that they ripped off from tourists, just like Robin Hood would hide away in Sherwood Forest with his rightful spoils. This is where local kids would divvy up their goods, then share them with their families or the community more broadly—the people who really needed it. Peering through the window of Kū'ike's pickup at the quiet, empty forest, I agree that it looks like a very good place to hide.

Kū'ike pulls the truck back onto the highway: there's one more thing he wants to show me. He makes a left and takes us down Laumilo Street, a residential, mailbox-lined road that's shaded by a generous number of palms and flowering shrubs. There are houses amid the greenery, but it's not always easy to see them: we drive past a series of stone walls, picket fences, and dense hedges, only occasionally catching a glimpse of the ocean, which lies just on the other side of the houses on our left. I see a man in flip-flops walking a small dog on a leash; a mother and son stroll by in their swimming suits. Kū'ike tells me that an empty lot on this street recently sold for $2.2 million.

My tour finished, Kū'ike drives back to the parking lot where we first met. I start to thank him and say goodbye, but he says he won't leave until my Uber arrives—it's getting dark, and he wants to make sure I don't get stuck out here. So we stand together in the dusky parking lot, goose bumps prickling on my bare arms in the evening air, and Kū'ike tells me a final story.

When he was about eight years old, his mother took him and some other children to a turtle pond a short distance from where we're standing. A sheltered lagoon, protected from the ocean beyond by a low stone wall, the pond is a sacred space where Hawaiians have traditionally raised turtles, a valued food for Hawaiian royalty. On this particular day, a *haole* couple motored into the lagoon in their boat—taking no care, showing no respect, just doing what they wanted, Kū'ike recalls. His mother, gentle but firm, asked the couple to leave. They shouted back at her, and he remembers the man, who was a big guy, being very rude. But his mother stood her ground, and the couple turned their boat and left.

When Kū'ike finishes the story, I remark that it must have been difficult for him, as a boy, to see someone treat his mother with disrespect. It was, he says, but that's not what struck him most from the experience.

"My takeaway is: I can say no. I can tell them, 'Beat it.' And we have every right to, as Indigenous peoples."

*   *   *

"Any city that sacrifices itself on the altar of mass tourism will be abandoned by its people when they can no longer afford the cost of housing, food, and basic everyday necessities." So wrote a thirty-nine-year-old activist from Barcelona in the pages of the *Guardian* in September 2014. It was at the tail end of a summer in which Barcelona had attracted a significant amount of international attention for its increasingly conflicted relationship with tourists. But the author of the op-ed argued that the answer for the city was not to attack tourism but to manage it: "We have to regulate the sector, return to the traditions of local urban planning, and put the rights of residents before those of big business," she wrote. "The way of life for all Barcelonans is seriously under threat. And the only solution is to win back democracy for the city."[11]

Less than a year after that essay was published, the citizens of Barcelona elected its author—who at that point had never held political office—to be the city's next mayor.

The election of Ada Colau in 2015 marked a turning point in Barcelona's relationship with tourism. Already famous in Spain for her work fighting housing evictions, Colau soon ushered in the city's first comprehensive efforts to regulate Airbnb and other tourist rentals. Under her leadership, City Hall banned the construction of new hotels in the city center and introduced neighborhood-specific rules to regulate the establishment of souvenir shops and other businesses that cater to tourists. Colau also enacted a moratorium on new tourist licenses for short-term apartment rentals and launched a major crackdown on illegal apartment listings to stop the glut of private apartments being taken off the residential housing market.[12] Legally, her administration couldn't revoke the roughly ten thousand tourist licenses that the previous administration had issued for apartment rentals. But they could regulate so-called home-sharing, the renting of a room inside a home. And in August 2021, City Hall hit with full force, prohibiting all private room rentals for stays of less than a month. In doing so, Barcelona became the only major city in Europe to impose such a ban.[13]

The rationale behind such policies went something like this: landlords in areas that are popular with tourists can earn a lot more from short-term rentals to visitors than from long-term rentals to locals, so many choose to remove their properties from the housing market. That reduces the supply of homes available and drives up rents. At the same time, people who rent out an extra bedroom of the home they own effectively increase the value of their property, which means that, if they ever want to put their home on the market, they can sell it for a higher price. Individual homeowners who earn money from short-term rentals tend to have a less pronounced effect on the housing market, because they are more likely to host tourists on occasion, instead of year-round. The bigger effects come from the professional operators and investment companies that use short-term rentals as a business opportunity. Not only do those players rent out more units, their units also tend to be busier, and to earn more money per available night.[14]

The effects of tourist rentals have shown up in Barcelona's housing market: a 2020 study published in the *Journal of Urban Economics* found that Airbnb activity in Barcelona had increased rents by 7 percent and housing prices by 17 percent in the neighborhoods with the highest levels of activity on the platform.[15] In the average neighborhood, the effects were a 1.9 percent increase in rent and a 4.6 percent increase in housing price. Other studies have drawn similar conclusions, both in the United States and elsewhere in Europe. A 2021 analysis of Airbnb activity in Reykjavík concluded that the platform perpetuates patterns of inequality in tourism-heavy areas.[16] A study focused on Athens, Lisbon, and Milan found that Airbnb fosters "a new form of urban displacement at a faster rate than traditional housing gentrification."[17]

In New Orleans, researchers found that, in ten neighborhoods, roughly 10 percent of the "long-term rental" stock had been converted into short-term accommodations, many of which were operated by companies, as opposed to individual hosts. "City planners' slow reaction and laissez-faire attitude, as well as ham-fisted lobbying by companies and private interests," the authors concluded, had allowed short-term rentals to contribute to "tourism gentrification" in the city, especially in historic, lower-income neighborhoods.[18] A recent overarching analysis of Airbnb data from across the United States found that the platform decreases the long-term supply of housing rentals and increases both house prices and rents, with the strongest effects coming in areas with fewer owner-occupiers, such as vacation towns.[19]

Many tourist destinations have joined Barcelona in taking measures to restrict short-term rentals in one way or another. Other prominent examples include San Francisco, Denver, Paris, Berlin, New York—and the Hawaiian Island of Oʻahu, which is home to both Honolulu and Kūʻike's hometown of Waimānalo. But this kind of tourist accommodation is just one example of the myriad ways in which tourism—whether in a city, a village, or a wild landscape—is crying out for regulation.

Without any government oversight and intervention, Butler is right that tourism will eventually harm residents' way of life and could even threaten the very attractiveness of the destination itself. The same can be said of any significant economic activity, but tourism is an area in which too many governments only get the memo that they should pay attention after too much damage has been done.

When governments do wake up, there are any number of steps they can take: Levy tourism taxes. Build parking lots, bathrooms, and other infrastructure. Impose access restrictions, or charge fees for visiting places at peak times. Smart, thoughtful policies that respond to and incorporate the voices of people like Mar, Kū'ike, and Rupesh can go a long way toward piercing the inevitability of the declining quality of life that Butler implies in his model. And as Rupesh and his colleagues in Kerala have proved, if a destination gets off on the wrong foot, it's not impossible to set it right again—although such a dramatic turnaround seems very rare indeed.

*   *   *

It's late 2023, two years after our Barcelona walking tour, when I reach out again to Mar, who is still hard at work in her home city. It's wonderful to reconnect with her over the phone, and I'm delighted to hear her updates on Max and Pablo. But when I ask about how tourism is doing in the city, her tone shifts.

"The situation is far worse than when you came," she sighs, adding that tourist numbers in the city have already exceeded their pre-COVID records. Ada Colau was voted out of office earlier in the year, and she tells me the city's new mayor is much more in favor of growth in tourism. But Mar's biggest concern is that Barcelona continues to operate according to an economic model that relies on attracting huge numbers of outsiders—whether as tourists or foreign tech workers—to keep its economy going.

But then Mar is excited about something, too: she's begun working with a network of ten European cities to help them revitalize their city centers. Some of the cities are struggling under the weight of tourism, while others are eager to welcome more visitors. It's a fascinating discussion, she says, and she hopes the cities in the network will be able to learn from Barcelona's experiences.

I ask Mar how things are going in their neighborhood in the city center, and she surprises me by saying that she and her family have moved—just like so many others before them. The tourist crowds got to be too much after COVID, she says; it felt like they were living in a "fake city." But they haven't gone far. Mar, Pablo, and Max now live near the old Olympic Village, in a part of Barcelona that was an industrial zone until the 1992 Summer Games came along and rejuvenated the area. Mar loves their new neighborhood, which is near the coast. Unlike when she was a kid, there are no more concrete walls blocking the Mediterranean view. Now she can go for a walk—and admire the sea.

Chapter Five

The Last Chance Saloon

I magine the kind of backhoe that you might see in the middle of a highway construction project, but instead of a shovel attached to its front, the backhoe is adorned with a sinister-looking ice pick that's affixed to the end of a mechanical arm that's longer than I am tall. And instead of digging its way along the edge of some sun-bleached interstate, this backhoe is drilling and picking—with an ear-numbing clatter—into a solid wall of cerulean, three-hundred-year-old ice. The ice surrounds the machine on all sides but one, which gives this backhoe the air of something conjured by Ms. Frizzle in *The Magic School Bus*: a fantastical vehicle drilling its way ever deeper into an unfathomable beyond. The wall of ice in front of the machine is dutifully falling away under the incessant grind of the ice pick, creating a drift of crushed ice below. Two hunched men shovel the ice out of the machine's way; their faces, red with exertion, are mere inches from the hammering metal rod.

It's a cacophonous and claustrophobic scene, and I'm observing it all from my delicate perch on one side of the backhoe, where

I keep a gloved hand braced against the ice wall next to me to prevent the machine from shaking me off with its shuddering. The backhoe operator, Benjamin Claret, is sitting comfortably in the driver's seat a few inches to my left, where he's deftly wielding the joystick-like controls. Benjamin takes a methodical approach to his work: he edges the hammering pick upward along a vertical line about eight feet long before shifting it to the left, then working his way back down. He repeats this movement several times, and within about five minutes he's created a window in the ice that's a few inches deep. He then edges the backhoe forward on its heavily chained wheels, gives a quick shout to the shovelers, and the process starts all over again.

The temperature here in the ice cave hovers right around the freezing point. Benjamin has no jacket and he works the controls with bare hands, but he wears a hefty wool sweater, slightly frayed, that looks as snug as the curly brown beard that warms his chin. Every so often as he works, Benjamin shouts instructions to the shovelers, or rises in his seat to get a better view of the ice on which he's working his magic. Even over the clatter of the machine, he exudes a kind of comfortable skill that comes only from years of experience, which is exactly what he has. Benjamin Claret is only twenty-nine years old on the snowy midwinter day on which he's invited me to observe him at work. But this world inside the ice has been a home away from home for him for nearly as long as he can remember.

It wouldn't be a stretch to say that Benjamin was born for this job. He's been coming to the glacier since he was a boy, when his father would sometimes bring him along for a day's work carving the ice. That was back in the late nineties and early 2000s, by which point the ice cave inside the Mer de Glace* glacier, which lies just outside of the city of Chamonix in the French Alps, had been a popular tourist spot for more than half a century. Like all glaciers, the Mer de Glace is a river of ice in constant movement. For this reason, the ice cave must be re-carved every year, in a process that takes up to five months to complete. It's painstaking work: not only do they carve out the cave for visitors to explore, they also cover the ground with a slip-free carpet, illuminate the interior with discreet light fixtures, attach information panels to the slick blue walls, and adorn the cave with ice sculptures—a polar bear, a windowed room, a throne that's perfect for everyone's photos. The scene has changed little since Benjamin was a child.

Benjamin's father inherited the job from *his* father, Georges Claret, who came up with the idea. It was just after the end of the Second World War, and Georges was working for EDF, the French energy company, which managed the flow of water that emerged from below the Mer de Glace. Georges knew that a natural cave formed at the base of the glacier, and he would sometimes bring friends along to show them around. At some point, it occurred to him that this icy wonder could be of interest to tourists. So Georges applied for a permit from the local authorities, who gave him a green light. There was no fantastical backhoe at that point, so the elder Claret and his comrades chipped out the cave with their shovels and ice picks, expanding it to accommodate a stream of guests. They called it the Grotte de Glace, and five thousand people came to see it the first year it was open.[1]

* This translates to "sea of ice."

To reach the Mer de Glace, most of today's visitors buy a ticket for the little red train that takes them from Chamonix up nearly three thousand feet in altitude to a place called Montenvers. They emerge at the top to find a gift shop and café, a hotel, and a broad viewing platform that overlooks the glacier, which fills the valley below. Because of that glacier, this spot—which lies about two and a half miles from the middle of Chamonix—has been attracting foreign visitors at least since 1741. That's when two young Englishmen made the trek up from the valley below and encountered the awesome view of the Mer de Glace, inspiring one to write an account that spread the glacier's fame in Europe. Plenty of famous visitors would follow, including Mary Shelley, who set the climactic scene of *Frankenstein* on the surface of the "tremendous and ever-moving glacier," which she saw in person in July 1816.[2] Subsequent visits by Alexandre Dumas, Napoleon Bonaparte, and Mark Twain helped to fix the Mer de Glace in the public imagination in America and Europe. Twain, writing in 1880, marveled at the glacier's crevasses, which "yawned deep and blue and mysterious" alongside the "huge round waves of ice [that] were slippery and difficult to climb."[3]

By the time Twain made his visit, the scene on the ice was far from wild and remote: tourists were "scattered far and wide over it, everywhere," Twain wrote, giving the glacier "the festive look of a skating-rink." By the late nineteenth century, the mule track that led up from Chamonix had become so crowded that local leaders decided—despite the protests of local hiking guides—to build a railway line to link Chamonix to Montenvers. The resulting steam-powered train, which opened in 1909, became the first major piece of human infrastructure to be built in the mountains above Chamonix. Many more would follow.

But as more people came to see the Mer de Glace, the glacier began to shrink: its tongue, which once reached nearly all the way to Chamonix, gradually pulled back toward its source: the high slopes of Mont Blanc. And, complicating matters for visitors, the glacier's surface dropped deeper into the valley below the viewing platform at Montenvers. By the early twentieth century, tourists had to walk down a narrow dirt path from Montenvers to reach the glacier below, and the path grew a bit longer every year. The distance grew so large that, in 1961, a new lift opened to whisk visitors down to the ice's surface, but its capacity of 450 people per hour soon proved insufficient. So in 1972, the seats were removed: now standing room only, the gondola could carry 700 people per hour down to the ice. But even that was soon unable to meet demand.

By the 1970s, gondolas and other types of mechanical lifts had sprouted up all over the mountains of the Chamonix valley. The gondola to the viewing platform at the Aiguille du Midi, which opened in 1955, whisked tourists up into the wild and frozen landscape at a breathless 12,600 feet. Ski lifts brought skiers to nearly similar heights on Brévent, Flégère, and the Grands Montets— high, treeless slopes that once served as grazing areas for local livestock. And at Montenvers, in 1988, the town of Chamonix built a bigger and faster gondola to whisk visitors down to the Claret family's ice cave. It served its purpose well, but its days were numbered from the beginning. When the gondola appeared, visitors had to walk down a mere three steps to reach the ice. By the year 2000, that staircase had grown to 118 steps. By 2023, the year in which I joined Benjamin in the cave, 580 steps separated the bottom of the gondola from the glacier below. And local leaders had decided that was too many.[4]

It's midday inside the ice cave, and Benjamin has just called a lunch break. He climbs down from his seat in the machine, while the shovelers stash their materials. We'll go to a heated shed nearby, Benjamin explains, for a *casse-croûte*—a cold picnic of torn baguette, cheese, sliced meats, and packaged salads. I'm looking forward to warming my fingers. We step outside, into the flat gray light of mid-January, where it's starting to snow. Standing on the metal walkway that leads to the ice cave's entrance, we can see a crane hovering above us: the crane that's being used to build the new gondola. The new structure will open in eleven months' time, and it will allow Benjamin to continue his family's line of work, at least for a while. The project was announced a couple of years earlier: the new gondola will be farther up the valley, anticipating the glacier's continued retreat. And it will be accompanied by a new interpretation center for tourists, in the form of a Glaciorium that will teach visitors about glaciers and climate change. The whole project is expected to cost €53 million, nearly half of which will go toward the new gondola.[5]

Benjamin tells me he's excited about the new lift: the stairs are too much for a lot of people, but the new gondola will allow everyone—children, seniors, anyone who struggles with steps—to share in the wondrous experience of walking inside a glacier. Perhaps anticipating a question, he reassures me that the new gondola has gone through all the required stages of environmental planning, and that it will be *démontable*—able to be dismantled. Because sometime soon, probably in the early 2030s, the days of the ice cave will be over for good. The glacier will have retreated so far up the valley that it will no longer be practical for tourists to reach it. By the 2050s, the Mer de Glace will have shrunk so much that it will most likely no longer be visible from Montenvers at all.[6]

In describing the all-but-certain demise of his family's line of work, Benjamin maintains a steady gaze and an even tone, which gives me the impression that he came to terms with this situation a long time ago. He's prepared for the change, in any case: he has another business. When Benjamin isn't carving out the insides of a glacier, he runs a popular cocktail bar in town.

*　　*　　*

In the mid-nineteenth century, cowboys who drove cattle between Texas and Kansas would follow the Chisholm Trail, which led them across a vast stretch of prairie that was then known as Indian Territory. But from the cowboys' perspective, at least, there was a big drawback to the route: federal law prohibited the sale of intoxicants in Indian Territory, which meant they couldn't get any booze along their trek. An enterprising barman named Curley Marshall saw an opportunity in this scenario: knowing that cowboys would be looking to drink their fill before they set off for Texas, he set up shop along the north bank of Bluff Creek in Kansas, the final stop along the trail before it passed into the vast, alcohol-free expanse of Indian Territory. He built a structure of thick logs and put a board out front, where all the cowboys would see it as they headed south. The sign read: "The Last Chance Saloon."[7]

It strikes me that twenty-first-century glacier tourists have something in common with those hard-driving cowboys. We know we're about to say goodbye to the thing we like to consume, but it's still available—at least for the most part, and at least for now. So we're bellying up to the bar, enjoying the warmth of the booze as it slides down our throats, knowing full well that the sensation won't last. Those Chisholm Trail cowboys had a "First Chance Saloon" to look forward to in Texas, on the other side of their journey. We, on the other hand, are just filling up—and trying to ride the buzz for as long as we can.

I've been a glacier tourist since 2009, when I first visited the Mer de Glace, and I've been to several other glaciers since. In this category, I'm in good company. Every year, about four hundred thousand people pay to ride the little red train up to the Mer de Glace overlook at Montenvers.[8] Switzerland's Aletsch glacier, which is both the largest glacier in the Alps and a UNESCO World Heritage site, attracts even bigger numbers: in the summer season alone, some 1.1 million people ride the lift up to the main viewpoints over the glacier.[9] Glaciers in New Zealand and Iceland also attract impressive numbers, but the biggest crowds are in China, where the glacial Yulong Snow Mountain attracted more than 3.8 million visitors in 2016.[10] In Argentina, the Perito Moreno Glacier won a Tripadvisor Traveler's Choice award in 2022, and the following year the travel site listed the glacier among the top visitor experiences in all of Argentina. "Must see natural wonder," wrote one Tripadvisor reviewer in February 2019. "If you get the chance go and see the glacier before it's too late and climate change melts it."

It won't surprise you to hear that most of these glaciers are disappearing, and quickly, too. Ninety percent of glaciers in the Alps—including the Mer de Glace—could be gone before the end of this century.[11] Globally, scientists predict that the world's glaciers could lose nearly half of their mass by 2100.[12] And many are already gone: scientists announced in 2009 that Bolivia's

Chacaltaya glacier, an eighteen-thousand-year-old ice field that was once home to the first ski area in South America, had disappeared entirely.[13] In 2019, a group of mourners mounted a memorial plaque at the site of Iceland's Okjökull glacier, which scientists had declared dead five years earlier. The same year, about 250 people gathered for a "funeral" of the Pizol glacier in eastern Switzerland, the first glacier to be taken off the country's official network of glacial surveillance. Public memorial services for moribund glaciers have since been held in Mexico, as well as in the Ticino region of Switzerland and the U.S. state of Oregon.

And glaciers aren't the only popular tourist destinations that are falling victim to climate change. The world's coral reefs are likely to disappear before the end of this century, primarily due to warmer and more acidic oceans. To take the most famous example of a reef in decline: in 2021, UNESCO's World Heritage Committee recommended that the Great Barrier Reef, which has been a World Heritage site since 1981, be added to the list of UNESCO sites "in danger," noting that the long-term outlook for the ecosystem was "very poor."[14] The government of Australia fiercely—and successfully—opposed the "in danger" listing, but that doesn't change the facts on the ground.[15] If and when life collapses in that reef, it will be both an ecological disaster and an economic one: tourism in the Great Barrier Reef supports sixty thousand jobs and contributes $3.8 billion to the local economy.[16]

The Maldives, where tourism accounts for 28 percent of the national gross domestic product, is another tourist spot that climate change could quite literally wipe off the map. "Our islands are slowly being inundated by the sea, one by one," the president of the Maldives, Ibrahim Mohamed Solih, told a UN climate conference in 2021. "If we do not reverse this trend, the Maldives will cease to exist by the end of this century."[17] The Marshall Islands and Kiribati could face a similar future, while in the Solomon Islands, at least five reef islands have already disappeared under rising seas. In some low-lying tourist spots in Tonga, climate change has already caused tens of millions of dollars in lost tourism revenue.[18]

Thanks in part to publicity stunts like glacier funerals, word is getting out about the beautiful destinations that climate change will soon drive to extinction. There's a good chance you've already heard about that funeral in eastern Switzerland, for instance: it was covered by CNN, the BBC, NPR, and *Time* magazine, among many other media outlets. This kind of publicity certainly raises awareness about the impacts of climate change, but it may also have the perverse impact of inspiring us to visit these places before they're gone for good. Recent surveys have shown that many people—and often a majority of people—who visit disappearing glaciers, for instance, are drawn by the fact that the glaciers won't be around for much longer.[19]

There's even a term for this phenomenon, one for which Curley Marshall could claim partial credit: last-chance tourism, also known as doom tourism, though the former seems to have gained more traction. The terms, which began cropping up around the turn of the millennium, describe a very postmodern approach to exploring the world: on our overcrowded, over-mapped, over-photographed planet, human beings are no longer racing to be the first to go somewhere extraordinary or do something exceptional. Now, we're racing to be the last. Through the eyes of a last-chance tourist, the ephemeral nature of a melting, sinking, or otherwise disappearing place makes the site significantly more alluring.

In some cases, people whose job it is to market tourist destinations have seized on the macabre appeal of the dying destination, playing on people's angst over climate change, in particular, to try to motivate them to come visit their tourist attraction before it's gone. We see this, for example, in the Canadian North, where as early as 2006, tourism operators were selling tours with the provocative title of "Polar Bears on Thin Ice," and where a 2010 study revealed that a majority of polar bear tourists were motivated by their understanding that the bears could soon succumb to climate change.[20] Academics have even concluded that growing awareness of global warming contributed to a "mini-boom" in tourism to the Arctic and Antarctic in the first decade of this century: when people realized these places were disappearing, they hustled to get there as quickly as they could.[21] Surveys have also shown that the allure of what is disappearing motivates people to visit the Great Barrier Reef, a crumbling Hasankeyf heritage site in Turkey,[22] and glaciers in New Zealand and the Swiss, Austrian, and French Alps—including the Mer de Glace. From this perspective, we might think of last-chance tourists as those whose voyeuristic instinct has been lit up: they want to get one last glimpse of the moribund patient—quick before he dies on the table.

But the situation might not be so morbid as it first appears. It turns out that the voyeurism of the last-chance tourist could deliver some tangible benefits—to the tourist herself and to the world at large. It's possible, but far from guaranteed. The constructive potential of last-chance tourism lies in the concept of cognitive dissonance, which will be familiar to anyone who has taken Psychology 101: this is the psychological discomfort that we experience when we realize that our behavior is out of step with our value system.

Sometimes the discomfort is so strong that it motivates us to make a change to bring these two incongruent things into alignment. From this perspective, last-chance tourism provides a potentially helpful paradox: researchers have found that visitors to glaciers usually have a good degree of environmental awareness, even as their travel to the glacier—and sometimes the mere fact of their presence in front of it—often increases the threat to its existence.

Herein lies a source of psychological discomfort that we might be able to use. Emmanuel Salim at the University of Toulouse and other scientists are now studying whether visits to disappearing destinations—particularly places that are threatened by climate change—can bring about a measurable change in awareness, attitudes, and ultimately tourist behavior with respect to their impact on the planet. In some cases, at least, the answer seems to be yes: many tourists come away from their encounter with a shrinking glacier with a strengthened resolve to protect the environment. A survey of visitors to the Mer de Glace found that nearly 82 percent said they would stop visiting glaciers if doing so would protect them. Another 80 percent said they would "try to learn more about the environment and how to protect it." The least popular behavior change intention on the survey, which was chosen by just under half of the respondents, was choosing vacation destinations that are closer to home.[23]

These were just measures of visitor intentions—more research would need to be done to determine whether last-chance tourists follow through. And not everyone in the study was equally affected: the researchers found that the more visitors understood that the disappearing glacier was an indicator of climate change, the more likely they were to show a willingness to change their behavior to reduce their climate impact. Therein, at least, lies a lesson: the managers of last-chance tourist sites can embrace the opportunity to educate their captive audience.

What about this argument: Can last-chance tourists become "ambassadors" for the place that's disappearing? You hear this one a lot with regard to Antarctica—a tourist destination that is at once incredibly fragile and shockingly expensive. Proponents of tourism to the frozen south argue that the small class of people who are able to afford the trip can serve as Antarctic emissaries by educating others, advocating for the continent's protection, and—in the words of the International Association of Antarctica Tour Operators—"making positive changes at home" to support the region.[24] However, a study published in 2015 raised questions about the validity of this proposition, concluding that tour operators in Antarctica would need to show "a more focused educational commitment" if they wanted to produce effective Antarctic emissaries. "Tourists returning from the Antarctic do not seem to play the role of ambassadors," the authors concluded, "because many visitors merely want a last chance to glimpse a vanishing world."[25]

There's a sentiment that Curley Marshall himself could probably get behind. It turns out that the original Last Chance Saloon lasted only five years, and its demise had nothing to do with cowboys losing their taste for liquor. The death of the saloon came at the hands of a group of people who deliberately—and unnecessarily—set the place on fire. A historical marker in Caldwell, Kansas, tells the story:

In 1874 a posse from Caldwell, while in pursuit of outlaws, thought badmen had holed up in the Last Chance and burned the saloon to

*drive them out. Though their suspicions proved to be unfounded,
the building had been destroyed.*

*   *   *

Between 2009 and 2013, about 8 percent of humanity's greenhouse
gas emissions came from tourism, and that share is expected to
grow significantly in the years ahead.[26] That's in part because
the growth of tourism will continue to outpace the growth of the
global economy, a trend that's well established. Researchers have
found that as people become more affluent, their demand for travel
tends to grow more rapidly than their demand for other products
and services. We want to see new places, or to visit that far-flung
family member, and we want to move around in the fastest and
most convenient way we can afford. So as we gain wealth, we swap
that bone-rattling bus journey for a comfortable ride in our own
car; then we swap the long car trip for a quick hop in a plane.

In economic terms, tourism is widely considered a classic luxury good: the more we earn, the more we're willing to spend traveling to the places on our bucket list—both in real terms and as a
proportion of our income.[27] And because our demand for tourism
is rising more quickly than tourism operations are decarbonizing,
the result of our growing appetite for travel is a net increase in
the sector's climate-warming emissions. At the same time, other
parts of the global economy are becoming less carbon intensive,
which is magnifying tourism's share of humanity's greenhouse
gas production. While our energy networks and vehicle fleets
are beginning to shift to renewable sources of power, aviation—
which represents one of the most important sources of tourism's

climate-warming emissions—will continue to be carbon heavy, at least for the next few decades. In the years leading up to the pandemic, aviation emitted roughly a billion metric tons of carbon dioxide annually, and the figures bounced back quickly as travel came roaring back after COVID.[28]

So what's a concerned traveler to do? For a while, "carbon offsets," a concept that gained traction in the late nineties and early 2000s, seemed to be a reasonable option for tourists who were looking to reduce their carbon footprint. In theory, at least, a carbon offset works like this: a traveler pays to support a tree-planting project, the restoration of a mangrove, or a similar initiative that promises to remove from the atmosphere the carbon the traveler emits during her trip. It's a nice idea, and for a while carbon offsets gained plenty of supporters—and investment. But the problem is that carbon offsetting hasn't proved effective: a study by the European Commission found that 85 percent of carbon offset projects failed to reduce climate-warming emissions. The problem, the report found, was that the projects either "made false assumptions" about what would have happened in the absence of the intervention, or the carbon-offsetting projects "were likely to have happened anyway."[29]

Offsets also raise the question of how they impact people's behavior. If someone travels more because her conscience has been assuaged by her purchase of offsets (which are probably invalid anyway), then the whole concept probably does more harm than good. David Victor, a codirector of the Deep Decarbonization Initiative at the University of California San Diego, said in an interview that the carbon offset market has been flooded with low-quality offsets, which has driven down the price of a carbon credit and made the whole system grossly ineffective at actually reducing the amount of CO_2 being released into the atmosphere. "Offsets were a magic wand because they were inexpensive and they made people feel like they were doing something," he said. "But they turned out to be almost entirely garbage."[30]

One obvious alternative to carbon offsets is to stop flying. The flight shaming movement gained traction alongside the rise in fame of the activist Greta Thunberg, who famously traveled across the Atlantic by sailboat to attend the UN General Assembly in 2019. While few concerned travelers would probably go so far as to re-create Thunberg's ocean crossing, it turns out that the idea of adjusting one's flying habits due to concerns for the climate isn't only for super hardliners. A 2019 survey by the Swiss bank UBS found that, of six thousand people polled in the United States, France, Britain, and Germany, 21 percent said that they had already reduced their flying on environmental grounds. UBS analysts predicted that such sentiment could halve the expected growth in demand for aviation—though even if growth is halved, it's still growth.[31] And we shouldn't think that aviation is the only way that tourism contributes to climate change: the food we eat while we're traveling, the goods we buy, the places we stay, and the taxis, shuttles, and bus rides that we take all play a role, too.

Dr. Victor told me that people who are concerned about the climate impact of their travels could use an online calculator to see how their flights contribute to their overall carbon footprint. But he said we can't rely on individuals to make the kinds of decisions that will actually move the needle: we have to transform the entire system. "The larger goal here is to have stewardship of the planet in the context of human and ecological happiness," Dr. Victor said.

Of people who choose not to fly, he added: "That's something that might make you feel good as an ascetic, but it's not actually replicable. And everything's about replication."

In October 2022, at a meeting of the United Nations agency dedicated to civil aviation, delegates from 184 countries adopted "net zero by 2050" as a "long-term global aspirational goal" for the aviation industry.[32] The announcement had been a long time coming. Many major airlines, including six of the largest U.S. airlines, had already pledged to achieve net-zero carbon emissions by 2050, if not sooner. So if the aviation industry gets its way, then commercial flying will result in zero additional carbon dioxide in the atmosphere by the middle of this century.

But the fact that the goal was described as "aspirational" is critical here, because there aren't currently any easy, market-ready technologies that can both quickly and drastically reduce the carbon emissions of aviation. And the "net" qualifier attached to all those 2050 goals means that airlines can account for any CO_2 they continue to emit either by using traditional carbon offsets—yes, the same ones that Dr. Victor called "almost entirely garbage"—or by capturing carbon dioxide directly from the atmosphere, which remains a very expensive process.

But there are new technologies in the pipeline that could help aviation make some important steps toward real carbon neutrality. The most promising of these include hydrogen-powered aircraft and fully electric planes, as well as a type of synthetic jet fuel made from carbon extracted from the atmosphere. Several airlines have already begun mixing in a small amount of cleaner-burning biofuel—which is widely known as sustainable aviation fuel, or SAF—to their normal fuel supply. These percentages are tiny, but they're expected to grow quickly in the years ahead. Many airlines are already investing in emissions-saving efficiency improvements; some are also investing in long-shot innovations that could deliver bigger gains down the line. Steven Barrett, a professor of aeronautics and astronautics at the Massachusetts Institute of Technology, and the director of the MIT Laboratory for Aviation and the Environment, said in an interview that the big challenge will be to make these changes as quickly as possible, given the enormous amount of inertia that's built into the system.

But airlines are already looking for short-term innovations that can deliver near-term benefits. They're retiring older aircraft, using more efficient flight routes, and instructing their pilots to taxi their planes with only one engine running. SAF—which is made from biomass like used cooking oil—is an important part of the short-term picture, though the biofuel accounts for less than 0.1 percent of the global supply of jet fuel. Over its life cycle, SAF has a smaller carbon footprint than conventional fuel, with which it can be mixed—but smaller doesn't mean nothing. When I interviewed Andreas Schäfer, the director of the Air Transportation Systems Laboratory at University College London, about this topic for the *New York Times*, he told me that the term "SAF" is inaccurate: "It should be *more*-sustainable aviation fuel," he said.

And SAF is expensive. As of 2023, it was more than double the price of conventional jet fuel, although that price premium has been dropping quickly. But given the high cost, airlines have been buying SAF in very small amounts and adding it to their fuel supplies at only a handful of airports. JetBlue flights that depart from the international airports in San Francisco and Los Angeles have some SAF in the mix. And since 2016, United Airlines has put some SAF into the tanks of all its planes flying out of Los Angeles International Airport; in 2022, the airline began doing the same for its departures from Amsterdam as well.

A coalition of airlines and other aviation industry players, led by the World Economic Forum, aims to make SAF account for 10 percent of the global jet fuel supply by 2030. But Dr. Barrett and Dr. Schäfer both told me that the world doesn't have enough biomass residues to produce anywhere near the amount of fuel that global aviation requires. Scientists are exploring new sources for the carbon that's needed to produce SAF—including animal manure, yard trimmings, food waste, and algae. And then there's the question of the quality and source of the biofuels: if SAF is made from oil derived from an oil palm plantation that has taken the place of a rainforest, then that fuel will ultimately do a lot more harm than good. So transparency here is critical. But even with high-quality SAF, this approach will only get us so far.

"Scaling up biofuels or biomass-derived sustainable aviation fuel over the next ten, twenty years is definitely the right thing to do," Dr. Barrett said. "But it's not going to be enough, ultimately. We need to start planting the seeds for what comes next."

One of the most promising technologies in the pipeline is jet fuel made from carbon from the atmosphere, which, as we all know, is full of carbon dioxide. This process, which is known as "power to liquid," works like this: enormous fans scrub carbon dioxide from the air; the carbon atoms are then extracted from the CO_2 molecules and combined with hydrogen produced from water electrolysis that's powered by renewable electricity. The result of this mash-up is a hydrocarbon fuel that can be used to power an airplane. The process is well established: in 2022, an unmanned U.S. Air Force plane completed a successful test flight running entirely on fuel made from carbon dioxide that had been extracted from the atmosphere. The key challenge here is the expense of all that renewable energy. But with the cost of renewables falling quickly, power-to-liquid fuels could be cheaper than most biomass-based SAF by as early as 2035.[33]

Hydrogen-powered aircraft is another innovation with promise, and one that's been around since the Cold War. But there's a good reason that we aren't all already flying on these aircraft: the engineering challenges—and potential safety issues—are significant. As a gas, hydrogen is too voluminous to be stored in useful quantities on board an airplane; instead, the hydrogen must be cooled to a liquid, which means storing it at minus 423 degrees Fahrenheit, the temperature at which hydrogen condenses. Pulling that off at airports around the world—let alone inside an aircraft—is no small feat. But, again, the technology exists. Airbus has announced three concepts for commercial aircraft powered by liquid hydrogen, one of which it hopes to launch by 2035. The European low-cost airline easyJet is also investing in hydrogen-powered aircraft technology.[34]

Electric-powered flight could also help the aviation industry get to "net zero" by 2050. Due to the current limitations of batteries, fully electric aircraft lack the energy required to get a large plane off the ground—let alone across an ocean. But for small planes on short-haul routes, electric flight could be an interesting option. In September 2022, the company Eviation Aircraft successfully completed an eight-minute test flight of a fully electric, nine-passenger plane above Washington State. At the time, the company said it hoped to have an FAA-certified version of the aircraft in operation by 2027.[35] This type of short-haul, carbon-free flying could soon take off in Norway, where the national airport operator has announced that all of the country's domestic flights should be fully electric by 2040.[36]

Airlines have focused on shrinking their carbon footprint to reduce the climate impact of flying, but Dr. Barrett of MIT said that, in doing so, they could be ignoring some much easier wins. He explained that contrails—those thin white streaks that sometimes appear in a plane's wake—alter the planet's temperature, perhaps even more than the CO_2 the planes emit. The science here is complicated because the effect of contrails varies from day to night. When the sky is dark, contrails trap heat radiating off the earth, leading to additional warming; when the sky is bright, contrails still trap heat, but they also radiate the sun's energy back into the atmosphere, and the net effect can actually be cooling. But studies have found that, overall, contrails warm the atmosphere—causing anywhere from half to three times as much warming as the carbon dioxide emissions from aviation, Dr. Barrett told me. When I interviewed him in late 2022, he was working with Delta Air Lines to study how making small adjustments to flight routes could reduce the warming impact of contrails. He said that because the vapor trails form only at narrow bands in altitude, and only when the air is cold and humid, aircraft can avoid those zones pretty easily—and without incurring too much additional cost for the airline.

"When you look at the state of the world today, I can't imagine we would want a less connected world with less cultural understanding and less economic interconnectedness," Dr. Barrett said. "We have to come up with the technical and operational and political solutions to make aviation such that it can continue to grow to connect more of the world—but get to net zero."

But even if all of humanity—the airlines included—stopped emitting greenhouse gases tomorrow, we'd still see a huge amount of warming over the next several decades. A 2021 study published in *Nature Climate Change* concluded that the greenhouse gases *that we've already emitted* could lead to as much as 4.1 degrees Fahrenheit worth of warming before the end of this century, which is beyond even the weaker goal of the Paris Climate Accord.[37] For children born in the latter decades of this century, glaciers will be like dodo birds or covered wagons—things you learn about in history class. Things that have no place in the world you know. With all but a few exceptions, in just a couple of generations, the living, breathing glaciers of the world will be gone.

* * *

Elvis legs. Sewing machine legs. The death wobbles. I'm not a big rock climber, but I've spent enough time among that crowd to know a handful of terms for the involuntary shudders that have just taken over the lower half of my body. And I've spent enough time halfway up a rock face to know that, once the shudders hit, it's very hard to get them to stop.

Another day, another outing to the Mer de Glace. Except this time, instead of going inside the glacier, I'm clinging to a metal ladder that's bolted to a sheer rock face a couple of hundred feet above the surface of the ice. It's not the most convenient spot to get hit by a case of the shakes, I think to myself, unhelpfully, as I try to calm my quivering legs. I'm willing myself not to look down, but my mind's eye is full of the sweeping, frozen landscape that lies below me. A river of ice, strewn with car-sized boulders and gaping crevasses, carves its way through a steep-sided valley, winding down from the snowy heights of Mont Blanc, which lies around the corner, just out of sight. On either side of the ice, steep piles of glacial debris angle up toward cliffs of granite that rise to the horizon, where they terminate in spiny pinnacles that are naked apart from a thin crust of windblown snow.

That vast, wild scene is the backdrop to my shaking legs, but right now I'm doing my best to focus on my fingers, which are starting to go numb against the iron rung that I'm gripping with as much force as I can muster. My ears are full of the wind that's gusting down from the fang-like ridge in the distance that marks the border with Italy. And my shaking legs are failing to respond to my brain's repeated attempts to calm them.

Did I mention I'm not attached to a rope up here? What the hell am I doing?

"Brad?" The wind whips away my voice, but my mountain guide, who is climbing steadily about a dozen rungs overhead, manages to catch the sound. He turns and peers down at me.

"You okay?"

"Maybe the rope is a good idea, I don't know." I try to sound nonchalant, but my legs are still going. The sweat on my palms isn't helping my grip on the cold iron rung.

"Okay, no problem."

With one hand, Brad reaches into his pack, pulls out a rope the color of a traffic cone, and eases it down the ladder to me. There's a carabiner attached to the end of the rope, which I manage to clip and lock into the belay loop on the front of my climbing harness. Brad is attached to the other end of the rope, which he threads through a metal clip that's bolted to the cliff face, just a short reach from the ladder. Now there's a fixed point between us: if either of us slips, the other's weight will counterbalance the fall, anchored by that bolt in the rock. A series of those metal clips runs alongside the ladder. From now on, we'll move together, with Brad threading the rope through the clips as he climbs, and me unclipping the rope as I come up behind him, always keeping at least two of those fixed points between us.

If Brad were out here with his climbing buddies, they wouldn't bother with this kind of safety measure on something as straightforward as a ladder. Standing at the base of the cliff, I thought I'd show Brad that I was cooler than the other tourists he guides in the mountains, so I told him I'd be fine without the rope. It didn't take long for reality to set in. But as soon as I see Brad thread the rope through that bolt on the rock, my breath calms—and my death wobbles disappear.

"It's okay, I'm more comfortable with the rope, too," Brad, being very generous, says when we reach a narrow ledge on the cliff, which we have to inch across to reach the next ladder in our long upward journey. We still have a few hundred feet of vertical climbing to do before we get to the spot where we'll stop for lunch, so we pause for a rest on this little patch of grass, which is about the size of a diving board. Here on the ledge, with one hand draped casually over a rung of the next ladder, Brad looks like a waiter taking a cigarette break between shifts.

"I mean, can you imagine the headlines?" he says, shaking his head: "'Journalist Falls to Her Death.'" I get the sense that he's teasing me now, ever so gently. Then he cocks his head, imagining the reactions of his colleagues: "'*Now who was it who was guiding her on that one?*'"

It's just another day on the job for Brad Carlson, a guide with the Compagnie des Guides de Chamonix, the world's oldest and (in France, at least) most prestigious association of mountain guides. If anything, my outing with Brad is less adventurous than what he's used to. On an average day, he might help tourists thread their way among the towering seracs and yawning crevasses of the Vallée Blanche, a backcountry ski route that runs over twelve miles and down nine thousand vertical feet, much of it along the Mer de Glace. He might lead-climb a multi-pitch route up one of those spiny pinnacles, managing the ropes while offering advice in reassuring tones to make sure his client doesn't get spooked. Or he might inch his way along the spine of the icy ridge that leads to the summit of Mont Blanc, holding a tourist on a short rope—always ready, if the client stumbles or slips down one side, to leap off the other side to counterbalance the fall.

But for Brad—who, in addition to his mountain guide certification, also has a PhD in ecology and works as an ecologist—guiding people in the mountains isn't just about the adrenaline, although he realizes that's usually a big draw for his clients. For Brad, to be a mountain guide is to be an ambassador of the natural world: to help people experience nature, but also to understand and appreciate nature in all its savage, and sometimes deadly, beauty. This approach, Brad says, is the future of his profession.

Brad is an American, a Vermonter, and he's a few weeks shy of his thirty-fourth birthday on the October day that I spend with him on—and above—the Mer de Glace. But Brad has lived in France since he was twenty-one years old, and in his bearing and habits, he strikes me as equal parts American and European. Brad will most likely be a French citizen by the time you read this: he and his American wife, the professional athlete Hillary Gerardi, were in the process of applying for French nationality when we met. But Brad held only his native American passport when he was inducted into the Compagnie des Guides de Chamonix, becoming the first non-European ever to be invited to join. As both an American and an ecologist, he is bringing a host of fresh ideas to the two-hundred-year-old institution: alongside two of his colleagues, Brad is leading a task force that's examining how Chamonix's mountain guides should adapt their work to the changing climate. It's a subject that he's spent a lot of time considering.

Brad thinks about this shift as occurring along a spectrum that ranges from immediate micro-shifts to long-term structural changes. On the near end of the spectrum, the micro-shifts are the kind of small adjustments to changing mountain conditions that guides have been forced to make for a while already. They adjust a climbing route to minimize exposure to rockfall, a sometimes lethal danger that climate change has made more frequent and more intense. Or they lead only one client instead of two or three, as they used to, on the snowy slopes of Mont Blanc, which warmer temperatures have made slicker, steeper, and more challenging to climb. But Brad tells me that these kinds of adjustments alone won't be nearly enough. More broadly, he says, he and his fellow guides need to change the myth that they're selling about the mountains.

Brad gives me an example: instead of offering to guide a client to the top of that one bucket-list summit—an objective that the increasingly erratic weather conditions may or may not allow—a guide could offer a four-day course of mountaineering skills, in which the client will do plenty of climbing, but may or may not make it to the top of Mont Blanc. The shift here is both subtle and profound. At a practical level, the client's experience may not be much different, but at a philosophical level, everything has changed: instead of selling a product for the client to consume (a tick mark next to the name of a summit), the guide is selling an education, an immersive natural experience that allows the client both to learn about the environment and challenge herself within it. In an ideal world, Brad says, mountain guides would encourage people to explore and understand the landscape—then help them find the courage to contemplate their own place in the scene.

This kind of approach is essential to what Brad describes as an urgent, dual crisis—climate change and the devastating loss of species that's happening simultaneously, but that is much less visible. Brad tells me that the disappearing glacier—which is what most people remember after a visit to the Mer de Glace these days—is just the most visible scar of a much deeper wound.

"The fundamental problems and solutions aren't just about carbon emissions," he says. "We have to fix our extractive, non-reciprocal relationship with the natural world."

At the top of the ladders, we step into an expanse of dry grass, strewn with boulders and straggly shrubs, that slopes gently down toward the cliffs we've just climbed, and the glacier below. We unclip from the rope, and Brad leads me a short walk away, where we settle in for our picnic lunch with a panoramic view. He gets out a pocketknife and begins slicing his bread and cheese. He offers me a piece of cured ham, a clementine. It starts to spit with rain, and I feel a chill crawl up the back of my spine.

The whole sweep of the landscape spreads out below us: the river of ice snaking its way down the bottom of the valley; the sharp, snow-plastered peaks that define the horizon; the low gray clouds framing the scene. Brad points to a grassy slope across the valley and tells me about how plant life has changed on that patch of ground with the glacier's retreat. These are the things that interest him most as an ecologist: the profound shifts that are visible only to a trained eye. Gazing out, I realize that Brad and I are the only two human beings in my entire field of vision. Everything in the landscape is fixed and unmoving, apart from the clouds skirting by overhead and the grass in front of us, bending in the wind. At the center of it all is the glacier, the inexorable force that has been drawing visitors to this valley—the valley it created—for nearly three hundred years. It's a wild and imposing landscape, and one that my grandchildren, if I ever have any, will probably never see.

An hour or so later, Brad and I are back at the bottom of the ladders, retracing our steps from the morning as we make our way down the glacier and toward Montenvers, where we started the day. The ice is so covered with gravel that I barely need the studded cleats that I brought along to prevent my hiking boots from slipping. We walk and talk, and Brad keeps remarking at how much the glacier has changed since he was last here, about two months before. The surface of the ice is in perpetual motion: crevasses—deep gaps in the ice—open and close, boulders emerge and are swallowed, streams shift and merge their way across the glacier's surface. The sound of running water is everywhere, though I can't always see it. This is not a place you would want to get lost in a fog.

When we're nearly at the end of our walk, Brad climbs to the top of a small swell in the ice, then gestures down the other side with his pole and calls me to come look. I inch up next to him and peer down into a yawning opening, the bottom of which I can't see. A series of small waterfalls spurt out of the cerulean walls of this deep gash in the ice, cascading into the unfathomable blue depths below. I feel like this could be a water feature in a fantastical ice palace, but Brad says that this is called a moulin: a vertical shaft in the glacier that's carved by the water melting on the surface. I remember Mark Twain's description of the gaps in the ice "yawning deep and blue and mysterious." It's still here, I think. And it still looks like a miracle.

Finally, we reach the metal staircase that leads up to Montenvers, where we will catch the train down to Chamonix. As we step onto the staircase, we encounter a string of tourists on their way down to Benjamin's ice cave, the entrance to which is just a stone's throw away. We pause to let them pass, and I look up at the crane that rises above us—the one that's building the new gondola farther up the valley. Another forty minutes of hiking and we make it up to Montenvers and all the trappings of modern tourist civilization: the well-curated gift shop, the heated bathrooms, the café selling espressos and Caesar salads.

As we wait for the red train to take us back to Chamonix, Brad and I strike up a conversation with a white-haired glaciologist who's also on his way down at the end of the day. He's just been at the glacier overlook, where he heard some tourists complaining about the number of people at the site.

"But I told them, 'You're here, too, aren't you?'" The scientist laughs and shakes his head, then recites a quote: "In an avalanche," he says, one finger raised, "no single snowflake ever feels responsible."*

I ask him what he thinks of the new gondola, already under construction. He sighs and gives a little shrug: "That's tourism in Chamonix."

---

* *"Dans une avalanche, aucun flocon ne se sent jamais responsable."*

Chapter Six

Tourist Trap

I t's ten o'clock on a balmy summer evening, and the crowds in
the alleyways of Amsterdam's Red Light District seem to have
reached their peak. I see couples walking arm in arm, parents
clasping the hands of their young children, a rowdy bachelorette
party in matching pink T-shirts, and packs of men of all ages,
laughing and shouting to each other as they peacock their way
around the neighborhood. Everyone is circling the alleyways, seeing and being seen, and occasionally stopping to refuel at one of the
many eateries where the lines spill out onto the sidewalk. People
are queuing up to buy pizza by the slice; ice cream cones; waffles
smothered in Nutella; a plate of french fries covered in bacon and
"warm cheese sauce." The sidewalks are strewn with empty beer
bottles, dirty napkins, plastic candy wrappers. Every so often, I'm
overwhelmed by a smell of piss so intense it makes me wheeze.

This could be a crowded tourist zone in any historic European
center—apart from a few telling details. I step into a corner store
to browse for souvenirs for my kids, and alongside the typical array

of key chains, mugs, and shot glasses, I encounter an entire wall of plastic tubs filled with "space cakes" and "magic cookies," whose packaging declares the goodies are laced with varying intensities of cannabis and psilocybin. Back outside, the summer sky is fading into night, and the windows in the alleyways are starting to glow a deep and alluring shade of red. When I walk past those windows and peer inside, I see women in towering platform heels, heavy makeup, and outfits that leave little to the imagination, many with breasts and lips of otherworldly proportions. It's 10:00 p.m., still early in the evening, and most of the women in the windows—and I see only women—are biding their time: pulling on a vape, adjusting a strap, sending a text, chatting with their neighbor, surveying the crowd. Every so often, I hear the tap of a long fingernail on a window, and turn to see a woman smiling and gesturing at a potential client, beckoning him over. The crowd seems full of easy prey.

I find a bar and nurse a beer until about half past midnight, when I follow some advice I've been given and make my way to a building whose front is adorned with neon lights that spell out "SEX PALACE" in capital letters. I join the mass of bodies moving toward the doorway, and follow them into a crowded, low-ceilinged room that smells of beer and sweat. The place feels like an arcade that's had all the video consoles removed: there's the black-painted walls, grim fluorescent lighting, and a gritty tiled floor adorned with yellow-painted arrows that everyone seems to ignore. The vibe is excited and a little rowdy, but mostly civil, very international—and very male. It feels like a United Nations of horny guys in here: I hear English in half a dozen accents, as well as French, Arabic, German, Hindi, Spanish, Italian, and several other languages I can't identify—but there's definitely no Dutch.

There's a peep show happening inside the SEX PALACE, and that's what I've come to see. This is a new experience for me. I'm a married mother of two and I'm embarrassed to admit that I've never even really watched porn before, let alone attended any sort of sex show. But here I am in Amsterdam's Red Light District, where this seems like the thing to do, and I feel a professional obligation to get the full experience. Plus, a sex worker I interviewed the day before strongly encouraged me to pay a visit to the SEX PALACE, where she said the owners are very good employers. The workers at this place can build real careers, she told me. Probably sensing my hesitation, she stressed that the peep show is low stakes: you pay two euros for two minutes in one of the viewing cabins. "If it's not your thing, just walk out," she said. "You should give it a shot."

So here I am, standing fourth in line in front of one of the cabins for the peep show, which is advertised outside with photos of women peeling off their bikini tops, clinging to poles, and licking each other's butt cheeks. There's a little pushing in line as I edge forward toward the door, but I'm impressed that the crowd isn't any rowdier. I look up and spot a handwritten sign above the door that issues a warning in English:

DON'T PEE IN THE CABIN
! FINE !
150€

I wonder how often that happens. My guess is probably a couple of times per night.

The line in front of me inches forward until, finally, it's my turn. I take a breath and step through the door and into a tiny room, almost like a closet, where I encounter a mild musty odor and a small window on the far wall. I put my coins in the slot and peer through the smudged glass, which offers a view into an adjoining room. Through the window, I see a blond woman, probably in her late twenties, wearing a black lace bra and underwear. She's maybe five or six feet from my face and she's lying on a round cushion that's spinning slowly as she rolls and thrusts her body to electronic music that thumps through invisible speakers. Just beyond her, peering through their own little windows, I see the faces of my fellow peep show viewers, who are feasting on her professional offerings with eyes that are fixed and unblinking. The woman moves and sways to the music in a way that strikes me as practiced, almost mechanical. Her face is neither blank nor emotional as she starts to strip: peeling off first her bra, then her underwear in short, efficient movements. She's naked within about thirty seconds. I marvel at the woman's sheer calm and confidence as she continues to execute the exaggerated movements of her routine, completely unclothed. Her face shows no signs of unease: she wears the sedate and aloof expression of a queen performing a routine ceremonial function in front of an audience of fawning subjects. Her viewers look like peasants begging for scraps.

The peep show feels transactional, sure—and bursting with lust, at least on one side of the equation. But the woman looks like a professional, and very much in control. I really hope that's the case. I hope she's dancing naked for paying customers because she wants to, not because she was forced to do so by poverty or intimidation. I don't know the woman's name, and I'm not about to interrupt her shift to ask for an interview. But from what I've learned over the previous few days, I know that she's required to register with the government. I know that she's obliged to pay tax on her earnings. I know that Dutch officials go to great pains in their interviews to try to determine whether she and her fellow sex workers haven't been trafficked and are indeed acting of their own free will. And I know that at least one other woman in her profession believes that this peep show is a very good place to work.

But then there's so much that I don't know. Whether the system is working as it's meant to; whether the woman's job brings her satisfaction, as well as a livable income; whether the mayor of Amsterdam is right when she says that human trafficking is still a serious problem in this historic corner of the city. I stay in the cabin for my two minutes, then step back out into the dim fluorescent lighting and hold the door open for the guy in line behind me.

Outside on the street, the scene has shifted. It's after 1:00 a.m. now and the crowds are still heavy, but the alleyways are no longer heaving like they were before. The ratio of men to women is even more pronounced—I would guess something like twenty to one. Nat, the sex worker I interviewed the day before, said that the workers always get the most business at the end of the night. Sure enough, as I stroll past the red-lit windows, I see even more men leaning in, having a chat, sometimes stepping through. Nat told me the sex workers have to pay about €200 to rent a window for the night. I wonder how many jobs it takes to make ends meet.

*   *   *

If you ask a resident of Amsterdam whether he ever spends any time in the Red Light District, there's a good chance he'll respond with a little grimace and a subtle shake of his head. That part of the city has nothing to offer people like him, he might tell you. The restaurants are bad and overpriced. The shops are full of tourist kitsch. The crowds are oppressive. It's a tourist monoculture. Even if you want to engage a sex worker in a window, there are nicer and much less touristy places in Amsterdam where you can find the same services. And anyway, our fictional Amsterdammer might say, why go to the Red Light District when there are so many other more beautiful and interesting parts of the city to explore?

It hasn't always been like this, as I learned from Geerte Udo, the CEO of amsterdam&partners, an agency whose primary function used to be the marketing of the city to potential tourists, but which now runs very different types of campaigns. In the late nineties, Udo told me, young Amsterdammers would still visit the historic city center to frequent its bars, boutiques, and restaurants.[1] There were tourists then, too, but the place was still hip. But, already in the nineties, a slow shift was in the works: lured away in part by the government's promotion of a business district outside the city, a growing number of businesses were leaving Amsterdam's historic center. Tourism, which was so deeply rooted in the place itself, expanded to fill the vacuum.

To today's typical Amsterdammer, the Red Light District and its surrounding area—which has been the economic and cultural heart of the city for more than seven centuries—has devolved into that thing that most people do their best to avoid: a tourist trap. And yet, despite the kitsch, despite the crowds, despite the prices, it won't surprise you to hear that some 2.5 million people visit the Red Light District every year. Of course, tourist traps can be found all over the world: the Taj Mahal, the Champs-Élysées, Fisherman's

Wharf in San Francisco, Hawai'i's Waikīkī, and Times Square in New York, to name a few classics. With the boom in international travel in the second half of the twentieth century, tourist traps began to sprout up wherever tourists began to congregate in any serious numbers. Their existence was probably inevitable.

The British writer Graham Greene is credited with the earliest recorded usage of the term "tourist trap," which he coined in his travelogue *The Lawless Roads*, published in 1939. The book recounts Greene's travels through Mexico, where he encountered what he described as "hideous" items on sale to tourists—painted clubs and walking sticks, stone mortars decorated in outrageous shades of red and blue.[2] To Greene, these tacky products were themselves the "tourist traps," not the zones or districts where they were sold—although the term he coined would soon expand to take on that broader meaning. Greene's travelogue also includes some keen observations of tourist behavior. He describes how Mexico's newspapers always included the latest news about local shootings, but this information never made it onto the single page of the paper that was translated into English, which was the only page he ever saw visitors reading. "They lived in a different world," Greene wrote of his fellow tourists, "they lived in a few square inches of American territory; with *Life* and *Time* and coffee at Sanborn's, they were impervious to Mexico."[3]

Alongside the tourism boom that followed the Second World War, the term "tourist trap" fixed itself in the vernacular, and its meaning continued to shift and expand over the years, matching the ways in which tourism began to mold much of the physical landscape of the twentieth century. The term continued to carry the tone of condescension with which Greene imbued it, and the negative connotations grew stronger over the years. By the late 1970s, "tourist trap" was so baked into the culture that it was used as the title of a low-budget horror film in which a group of friends finds their way to an abandoned roadside museum of animated waxwork mannequins. After ninety minutes of bloodstained horror, only one in the group survives; the rest have been transformed into mannequins themselves. The narrator of the movie's trailer goes so far as to provide us with a new definition of Greene's term: a tourist trap is a place "where beautiful young people looking for excitement are tricked, terrorized, trapped."[4]

Modern dictionary definitions of "tourist trap" aren't quite so melodramatic. These tend to include references to large crowds and overpriced goods and entertainment, sometimes with an overtone of tourist exploitation. I don't see this nuance in dictionary definitions, but I would add that, in our modern understanding, a "tourist trap" tends to imply a level of falseness or cheap display—a place that presents a version of a culture that those working in tourism have purposefully dumbed down so it's easier, faster, or otherwise more pleasurable for the passing tourist to consume.

I'm thinking, for instance, of a "luau" performance that I attended inside a shopping mall in Waikīkī—on the same Hawai'i trip that had me driving around Waimānalo with Kū'ike and sitting in on the board meeting with John De Fries. But there in Waikīkī, for a mere $118, I got a seat at a crowded plastic table, a very watery mai tai, a disposable plate full of lukewarm buffet food, and the chance to embark on a "journey through Polynesia" that consisted of a series of dances and cultural displays from several Pacific Islands. The evening included plenty of cheesy jokes from the emcee, a series of highly skilled displays from the performers, a whole array of shiny, neon-hued costumes, some very lively audience interaction—and, unsurprisingly, zero mention of colonialism or exploitation.

The show, which was billed as "the most authentic luau show" on the whole island of O'ahu, ticked every single one of my "tourist trap" boxes: overpriced, crowded, a cultural representation that's streamlined and packaged for easy tourist consumption. But everyone around me seemed to be having a wonderful time. By the end of it, I was on my feet right alongside them, applauding the mind-numbing speed at which the performers were able to vibrate their hips to the sharp and incessant beat of the drum being played by the bare-chested and heavily tattooed man who had scooped chicken teriyaki onto my plate a couple of hours earlier. Because here's the thing: the "luau" wasn't an education; it was a piece of escapist entertainment.

I think that's what most of us are looking for in these places. It's easy to think that tourist traps lure in unsuspecting tourists, only to fleece them of their money and subject them to bad food and overpriced items or entertainment. But if tourist traps are as purely negative as this, then why haven't we tourists learned to avoid them? And yes, I'm using the first-person plural here because I'm talking about you and me both. I've been to plenty of tourist traps over the years, and I'm guessing you probably have, too. If we're the high-and-mighty type, we might have told ourselves that we were visiting these places ironically, or perhaps for deeper reasons than "most people," or that we only went to those places when we were younger, or because a friend wanted to go, etc., etc. Sure, any or all those things might be true, but that doesn't change the fact that we've been one of those bodies in one of those places.

It makes me think of the 2010 advertising campaign by the Dutch satnav maker TomTom, which struck such a chord that it later became a meme. "You are not stuck in traffic," read the TomTom billboard, in all caps. "You are traffic."[5]

So too with tourism. As tempting as it is to pin the "tourist" label on other people, it's even more tempting to think that we're not the type who would ever go to a tourist trap. Sure, we probably avoid the tourist traps in our own cities and regions—but probably not so much when we're abroad. Even Graham Greene admitted that he wasn't immune to the allure of the tourist trap, at least in our modern understanding of the word. In the same travelogue in which he coined the term, and in which he sighed about the "tourist junk" and "tourist trophies" on sale at the spots frequented by tourists (himself included), Greene also acknowledged the power of the tourist trap's siren call. "I was back where sometimes I had longed to be—on the tourist track," Greene wrote on his arrival in Oaxaca, after a sojourn to less-visited corners of Mexico. "At any moment I expected to see my old friend from Wisconsin coming round a corner, eager to introduce me to a porter or a waitress who had looked after him. This was a city described in guidebooks where you could hire a taxi and see the sights."[6]

Tourist traps can be deeply problematic, especially when it comes to representations of cultures that have been exploited by visiting Westerners. At the same time, these places hold a huge appeal. As Greene appreciated, "the tourist track" offers us the comfort and ease of the familiar: menus in a language we can understand, free Wi-Fi, food that we at least recognize, even if it's bad and overpriced. Like Greene looking for his Midwestern friend, we also use tourist traps to locate a temporary community when we're far from home: an enclave of fellow humans who, like us, are looking to explore and enjoy a new place, but who are struggling to manage the challenges and inconveniences that we've been wrestling with, too. And the world's most iconic tourist traps also offer us the opportunity to stake our own personal claim on a sight or experience that the rest of humanity has deemed somehow worthy or exceptional. So we get a selfie in front of Niagara Falls; at the top of the Eiffel Tower; in the shadow of the Burj Khalifa. And in so doing, we forge a connection, however flimsy, between our fragile human egos and something much bigger than ourselves—a deep craving for us all.

Tourist traps also respond to another basic human need, something that we spend billions of dollars chasing: an escape from reality. Because whatever stripe of tourist trap you might find yourself in, these places have one underlying truth: they have very little to do with reality, at least the kind of reality in which most of us live our daily lives. Tourist traps are places of escape and entertainment. They are also places where we feel like the normal rules of life don't apply, which is certainly the reason why I, at the age of forty-one, attended my first sex show—all two minutes of it—right in the heart of a tourist trap. I would never have done that at home. I would never even have done that in a "normal" part of Amsterdam. It was the otherworldliness of the Red Light District that allowed me to give myself permission to pay to watch a woman dancing naked. It was the sense that I was among others who were like me: pretty much normal people who were temporarily, and knowingly, occupying a place of fantasy.

Because it's easy to give ourselves permission to do new—and riskier—things when we're inside a tourist trap and the real world feels so far away. This is one of the reasons tourism has come to be the source of so many problems in Amsterdam, where city leaders have launched a campaign to reduce tourist growth in the city (more on that shortly). Taken to a not-too-distant extreme, the same spirit that gave me the courage to visit a peep show might inspire one of my fellow tourists, whether in Amsterdam or otherwise, to do something beyond the bounds of the law.

We've all heard of those misbehaving tourists who urinate in the street, etch their names onto ancient stone walls, steal a tile from an ancient mosaic floor. But even if we don't go so far as to commit a crime, the sense of being in a fantasy world can very well take us outside the bounds of public decency and a general sense of respect for the people whose home we're visiting. In Amsterdam, I was told that it's not unusual for residents of the Red Light District—which has a permanent population of about five thousand—to wake up on a Saturday morning to discover fresh vomit on their front step. And I'm sure they must encounter the intense odor of urine on a regular basis as they go about their day. We tourists bring a lot of money into the neighborhood. When we fall too deep into the fantasy, we also bring plenty of chaos.

So part of our jobs as tourists is to keep one foot firmly planted on the rocky shore of reality, even as we dip the other into the inky waters of the tourist fantasy. But that's not to say that we should never let ourselves escape. Psychology tells us it's important to slip away from reality every so often, because doing so can help us manage the strains and constraints of everyday life. The American Psychological Association defines escapism as "the tendency to escape from the real world to the delight or security of a fantasy world," adding that fantasy "may reflect a periodic, normal, and common impulse."[7] Taken to an extreme, this can slide into neurosis or pathology, even if it doesn't inspire rude or lawbreaking behavior. But sometimes the right dose of fantasy can be exactly what we need. We just have to make sure it happens within the right framework.

*   *   *

It's just past eight thirty on a bright June morning in 2021, and I'm waiting among a gaggle of television and print reporters in the manicured "Town Square" of Disneyland Paris, a theme park that occupies some hundred and twenty-four acres of former beet and potato fields a short train ride east of the French capital. But there's no sign of farming going on anywhere this morning. There's not even much that would tell you we're in France, apart from maybe the trim-fitting suits and dark, narrow ties on the handful of security guys who are milling around, keeping an eye on things. Otherwise, I feel like I'm standing in the middle of a Norman Rockwell painting: American flags fly from the tops of the quaint buildings that line the square—the train station, the city hall, the bookstore, the toy store, the candy shop. Tidy lawns are dotted with immaculate flower beds; bulbous old-fashioned lampposts punctuate the scene; the morning sky is even playing along, showing off in a perfect shade of canary blue.

Disneyland Paris has been closed for the last several months because of COVID, but it's reopening this morning, and the Disney media machine is pulling out all the stops for the official moment. When I got wind of this a few weeks earlier, I pitched a story about it to my editor at the *New York Times*, and she was interested. I thought I would use the news hook as an opportunity to write a piece that would explore the park's place in French culture and society, as well as the complexities of managing the tourist masses amid a global public health crisis. I wasn't expecting to get a lesson in human psychology—and image management.

But I'm already starting to get a sense of these things here in the Town Square, where I'm accompanied by the photographer whom the newspaper has assigned to the story, a man I've just met and who's already busy snapping photos of the scene. Things are livening up as the expected moment approaches: an exuberant Mickey and Minnie Mouse have just appeared on a balcony above us, alongside Goofy, Pluto, and the human-sized chipmunks Chip and Dale. Disney "cast members" in period costumes are emerging from nowhere onto the sidewalks that line the Town Square. Everyone—apart from the security guys, and the clutch of loitering journalists—is dancing, pumping their fists and singing along in English to some up-tempo music that's just begun to reverberate through the still morning air: "This is your world, come play inside / This is the story that we'll write!"

As the music crescendos, the news crews train their cameras on the inside of the park's main entrance. A dozen children from a local charity skip into the scene as a television crew runs alongside them, capturing the moment. Seconds later, a herd of parkgoers trample into the Town Square, and the park is officially open for business. There are parents pushing strollers and plenty of kids jumping with excitement. But perhaps because it's a Thursday morning and French schools are still in session, I see a lot more adults than children streaming in, and many are dressed for the occasion. I spot a young woman in a billowy, bubble-gum-pink princess skirt, a pair of middle-aged women in head-to-toe outfits inspired by Minnie Mouse. I scan the crowd of mouse-eared headbands, looking for a target; I need to get a quote. My voice recorder will be useless with all this music blaring in the background, so I pull out my notebook and pen as I jog over to a young woman in silver-sequined mouse ears who seems to be gazing in awe at the scene around her.

"It's just so nice to be back," the young woman says, shouting to be heard over the music and wiping away the tears that are wetting the top of her face mask. Her name is Tamara, she's twenty-four years old, and she's traveled about four hundred miles from her home in Germany to attend the park's reopening. "It's unbelievable," she says, adding that this is probably her tenth visit to Disneyland Paris, the park formerly known as Euro Disney, which opened about five years before she was born. "Disney has been my big love since childhood."

Before I stepped into the Town Square of Disneyland Paris half an hour earlier, I had been to a Disney theme park only once in my life, on a family trip to Orlando in 1987. The conditions of my Disney visit are a little different this time around. I'm here for work, of course, and I'm full of questions that wouldn't have occurred to my five-year-old self. I also have different companions on this visit. I don't get to hang out with my parents and grandparents like I did the first time. Rather, the photographer and I are companions for the day—and Disney assigns us a babysitter from the company press office, completely free of charge.

The babysitter turns out to be an overtly friendly American guy about my age, and he never leaves my side over the course of my official visit. After that grand reopening moment, he escorts me and the photographer throughout the park, swiping a little pass he carries that magically allows us to jump to the front of every line we encounter. So we zip around Big Thunder Mountain and the *Cars* ride, an attraction he's eager to show us in the newer section of the park. Our babysitter is incredibly attentive: he suggests people for me to interview, and always hovers as I ask my questions. He tells me about the history of Disneyland Paris, the details of the renovation work that's underway, and the number of Purell hand-sanitizing stations that have been installed throughout the park as a pandemic precaution (nearly two thousand). He makes sure I have enough water to drink and that I'm not too tired from walking. But most of all, he reassures me, he's there to make sure I get everything I need for my story.

The babysitter is equally attentive to the photographer and what he's up to. As the babysitter leads the two of us down Main Street, U.S.A. in the direction of the Sleeping Beauty Castle, he notes that the iconic structure is under construction. That's why its spires, which would normally be gleaming in the morning sun, are all boxed up under scaffolding that has been painted to resemble the normal castle exterior. Our babysitter openly expresses his certainty that the photographer will understand that the castle shouldn't be photographed while it's in this state. The photographer, who seems to be a man of few words, doesn't offer a clear response. Later, near Space Mountain (recently rebranded as Hyperspace Mountain), I interview a family visiting from the United States, some of only a handful of Americans I notice in the park that day. After I finish my brief line of questioning, the photographer snaps a few photos of the smiling family. As soon as we walk away, our babysitter makes a quiet comment to the photographer: One of the teenage children in the group wasn't wearing a face mask, as per the park's rules at the time. Could he please delete those images?

I don't know if the photographer and I are being afforded special treatment because we're there on behalf of the *New York Times*, or if all visiting journalists get the same deal. Either way, our babysitter treats the two of us to a visit to Disneyland Paris that's very unlike what anyone without a media badge would experience. After several hours together, our babysitter passes off the photographer to one of his colleagues, then escorts me to the park's exit. I say goodbye and tell him I'm looking forward to heading home to my village the next day. Which is exactly what I do, right after I buy my own ticket to the park and spend another six hours inside—this time, on my own.

If we return to our original definition of a tourist trap—a crowded, overpriced place that presents tourists with a falsified or dumbed-down version of reality—then it seems clear that theme parks are tourist traps in their highest manifestation. You wait in line for two hours to go on a ninety-second ride. You pay well over a hundred dollars just to get into the place, then fork over double that amount to feed your family for the day. You explore a whole colorful array of fantasylands, which are all sandwiched together in a tight, walkable space, complete with cartoonish maps and themed signposts that guide you from one fake world to the next. Theme parks have nothing to do with reality, which is precisely the point—and precisely why my Disney babysitter and the other people who manage these places go to such pains to ensure that the fantasy bubble doesn't burst, a calamity that would surely bring the whole enterprise tumbling down.

We tourists are game to play along here, as evidenced by the more than 175 million of us worldwide who spend a day inside one of these fantasy worlds every year.[8] But it's easy to see why we're so eager to pay for the privilege. Explicitly false versions of reality that we find inside theme parks have a whole lot to offer, just like Amsterdam's Red Light District and tourist traps more broadly. These places promise us a glorious break from the everyday, and the chance to connect with fellow seekers of an earthbound paradise.

On my second day in Disneyland Paris, when I'm wandering around on my own, I bump into a pair of German sisters, Sara and Petra, as I wander past the fake Moroccan archway that leads to Adventureland. I first encountered the sisters the day before, on the fringes of the reopening ceremony, which they attended in coordinated outfits. The sisters still look exhilarated midway through their second full day in the park, and they're eager to unload all the details of what they've seen and done, and eager to ask me if I've been having a good time myself. They can hardly believe it's my first visit to Disneyland Paris, which they tell me they've visited hundreds of times since their first visit as girls in 1992. I ask them what it's like to be back now that the park has reopened. Sara, the younger sister, says the park feels the same as ever. Then she gives me the quote that my editors end up using in the story's headline: "It's like coming home to family."[9]

When the article runs in the paper the following week, I send my babysitter the link, a courtesy I extend to anyone who helps me with a story. Soon after, when I see his name pop up on my phone, I know something must be up. Sure enough, my babysitter's voice sounds annoyed and disappointed on the other end of the line.

I get the sense the general tone of the story wasn't what he was expecting, but there's nothing he can do about that. However, he does have a specific request: The story includes a photograph of the Sleeping Beauty Castle, all boxed up for renovations—something that I also noticed when I saw the piece online. (I never see the photographs before a story runs.) Could I please ask my editor to take the photo down, my babysitter sighs over the phone, or at least add a line to the caption saying it's undergoing renovations? Maybe they could even mention that the work is being done by the same French company that's leading the restoration of Paris's Notre-Dame Cathedral?

I'm a little annoyed at the request, but I also feel for the guy, who's just trying to do his job. I shoot off an email to my editor to pass along the message. No change is made.

For people who aren't really into theme parks (and I would count myself in this group), it can be tempting to look down our noses at Disneyland Paris and its ilk, precisely because of the park's wholehearted embrace of everything false. But this sort of attitude is shortsighted: we don't always need to strive for our experiences as tourists to be as "authentic" as possible. Sometimes it's better for everyone—children and adults alike—when we make the search for *in*authenticity the focus of our tourist explorations. If we all chose to embrace fantasy, but only under the right conditions, we could probably do the world of tourism a whole lot of good.

I'm thinking here of the Lascaux Cave in southwestern France, one of the world's most important examples of prehistoric art. The cave gets about a quarter of a million visitors every year;[10] except it doesn't. The cave has actually been closed to tourists since 1963, when the daily flow of more than a thousand living, breathing, and spore-toting visitors was found to be causing irreparable damage to the ancient wall paintings. But twenty years later, managers of the site opened a replica cave that was designed explicitly with tourists in mind, and the facsimile has proved very popular indeed.[11] "I wasn't sure beforehand whether it was worth visiting a reproduction, but in hindsight it totally was," a British tourist wrote on Tripadvisor of his family's visit to the site. "It brought cave paintings to life in a way that you can't appreciate from a small, flat photo. . . . The reproduction is like being in the real cave, from the look and feel of the 'rock' to the temperature, acoustics and atmosphere. It's not at all like looking in a glass display box at a museum." And while tourists admire the replica, the real cave is preserved for scientists, safe from the masses.

Or I think of the fake "ice cave" that I walked through on the same Iceland trip on which I met Eliza Reid and paid a visit to the very real—and very crowded—Justin Bieber canyon. The cave lives inside the impressive "nature museum" that sits atop a hill in Reykjavík, and it offers visitors the chance to get a taste of the chilly claustrophobia that I experienced inside the genuine ice cave that Benjamin Claret still carves into the Mer de Glace. I visited the fake cave in Reykjavík with my family just a few months after I spent the morning clinging to the edge of Benjamin's ice-drilling machine. Compared to the real ice cave, the fake one was much more peaceful—and infinitely more educational.

At the museum in Reykjavík, we stood in line in a carpeted corner for about fifteen minutes before entering the ice tunnel and marveling at its frozen walls; the temperature was so cold that we could see our breath. We emerged from the cave into a high-ceilinged gallery that hosts an interactive exhibit on glaciers and climate change. Fake though it was, the museum's version of a glacial cave was a compelling way to experience and learn about an important feature of our natural world. Soon, this kind of fake experience of a glacier will be the only option available.

Continuing the theme, it's easy to see how tourism's embrace of falsehood leads directly to virtual reality, which has already become popular. Virtual reality allows visitors to "experience" Mount Fuji, China's famous terra-cotta warriors, or St. Peter's Basilica—without contributing to problems of overcrowding or damage brought about by visitors' presence. In April 2020, with many of us in full pandemic lockdown, my fellow journalist Debra Kamin and I cowrote a story for the New York Times that was given the headline "52 Places, Virtually," in which we described how all of us who were stuck at home could get a digital taste of some of the year's most interesting tourist sites.[12] For people who are content with a brief experience of a "must-see" place, this brand of falsity could be just what they're looking for.

And, in some cases at least, that's great. The fact that people can scratch an itch through a VR tour, a fake cave, or a day in a theme-park version of Europe might mean they won't impose their bodies or project their fantasies onto real-world places where normal people are just trying to go about their daily lives: places like Barcelona or Hawai'i—or Amsterdam's historic center. The deeper problem with tourist traps, perhaps *the only* significant problem with tourist traps, arises when the fantastical, rule-bending world they represent begins to trespass on everyday life.

✽   ✽   ✽

The visitor industry has been a part of life in Amsterdam for centuries, starting with the religious pilgrims who traveled to the city in the Middle Ages and expanding to include the many sailors who paid short visits to the city center (and its sex workers) in the seventeenth and eighteenth centuries, at the height of Amsterdam's power as a global hub of commerce and shipping. But it wasn't until after the Second World War that the city's tourism industry really began to take shape, alongside the rise in international tourism more broadly. Fueled in part by the social and cultural radicalism that began to take root in the city in the 1960s, Amsterdam soon became known as a haven for the free-spirited, a reputation that would increasingly shape its image abroad in ensuing decades. But tourism in Amsterdam really began to take off following the financial crisis of 2008, which hit the Netherlands hard. As most of the country's banks were nationalized or otherwise bailed out, leaders in Amsterdam, by far the nation's biggest tourist destination, turned to visitors to revive the flagging economy.

The good news was they already had their product: Amsterdam's historic center, and its infamous Red Light District. And they already had a branding strategy for the city: I amsterdam, which the city launched in 2004 with the primary goal of attracting both tourists and foreign investment. But the marketing campaigns picked up following the crash of 2008. The tone of some of the ads also shifted away from the values and aims that the original I amsterdam branding strategy had espoused, which included a desire to *reduce* the city's reputation as a place of sex, drugs, and rock and roll. In 2010, I amsterdam launched a tourism marketing campaign featuring a two-minute video that depicts the ultimate sloppy night out. The video—titled "How to Spend €1,000 in Amsterdam"[13]—shows a visitor to the city ordering rounds of shots, crashing a bike on the street, bribing a police officer to get out of a fine for public urination, and ending the night with an amorous encounter with a very attractive woman. The video, which went live on YouTube in September 2010, seems to have motivated plenty of tourists. "Dude. I wish I saw this for inspiration before I went," wrote one YouTube commenter, adding: "Awesome that it's made by the country's tourist program itself. Respect." Another was equally inspired: "i need to go there before i die . . . and live that . . . at least, just once!!!!" Several others asked for the name of the actress hired for the shoot.

It's hard to know how much of Amsterdam's tourism growth to attribute to marketing campaigns and how much to the steady growth in tourism worldwide—particularly in Europe—that happened throughout the 2010s. Either way, Amsterdam's leaders got what they were looking for: hotel visitor numbers grew from 5.3 million in 2010[14] to 9.2 million in 2019[15]—and that's not even counting Airbnb stays. But it didn't take long for local attitudes toward tourism to shift dramatically, and the government wasn't far behind.

The first signs of a change in mood came in 2013, when local newspapers started reporting that residents of the city center were unhappy with how things were going in their neighborhood. Tourists were leaving all sorts of unseemly things behind them in the streets—litter, urine, vomit, excrement. They were also making way too much noise at night, and crowding the streets so much that residents could barely pass. Before long, the cool boutiques and bars that Amsterdammers liked to frequent were replaced with places that sold bad food and cheap tourist bric-a-brac. Tourism was an invading army, and the residents were being pillaged.

Within a couple of years of those first grumblings against tourism, the outcry grew so loud that Amsterdam's tourism marketing board made an about-face: instead of *marketing* the city to potential tourists, the agency began to spend its budget on *managing* the visitors who were already there. (This shift put Amsterdam at the forefront of a trend in urban tourism that would accelerate in Europe and beyond in the years that followed.) Amsterdam's reversal on tourism promotion culminated in 2023, when City Hall launched an anti-marketing campaign called "Stay Away," which was targeted at young men from Britain. In what can almost be seen as a mirror image of the I amsterdam video from thirteen years earlier, the 2023 campaign featured videos depicting drunk tourists being handcuffed, taken away by police, and fingerprinted and photographed at the local station. "Coming to Amsterdam for a messy night?" reads the closing caption of one of the thirty-second spots. "Stay away."[16] (A twenty-four-year-old Dutch bartender working in the Red Light District told me the campaign was "totally cringe," echoing the sentiment—if not the exact phrasing—that I heard from each of the half dozen or so people in Amsterdam I asked about the campaign, one of whom was an elected city official.)

But the changes weren't all just talk. While Amsterdam's leaders were overhauling how they portrayed the city to potential visitors, they also imposed strict regulations on tourist activity, particularly in the Red Light District. In the decade following 2013, city leaders raised Amsterdam's tourist accommodation tax; introduced a tax on cruise ships; banned smoking cannabis on the street in certain areas; forbade guided group tours in the historic center; banned organized pub crawls; and enacted some of Europe's strictest regulations on Airbnb and other tourist rentals. They also introduced controls on visitor behavior in the city center, which I saw in action on the night that I stopped by the SEX PALACE. From the early evening, red-shirted staffers were on hand to guide the pedestrian traffic flows, using metal barriers to make a one-way system in the tightest spots; I didn't see anyone disobey. Police officers were also patrolling on foot, and I saw one man being issued a fine on the spot for walking around with a glass of beer. But despite all the measures the city adopted, when I visited Amsterdam in the summer of 2023, everyone I spoke to agreed that serious problems with tourism persisted in the Red Light District. And the specific complaints were largely unchanged: crowding, litter, street noise in the wee hours of the morning.

The mayor of Amsterdam, Femke Halsema, is pushing for a drastic solution: having already transformed the way the city both markets and regulates tourism, she thinks it's time to overhaul the product they're selling to tourists in the Red Light District. To that end, she's proposed a ban on the sale of cannabis to anyone who can't prove that they reside in the Netherlands. She also wants to close the "windows" and move all the neighborhood's sex workers to an "erotic center," a sex hotel that would sit on the city's outskirts. (Halsema, through a spokesperson, declined my requests for an interview, so I'm drawing on public information here.)[17] This approach would effectively rid the Red Light District of the two essential elements of its tourist fantasy: sex and drugs. By bursting that fantasy, perhaps the mayor could make the neighborhood's problems with tourism disappear.

Or perhaps not. Lennard Roubos, a thirty-year resident of the Red Light District, isn't thrilled with the mayor's approach.

Lennard works for an organization called We Live Here, which aims to make visitors aware of the fact that the Red Light District isn't just about sex, drugs, and rock and roll—it's also a place where people live. Lennard agrees there are problems with tourism, but he doesn't think they stem from the sex workers or coffee shops selling weed, which have been around for decades. The mayor's approach would extinguish the spirit of the neighborhood, he told me, adding that the real source of the problem is the sheer growth in tourist crowds, which he said was far from inevitable.

"It was really because of the promotional campaign executed by the municipality," Lennard said, noting that the I amsterdam campaign was "much too successful" in attracting too many of the wrong type of visitor to the city. "We are always trying to propagate a balance between tourist and local interest," he said. "But the balance is very hard to find these days."

To what extent can tourist traps and reality coexist? As long as the tourist numbers stay low enough, the friction is minimal, and we can all enjoy the many benefits that tourist traps can provide. But when tourist numbers get too high—and too many of those tourists fall too deep into the tourist fantasy—then the strains become untenable. A threshold is crossed, and the no-rules fantasyland spills over into everyday life. As tourism numbers globally rise in the years ahead, many more destinations will become inundated—with or without the assistance of tourism marketing campaigns. The challenges of Amsterdam's Red Light District are most likely a sign of things to come.

Governments will have a lot of work to do here, but part of the answer lies with us as well. Because we tourists have more power than we think. Let's return briefly to the definition of an "old tourist" that I offer in the introduction: this is a pure consumer who sees the people and places he encounters when he travels as nothing more than a means to some self-serving end; he confines his destination and its inhabitants to a preconceived story, and fails to consider them with any real empathy; he projects his fantasies onto the place and its people, and reacts with disappointment or outrage when the reality fails to match his romanticized vision.

An old tourist and a tourist trap make for a dangerous combination, as any resident of the Red Light District can probably tell you. But I wonder about the possible impact of our new tourist, the person who strives to understand his impact on the place he visits, and who even hopes he might leave the place better than he found it. Can he have a say here, too?

* * *

It's a sunny Saturday in the Red Light District, about twelve hours after my peep show experience, and an entirely different scene is playing out on the sidewalk in front of the SEX PALACE. A small but riotous parade is passing by, and half a dozen of the establishment's employees have stepped out onto the sidewalk to cheer it on. The parade consists of a small marching band in mismatched red T-shirts, a few costumed entertainers on stilts, an enormous puppet version of what looks like a llama, and a clown on a unicycle careening toward his laughing spectators. It's a joyous procession, and it seems to fit the mood on the streets: light and bright and exuberant. The only remnants of the night before are the empty beer bottles and discarded to-go containers that litter the sidewalk underfoot, but no one seems to be looking down anyway.

The parade is part of a festival being put on by a local arts and culture association, and it's happening throughout the Red Light District over the next two days. There are concerts, lectures, photo exhibitions, cooking workshops, and sports activities, all hosted by local artists, musicians, businesses, and nonprofits. The festival is aimed at Amsterdam residents, Elena Simons, one of the organizers, told me, which is why its official program and flyers are printed only in Dutch. Tourists are welcome to join in, she added, but the real point is to help Amsterdammers rediscover their historic city center and what it has to offer—which, from the looks of things, seems to be quite a lot.

I take a stroll through the neighborhood in the Saturday sun and end up in the area around the Oude Kerk, the soaring medieval church that occupies prime real estate in the Red Light District. On the far side of the church, I stop by the Prostitution Information Center, where I interviewed Nat, a sex worker, a couple of days earlier. Nat is there again today, alongside Brenda, a fifty-nine-year-old window worker, who invites me to join her at a table outside. As part of the festival, a free lecture is underway inside the center—this one is about what it's like to become a "cam girl," a sex worker who sells her images and videos online. I linger outside, chatting with Brenda, then continue my stroll to the south side of the church, where I encounter a local choir singing oldies songs to a delighted crowd. Then I round another corner of the church and reach my final stop: a stand just across from a café with the apt name of Quartier Putain—which means "whore quarter" in French. Stefanie Caton is standing in a patch of shade nearby, next to some picnic tables and a string of small colored flags that have been tacked up for decoration. In front of her, there's a blackboard sign on which someone has written in rainbow-colored chalk: "Make Your Pledge to Amsterdam." A handful of people are sitting around the picnic tables, using the paper and markers provided to write and decorate their own promise to the city.

With her salt-and-pepper pixie haircut and rainbow flag T-shirt, Stefanie, who's running the stand this afternoon, looks very much like the social entrepreneur she is—and she's eager to tell me how things are going. One recent interaction seems to have left an impression on her: three men—from Libya, Iraq, and Malaysia, respectively—stopped by shortly before I did to make a pledge. She describes how the three men took their time thinking about what they'd write. They started by talking about what they love about the city, which they've now visited four times together: the diversity, the urban mobility, and the linguistics they encounter. Then they made their pledge, which was to find ways to embrace and support all those things that they love about Amsterdam—both during and between their visits.

"Those are the tourists we want here," Stefanie says, beaming. She adds that she hopes to introduce an Amsterdam pledge to hotels all over the city. As tourists check into their accommodation, they'd be presented with an array of pledges from which to choose—to help keep the city clean, to maintain a respectful noise level in the street, or simply to keep in mind that the city they're visiting is also a home for many people.

Such gestures may smack of tokenism. Would a tourist really change his behavior just because he ticked a box or signed his name to a little piece of paper? But this approach has been tried with relative success in other places popular with tourists, including Iceland, New Zealand, and Finland, as well as Aspen, Colorado, and Bend, Oregon. Perhaps Stefanie's pledge might serve as a little nudge, a timely reminder that it's possible to be more than a pure consumer in search of a fantasyland in someone else's backyard; that it's possible to aim for better, even if we don't always reach it; that it's not too presumptuous for us to aspire to do something good for a place we visit.

I ask Stefanie what she thinks of the mayor's proposal to move sex workers out of the neighborhood, and she cuts me off before I finish the question. "I dislike it," she says: the sex workers are part of the neighborhood, and they need to be protected and treated with respect. There's a place for them here, too. "We have to make this community work again, together—and help our guests, the tourists, look at this community another way," Stefanie says. "I already see a lot of positive-minded people, but if I could wave a magic wand, there would be even more positive thinkers. The negativity would go away, and this community would be a community again. And that community would include the visitors."

Stefanie returns to the Libyan, Iraqi, and Malaysian tourists and the pledge they made just before I stopped by. "It's so heartwarming," she says, noting that the Libyan man complimented her rainbow flag T-shirt, saying it represents the openness and diversity that he so appreciates about Amsterdam.

"I mean, those guys love this place. They're invested. And we need those people, right? So let's look at those guys and let's ask *them*, 'What can we do? Can you help us? Can you think with us?' And they already do. Those are the tourists we want here."

Chapter Seven

The New Tourist

On June 24, 2023, which happened to be the very day that I met Stefanie Caton in Amsterdam, the *New Yorker* published a "Weekend Essay" by the philosopher Agnes Callard that was titled "The Case against Travel."[1] Citing Emerson, Socrates, and Kant, among other luminaries, Callard argued that we'd all be better off if we opted out of the tourist exercise. Travel is a noble sounding but "self-undermining" pursuit that transforms us "into the worst version of ourselves while convincing us that we're at our best," a phenomenon she dubbed "the traveler's delusion." Travel dehumanizes us, Callard added, forcing us into the role of spectator to the spectacle of the people and places we encounter. She described the tourist as "a deferential character" who ignores his own values and impulses and relies on external sources—experts, postcards, "conventional wisdom"—to figure out what he ought to do when he's visiting a place. This very outsourcing "renders the tourist incapable of experience."

To illustrate the vapidness of the tourist exercise, Callard described a trip she took to Abu Dhabi in which she visited a falcon hospital, solely because the place was "one of the answers to the question, 'What does one do in Abu Dhabi?'" The resulting visit was as meaningful as you might expect: she walked away underwhelmed. "If you are going to see something you neither value nor aspire to value, you are not doing much of anything besides locomoting," she concluded. While we all like to think that we come back transformed or otherwise improved by our vacations, this is a delusion. "Travel is a boomerang," she wrote. "It drops you right where you started."

There was some pushback against Callard's essay after it was published, including in the *Guardian* and the *New York Times*. But the public reaction to the piece wasn't as strong as I expected, given how close to home Callard's essay would've hit for so many of us. Chalk it up to "the case against travel" being a pretty easy argument to make in the summer of 2023. With the disappearance of the lockdowns, travel bans, and testing requirements that had tried everyone's patience under COVID, tourist numbers were surging. In the summer of 2023, Barcelona, Venice, Dubai, and other top tourist spots broke records they'd set in 2019, and the news was full of stories about the damage all these visitors were causing.

In the weeks after Callard's essay was published, news stories appeared about the tourist who used a key to carve "Ivan + Haley '23" into a wall of the Colosseum in Rome; about a group of young Germans who toppled an ancient Italian statue while posing for a photo for social media; and about a Canadian teenager who carved his name into the wall of a 1,200-year-old temple in

Japan. Also that summer, the climate reared its head. "Tourists Flee Rhodes Wildfires in Greece's Largest-Ever Evacuation," ran one headline from CNN. "Maui Tourism, an Economic Mainstay, Sparks Anger amid Fire Ruin," Reuters reported a few weeks later. "Wish You Weren't Here! How Tourists Are Ruining the World's Greatest Destinations," sneered the headline of an essay that ran in the *Guardian* in August, a piece that quickly shot to the top of the paper's "most viewed" list. The same month, a *New York Times* story described how the summer's thunderstorms, fires, heat waves, and tornadoes had been wreaking havoc on people's travel plans. "Is This the End of the Summer Vacation as We Know It?" asked the headline. At that point, it seemed like a rhetorical question.

Against that backdrop, Callard's essay made a whole lot of sense. It may have struck some as the inevitable end point of the trajectory on which we all appeared to be hurtling during the summer of 2023. Every day, we were presented with new evidence that travel was not only self-indulgent but destructive—to the people and places we were visiting as well as to the very integrity of our earthly home. Callard's essay didn't reference the climate impacts of tourism, or any other negative externalities; her focus was on the ways in which we tourists are the victims of our own delusions. But to readers of her essay, the jump from *self*-destruction to *world* destruction would have been an easy one to make.

With only a couple of exceptions, which I'll get to shortly, I agree with all the points in Callard's essay. I especially appreciate her description of tourists as "unchanged changers"—people who inflict their presence on a place without pausing to open their hearts, minds, or souls to the experience. And I'm grateful for any self-reflection that Callard's essay may have inspired among her readers. But Callard goes wrong in assuming that what she describes is the whole picture of tourism. Her essay portrays only a single cross section of an enormous landscape, and the cross section she has chosen is among the worst of them all. The piece reads like a 2,400-word definition of an "old tourist," which, as narrowly focused as it may be, is nonetheless a valuable and constructive contribution to the public conversation.

There are plenty of old tourists in the world, of course. It's important we understand them—and learn to recognize them when they show up in the mirror. Because, just like Callard at the falcon hospital, most of us have probably been an "unchanged changer" at some point, if not at many points, during our travels. I know that's certainly true for me. I also know that I can be—and, I would venture to say, that I often *have been*—something a whole lot better than what Callard describes. I'm guessing you probably have, too.

Call me an idealist, but I believe it's well within our power as tourists to rise above the soulless, consumerist exercise that Callard rightfully condemns. Not only are we able to do this; a lot of us really *want* to. And given the existential and fundamentally transnational nature of the crises that our species may face in the years to come—catastrophic climate change, ecological collapse, global thermonuclear war, runaway artificial intelligence, a pandemic even more lethal than COVID—our willingness to strive for our highest potential as tourists may soon be nothing short of essential.

* * *

On the day I meet Fatimah Al Zimam in Riyadh, the capital of her home country of Saudi Arabia, she appears in the lobby of my hotel wearing black athleisure tights and a lightweight button-down shirt that hits just below her hips. Her sleeves are rolled to her elbows, and her tight black curls are half swept up with a clip that keeps her face clear and open to the world. Fatimah is a Saudi woman—she has never lived anywhere else—and she isn't wearing any sort of headscarf. When I remark on this, shortly after she shakes my hand beneath the hotel's enormous portrait of the Saudi crown prince, Fatimah tells me she hasn't covered her hair in years.

I'm six days into my first-ever trip to Saudi Arabia, and it's no stretch to say I'm feeling a little out of my depth. I've done plenty of solo travel over the years, but never to the Middle East. Solo or otherwise, I've never been anywhere on the Arabian Penin-sula, unless you count changing planes in Doha. Before I started planning this trip, I didn't speak any Arabic; I had only a passing understanding of Islam; and everything I knew about Saudi Ara-bia I'd either read on the news or gleaned from friends who last visited the country a generation before. As a tourist destination, Saudi Arabia was about as foreign to me as any place on the planet.

So my trip wasn't inspired by a deep personal connection to Saudi Arabia; I'd embarked on it more out of a profound profes-sional curiosity. I'd heard some fascinating things about tourism in Saudi Arabia, which is at once one of the world's oldest and newest travel destinations. Millions of Muslim pilgrims have made the trek to the Arabian desert since the seventh century, when the Prophet Muhammad made the hajj to Mecca one of the pillars of Islam. But modern, non-Muslim tourism in Saudi Arabia only started in September 2019, when the government began issuing general tourist visas while pumping billions of dollars into secular tourism, which at the time was a minor activity indeed.

The shift was part of a broader trend of Middle Eastern countries opening up to Western tourists, which began with the United Arab Emirates in the 1990s, and later spread to Oman, Qatar, Kuwait, and Bahrain. Saudi Arabia was the last, biggest, and most conservative player to enter the game. And when it did, it dove in headfirst. In its Vision 2030, the Saudi government identified tourism as one of the key drivers of its economy, and the government announced that it hoped to attract a hundred million international visitors.[2] I interviewed an academic who told me that Saudi Arabia was the single most important place I should visit for a book about tourism at this particular moment in history. My book editor was intrigued. The flights were reasonable, and the dates worked. What the hell, I thought; let's do it.

But I'll be honest when I say I was scared to go—more scared than I've been ahead of any trip in recent memory. I'd read about the Saudi government's human rights record, its treatment of journalists, its oppression of women. I'd also heard that the government—keen to project a favorable image of Saudi Arabia on the world stage—was actively working to manage the media narrative about tourism in the country. From my perspective, none of these things seemed particularly auspicious. So I decided to visit the country purely as a tourist: I would request no official interviews, put my voice recorder away, and document the experience as any tourist would: through photos and videos taken on my phone and scribbles in my notebook back at the hotel at the end of the day. I wanted to get the same experience that any other Western visitor would have in Saudi Arabia. I didn't want the government to assign me a babysitter; I also didn't want to end up in a Saudi jail. So I scoured the internet for blog entries written by women who'd traveled alone to the country. I reached out to friends of friends who'd been there recently, asking them for contacts and advice on where to go, what to see, how to behave, how to dress. I downloaded an Arabic-language audiobook and ordered a couple of burkas on Amazon. I booked my flights. I took a deep breath and told myself it would all be over in a week.

So here am I at ten o'clock on a Friday morning in Riyadh, and Fatimah—whom I've hired as my tour guide for the day, on the recommendation of a friend of a friend of a friend—has a full slate of activities planned for us. She's going to take me to a UNESCO World Heritage site on the outskirts of the city; to the Saudi national museum; and to an ancient fortress that sits in the middle of modern Riyadh. Our mode of transportation is Fatimah's silver pickup truck, a battered old GMC Sierra whose glove compartment is adorned with a fading Bart Simpson sticker. As she zigzags through the heavy traffic on our first foray of the morning, Fatimah, who is thirty-three years old, describes her childhood in Saudi Arabia's lush south, where she grew up in a household with her mother and father, along with her father's second wife and her twenty-five siblings and half-siblings. Fatimah says she refused to wear a headscarf in public when she became an adolescent. And she tells me how she discovered her passion for rock climbing in her late twenties, after she took a free course offered by the Saudi government.

The museum and historic sites we see together are interesting and educational, but by far the most captivating aspect of the day is my conversations with Fatimah, which start that morning in her pickup truck and continue pretty much unabated for the next twelve hours. For lunch, we end up at a restaurant in Diriyah, a sprawling, open-air network of shops, eateries, and tourist attractions that's one of the Saudi government's "giga projects." These are places where the government is investing somewhere north of a billion dollars to build a fresh future for the country's oil-based economy. Other giga projects include NEOM, a futuristic megacity that's due to cover an area the size of Massachusetts in the middle of the desert, and the Red Sea Project, a luxury development that includes a new international airport, fifty resorts, and some eight thousand hotel rooms. Here in Diriyah, which sits next to a historic site that's considered the ancestral home of the Al Saud dynasty, the focus is on heritage tourism—but there's plenty of shopping and dining to do, too.

Around midday, Fatimah and I take a table for two in a restaurant whose air-conditioning is so intense that it instantly gives me goose bumps. The dining room is bright, airy, and overflowing with a small greenhouse's worth of plant life; the menu features "Next-Level Avo Toast," crispy calamari, and wild mushroom risotto. Between sips of Perrier, Fatimah says matter-of-factly that she's in the process of splitting up with her husband. He never provided her with a house or even got a real job; she's always paid their rent, with the income she earned first as a math teacher then as a tour guide. She's been living alone for years, but hasn't ended the marriage because she was waiting for the rules to change, which finally happened just a few days before. Fatimah's planning to file the papers the following week; she's looking forward to making it official.

That night, Fatimah offers me a lift to the airport, and we end up stuck in one of the top ten traffic jams I've experienced so far in life. But we have plenty of ways to pass the time. As we wait for the line of cars to inch forward, Fatimah coaches me on how to introduce myself in Arabic and tries to teach me how to count to ten. She passes me her phone to show me her favorite TikToks and Instagram memes, and tells me about the time she peed on a nest of rattlesnakes when she was camping in the desert. She asks about my family, my upbringing, and life in France. I ask what she thinks of her country's leaders, whose images appear everywhere: on billboards along the highway, above the reception desk of every hotel and office building, in the ads that show up on my social media feeds. I ask whether she believes women in Saudi Arabia have all the freedoms they deserve, and I ask what she thinks of the assassination of the journalist Jamal Khashoggi, an incident that—judging by her response—she's clearly spent some time considering. Her answers are thoughtful; many surprise me, and I find myself disagreeing with several outright. I push back on some of her answers, and she responds accordingly—but we never come close to an argument. Mostly, Fatimah and I watch the booming megacity of Riyadh creep by outside the windows of her pickup truck, and we talk about our lives.

After I get home, I pitch a Q&A with Fatimah to my editors at the *New York Times*, and I'm delighted when they say yes. I reach Fatimah again over Zoom a few weeks later to conduct the official interview, which I then write up, adding important context at the top. I describe Saudi Arabia's recent opening to secular tourists, and I note the country's dismal human rights record, adding that Saudi Arabia has been ranked the world's second-most-dangerous destination for LGBTQ travelers. But I try to place Fatimah in the context of her country and the rapid changes it's experiencing, and how tourism ties in with that evolution.

When the piece goes online, the comments section isn't quite as sunny as it was for the Q&A with Eliza Reid. Several commenters reference the crown prince, Mohammed bin Salman, commonly known as MBS, the de facto ruler of the country and the one who the U.S. government says ordered the assassination of Khashoggi in 2018. A couple of days after the Q&A is published, I get an email about the crown prince, too.

"Just curious—how much did MBS pay you to tourism-wash his country? Or was the payment done strictly in bonesaws?" one reader, who calls himself John, writes me in an email. "I'd say you should be ashamed to write pieces like this but clearly your conscious [*sic*] is for sale."

*　　*　　*

As an American who's lived outside the United States for most of my adult life, I've met several people over the years who've told me that—"no offense, but"—they refuse to set foot in my home country. Their concern is sometimes practical: they're afraid they'll be shot, or that they'll trip on the sidewalk and end up with a $50,000 hospital bill. More often, though, their refusal to visit the U.S. is philosophical: they're disgusted by my home country's policies on abortion, race, immigration, policing, or the vicious nature of American bipartisan politics. They've seen the headlines and—no, thank you—they don't want any part of it.

I don't fight people on these things. They can think what they want, and I usually see where they're coming from, in any case. But those conversations always break my heart. I wish all my foreign friends could see past the thin shell of their prebaked judgments of my home country, as accurate as some of those judgments may be. Those people who refuse to visit see the United States as a potent symbol of something that scares or disgusts them. I, on the other hand, see my home country as a deeply flawed and beautiful place that's home to millions of diverse souls, including many of my closest friends and family members. I usually don't say this out loud, but I always hope the naysayers might one day visit the U.S. and see there's a lot more to it than the politics and crises they read about in the news. Maybe, someday, they will.

I wouldn't say the week I spent as a tourist in Saudi Arabia at the age of forty-one changed me as a person. But it did transform my understanding of a part of the world I'd known very little about prior to my trip. Did my time in Saudi Arabia make me think *better* of the country? I wouldn't say so. I was taken aback by many things: the stark beauty of the desert landscape; the immensity of the infrastructure development in the middle of that desert; the fact, as I learned in preparation for my trip, that homosexuality in Saudi Arabia is a crime punishable by death;[3] the looming omnipresence of the country's leaders in both the physical environment and the minds of many Saudis. ("There are no protesters in Saudi Arabia," one business owner told me.)

Mainly, though, my week as a tourist in Saudi Arabia gave me a glimpse of the breadth and depth of my ignorance of the place. My experience as a tourist there cracked open my thin shell of a judgment about Saudi Arabia and gave me the chance to build something more substantial in its stead. My opinions of the country's politics haven't changed. But I now know that Saudi Arabia is a deeply flawed and beautiful place that's home to millions of diverse souls, including my fun and courageous tour guide, Fatimah. Had I let my fear prevent me from visiting, I would've denied myself the chance to experience that shift in perspective—which was a valuable gift indeed.

I'm guessing that you, dear reader, have probably had a similar mind-opening experience when you've ventured away from home. If you spend any time speaking to the people you meet when you travel, it's very hard not to.

*   *   *

So there you have my anecdote from a trip to the Middle East, which I offer as an extended counterpoint to Callard's story of her visit to the falcon hospital in Abu Dhabi. But there's more to explore here, too. We need to examine the assumptions that underlie many of Callard's critiques of the modern tourist. Because, at a fundamental level, Callard's understanding of what a tourist is—and isn't—is baked into a particular conception of tourism that now predominates in the West, but which is hardly the only way of seeing things.

Human beings were crossing borders, and spending money while doing so, for thousands of years before the notion of a "tourism industry" came along. We traveled as migrants, merchants, pilgrims, invading armies, and, occasionally at first, as pleasure-seekers. Etymologically speaking, the first "tourists" appeared in

Europe in the second half of the eighteenth century.[4] The word was first used to describe wealthy young men on "Grand Tours" of the Continent, extended expeditions that were considered essential preparation for life in the highest echelons of society. But it wasn't until the nineteenth century that those kinds of experiences started to become available to anyone outside the upper classes. The word "tourism" made its first appearance in the written record in 1811, and the next hundred years would see the small but growing population of tourists, mainly originating in Europe and North America, begin to define what the term could mean.[5]

Things got off to a quick start. The rapid spread of steamships and railroads in the first half of the nineteenth century made it easier and cheaper for people to traverse long distances, while popular travel accounts spread the word about these wonderful new ways to see the world. In 1841, an enterprising British missionary named Thomas Cook began charging his fellow teetotalers one shilling per head for local journeys by rail. Over the next two decades, Cook expanded to weekslong group excursions to France, Switzerland, Italy, Egypt, the United States, and beyond—an innovation that would later earn him the nickname "the father of modern tourism." Tourism was growing on the other side of the Atlantic, too, as early-nineteenth-century hotels sprang up in the Catskills, the White Mountains, and Niagara Falls, attracting wealthy city dwellers in search of a brief taste of the sublime in nature.[6] New beach resorts from Maine to New Jersey transformed the United States' northeastern coastline into a summertime playground.[7]

Would-be American tourists were looking farther afield, too, thanks in part to the writings of Mark Twain, whose popular and irreverent dispatches from Hawai'i, Europe, the Middle East, and North Africa helped propel the Midwestern writer to fame years before he published anything about Tom Sawyer or Huck Finn. *The Innocents Abroad*, which appeared in 1869, was Twain's account of the five-month group trip that took him from Paris to Damascus, from St. Peter's Basilica to the Pyramids of Giza. "It would be well if such an excursion could be gotten up every year and the system regularly inaugurated," Twain wrote in the book's conclusion, then explained his reasoning, in what would become one of his most famous lines: "Travel is fatal to prejudice, bigotry and narrow-mindedness, and many of our people need it sorely on these accounts," he wrote. "Broad, wholesome, charitable views of men and things can not be acquired by vegetating in one little corner of the earth all one's lifetime." The book, whose alternate title was *The New Pilgrims' Progress*, sold seventy thousand copies in the year it was published. It would go on to become Twain's bestselling work during his lifetime.[8]

But it didn't take long for tourists to begin attracting derision from within their own well-to-do ranks. Fyodor Dostoevsky, traveling in Western Europe in 1862, bemoaned the "self-satisfied and perfectly mechanical curiosity of British tourists . . . who look more into their guidebooks than at the sights."[9] E. M. Forster's *A Room with a View*, published in 1908, satirized the well-to-do English tourists in Florence who looked down on the somewhat less privileged tourists who traveled by way of Thomas Cook—a man whose name and eponymous business had by that point become synonymous with package tours. ("I knew he was trying it on," fumes one Englishman, complaining of a perceived slight from an Italian carriage driver. "He is treating us as if we were a party of Cook's tourists.") Even Twain, an outright supporter of the tourist enterprise, recognized the comedy inherent in the tourist's earnest desire to travel, at one point calling himself and his companions "a pack of blockheads . . . galloping about the world, and looking wise, and imagining we are finding out a good deal about it!"

But gallop about they did. A hundred years after its etymological birth, tourism was still the domain of the rich—though it was no longer the exclusive domain of the superrich—and it was beginning to take on some of the structures and attitudes whose echoes we can still see today. But tourism before the world wars was still something of an oddball activity—a quixotic quest for those "new pilgrims" who could afford it. No one was talking about tourism as "an industry," at least not yet. But that would change soon.

*　　*　　*

Between 1950 and 2019, international tourist arrivals grew from 25 million to nearly 1.5 billion. By the time international travel came to a screeching halt with the border closures and lockdowns that took effect in March 2020, tourism had grown from a niche pastime to the world's most important mover of human beings. On the eve of the COVID-19 pandemic, tourism was driving roughly 10 percent of the global economy and underpinning 10 percent of the world's jobs. Tourism had spread to cities, villages, and wild, remote landscapes on every continent, leaving hardly any person or place untouched. And in ways that are impossible to quantify, tourism had fundamentally shaped our impressions of our fellow human beings and their languages and cultures. The tourism boom that began in the peace and economic prosperity that followed the Second World War had, by March 2020, left a profound, pervasive, and enduring imprint on the modern world.

To the extent that people were aware of this shift as it was happening, they developed competing frameworks to understand what this force was and what it meant. One of these frameworks was championed by a small but vocal group who held that tourism was primarily a force for peace—and even a human right. In May 1925, with the ravages of the Great War still fresh in Europeans' minds, fourteen national tourism organizations from across the Continent gathered in The Hague to "work for a lasting peace" by promoting tourism among the countries that had recently been at war. On July 5, 1941—less than two months after the most intense German bombing raid of the London Blitz—the *Times* of London predicted that Thomas Cook's company would be critical to a post-war future: "When peace comes, [Cook's] will have a great work to do for civilisation in helping to reopen the channels of intercourse between the nations," the editors wrote. The first issue of the *Tourist Review*, which appeared in 1946, drove the point home. "There is one easy way by which nations may come to understand each other," wrote Douglas Hacking, a member of the British House of Lords, "and that way is reciprocal interchange of tourists." Before the end of the decade, the United Nations would enshrine several facets of tourism within the Universal Declaration of Human Rights, which stated that all people have the right to cross international borders, and enjoy rest, leisure, and paid holidays from work.

The Cold War provided a new impetus for this idea of tourism as a force for peace. Khrushchev embraced tourism as an element of his policy of "peaceful coexistence," allowing tourist exchanges between the Soviet Union and the West beginning in the 1950s. And in 1957, the travel bureaus of the socialist states agreed that "the most effective path to mutual understanding and comprehension is for nations to speak to nations in the most direct manner, by tourism."[10] Later the same year, an international tourism conference in Prague brought together diplomats and travel industry officials from two dozen countries on either side of the Iron Curtain to make progress toward "the ideal of peace and undisturbed work for us all."[11]

The momentum behind this idea of tourism as a force for peace began to slow in the 1960s and '70s as the economic benefits of tourism became increasingly obvious—but it didn't disappear. The UN General Assembly declared 1967 the International Tourist Year, under the motto "Tourism, Passport to Peace."[12] In 1988, a thousand delegates gathered in Canada for a conference with the lofty title "Tourism, a Vital Force for Peace." Pope John Paul II sent the conference a prerecorded message, while President Ronald Reagan and Soviet leader Mikhail Gorbachev declared in a joint statement that "there should be greater understanding among our peoples and to this end we will encourage greater travel." After a lull in the 1990s, the concept gained traction again in the wake of the 9/11 attacks. In November 2001, the World Travel Market—one of the travel industry's biggest and most influential annual conferences—adopted the theme of "peace through tourism" for its opening ceremony.[13] The concept has seen something of a renaissance in the years since, in academia as well as in the tourism marketplace. But cynicism around this view has rightfully emerged, because the promise that your vacation can solve the world's problems is not only a lofty ideal; it's also a potent sales tool.

The people launching those critiques most likely fell into the camp that began to emerge in the 1960s: those who held that tourism is, first and foremost, an engine of capitalism. It was in the 1960s that people first started to talk about tourism as an "industry" in its own right: an export sector that creates jobs, generates revenue, and that can underpin powerful and sustained economic growth. This understanding of tourism might seem obvious to us now, but it was hardly inevitable. For one thing, academics debated whether tourism could even rightly be defined as "an industry," given how fragmented and diverse tourism activities can be, and the fact that only a portion of them can be considered "industrialized."[14] But that was beside the point to many who worked in tourism—people who had a powerful incentive to present their operations as contributing to a vital sector of the economy. As the academic Freya Higgins-Desbiolles has argued, the presentation of tourism as an "industry" allowed those who worked in the sector to gain clout and acceptance among those in power, and "to access support and resources that would otherwise be unobtainable."[15]

The new industry of tourism organized itself into professional associations complete with lobbyists, statisticians, and annual economic impact reports. It scored minister-level appointments in many governments; academic departments within universities (often inside the business school); and its own agency within the United Nations. Along the way, tourism became synonymous with hotel chains, cruise lines, airlines, and later the online platforms that accounted for much of tourism's economic contribution. These were people who had succeeded in monetizing humanity's impulse to move—in overlaying a capitalist meaning onto what for many had been primarily a heartfelt, wisdom-seeking pursuit.

And the product the industry was selling wasn't a laptop or a haircut or an expert's help on our tax returns. The product was the "destination" or the "experience" that the tourist would have there. While the proponents of tourism as an industry may have spoken of the social, cultural, and later environmental benefits of tourism, the overall goal for most of them was simple: they wanted to grow.

Alongside those who saw tourism primarily as a force for peace and those who considered it first and foremost an economic engine, there's a third group, which probably includes most of us. These are the people who thought of tourism as pure pleasure, a frivolous activity that doesn't merit any serious thought, let alone scrutiny. This kind of thinking is an easy trap to fall into, but it can be an insidious one. The "tourism as a frivolous pursuit" mindset can look like a city government that neither supports its tourism industry nor does anything to regulate it. It can look like a magazine editor who wants an article about the "top ten" beaches in a country and assigns the piece to someone who *has* never—and probably *will* never—set foot in the place. And it can look like a tourist who books a flight to one of those "top ten" spots just because she likes the look of the stock photos the editors picked to run alongside the text, and who wants to get the same shot for her Instagram feed. The recent headlines about the impacts of tourism have woken many of us from our slumber on this point, but the idea that tourism is a lightweight subject that requires no scrutiny or self-reflection has proven stubbornly persistent.

All three of these things are true. Tourism is at once a powerful social movement, an industry, and a frivolous pursuit. But by the summer of 2023, when Callard's essay appeared in the *New*

Yorker, it seemed clear that only two out of three of those conceptions of tourism had managed to stick in the public imagination. With some important exceptions, we tourists saw ourselves as unthinking pleasure-seekers and consumerist cogs in an industrial machine. We'd forgotten about the power we hold as contributors—however unwitting—to a vast and potent social force.

There's a danger inherent in this tourist mindset that we've slipped into. When we tourists view ourselves through a hedonistic or a capitalist lens, it's all too easy for us to inflict a huge amount of harm—on ourselves, as well as on the people and places we visit. We become unadulterated consumers who insist on getting "our money's worth" when we pay to consume the product we've selected: our destination of choice. When we see ourselves as consumers, we cast ourselves in the role of the dominant actor, the one who calls the shots. We objectify and commodify and, in so doing, belittle the human beings and landscapes we've come to "consume." And when we see ourselves as pure pleasure-seekers, we willfully blind ourselves to the impacts that our presence has on the people and places we visit. We become Callard's "unchanged changers."

In so many aspects of our lives, we stoop or rise to the expectations that we set for ourselves. When it comes to tourism, our expectations need a serious upgrade.

One of the many luminaries whom Callard rallies in support of her argument is the prolific British essayist, novelist, and social commentator G. K. Chesterton, born in 1874, who was indeed skeptical about the benefits of travel. Callard quotes Chesterton's belief that "travel narrows the mind," but she doesn't give him the chance to complete the thought. "I have never managed to lose my old conviction that travel narrows the mind," Chesterton writes in the opening line of a collection of essays from his travels in the United States in the 1920s. But then he continues: "At least a man must make a double effort of moral humility and imaginative energy to prevent it from narrowing his mind." Chesterton goes on to tell us that he believes in "a better way" for people to meet each other across their national boundaries, and he admits that "to hint at some such better way" is the real purpose of his book. This "better way" is a form of communion that "largely consists of laughter," Chesterton explains. It's an even exchange in which no one considers himself superior—"a form of friendship between nations which is actually founded on differences."[16]

If we tourists are looking to rise above the low expectations and limited mindset of the "unchanged changer," then striving to embody Chesterton's "double effort of moral humility and imaginative energy" is an excellent place to start. We need to encounter each other on an equal footing and offer up something of ourselves, even as we ask something of the people and places we visit. And we need to remember that, yes, we are consumers, and yes, we are looking to enjoy ourselves when we travel. At the same time, we are also powerful agents of social change, whether we like it or not.

There's one more moment from my day with Fatimah that I want to tell you about. And it went like this:

It's around 8:00 p.m. in central Riyadh, and nearly time for me to head to the airport to catch my flight home. Fatimah and I have been enjoying a stroll through the area around the Al Masmak Fortress, an imposing structure that played a key role in the unification of Saudi Arabia in the early twentieth century. It's a warm and breezy evening, and the scene around the fortress is alive with parents pushing strollers, kids playing soccer, clusters of women chatting and laughing. But Fatimah already knows the traffic is going to be bad on the road to the airport, so she suggests we get going. We climb into her pickup truck, which is parked in a busy lot alongside the fortress, and she turns the key in the ignition. But nothing happens: the battery is dead.

Fatimah and I jump out of the car, and she peers under the hood. She'll get the cables from the back of the truck, she says; we'll need to find someone to give us a jump. But before Fatimah even steps away from the innards of her truck, a young man approaches and greets us in Arabic. He has a friendly face and dark, short-cropped hair; I would guess he's twenty-three or twenty-four, and he's wearing the traditional garb of a Saudi man: a simple white robe, called a thobe, that reaches past his knees. I listen without understanding as Fatimah speaks to him in Arabic and gestures toward the truck; at one point, I catch the word for "American." The young man looks at me and his face lights up; he immediately switches to English, which he speaks very well. His name is Abdullah, and he says he can help us fix the truck. Abdullah runs to get a portable battery pack from his own pickup truck, parked a stone's throw away, and within minutes Fatimah's engine is once again humming happily.

We thank him profusely and move to leave, but Abdullah is eager to chat. He wants to tell me about his recent trip to the United States. He and a friend recently finished their architecture exams, he says, so they splurged on a vacation to Orlando and New York City to celebrate. He tells me that he was scared to go—especially to New York, given what he'd heard about guns and crime in cities in the United States. But he came away with a very different impression of the country. "America is nothing like what you see on the news or social media," he tells me with enthusiasm. "I couldn't believe it—I felt so safe the entire time."

*   *   *

The tone of Callard's essay turns a little dark toward the end. She concludes by arguing that the real reason so many of us like to travel is that it distracts us from the "certainty of annihilation," the inevitability of our own death. "You don't like to think about the fact that someday you will do nothing and be nobody," she tells us. So instead of ruminating on death, we book a flight to Rome.

Maybe that's true for Callard? I have no idea how many people will join me in this opinion, but I'm deeply comforted by the knowledge that, a hundred years from now, the whole world will most likely have forgotten me completely, except perhaps for my immediate descendants. I find this liberating. So what if I embarrass myself in a radio interview or attract ridicule for something I write? The whole idea of this particular Paige McClanahan exists for only a brief, flickering moment. My life will soon be extinguished; I may as well shoot my shot.

Here, too, though, Callard gets something right, because—even if we don't fear death—"the certainty of annihilation" does provide us with a powerful motivation to venture away from home. But it's not because we have to distract ourselves from our impending doom. It's because one of the most constructive things we can do in our flickering moment of life is to embrace the chance to leave our comfort zones—those dangerous lairs where we learn to languish—and seek out the unfamiliar.

For the new tourists among us, tourism is a powerful means toward this end. Tourism compels us to reach beyond the languages, cultures, religions, and landscapes in which we feel most at home. Tourism asks us to find the courage to connect with the humanity in people who look, speak, dress, and pray in ways that may, at first glance, appear completely alien to us. Tourism inspires us to demand that our governments and the companies we patronize work to protect the people and places that we are so privileged to visit. And tourism compels us to recognize and confront the prejudices that continue to blind us, despite our best efforts. For the new tourists among us, tourism is a challenging—and often pleasurable—path toward a fuller and more compassionate life. Because the moment we make ourselves uncomfortable is the same moment that our souls begin to grow.

So does tourism narrow the mind or expand it? Does tourism build up our world or tear it apart? The only answer to those questions is "Yes." Our job, as tourists, is to wake up to the stakes of what we're doing, then use that knowledge to light our own path through the fog.

Epilogue

Seen from a few thousand feet aboveground, the waters off Waikīkī are about a dozen iridescent shades of blue, each somehow bluer than the last, and the hulking, jungle-covered mountains that serve as a permanent backdrop to the sprawl of Honolulu completely dwarf the high-rises that line the coast. From the air, the island of Oʻahu looks like a jagged, moss-covered rock jutting out of the ocean, with just a strip of concrete-loving humanity clinging to the coast.

It's a few days after Kūʻike showed me around Waimānalo, and my family and I are aboard a flight that's headed from Honolulu to the Big Island of Hawaiʻi. We've spent the past three weeks on Oʻahu. As I chased interviewees and sat in conference rooms, my husband worked remotely while our kids went to day camp and had playdates with their grandparents and Honolulu-based aunt, uncle, and cousins. Apart from my solo outing to a "luau" one night in Waikīkī—which was for research purposes, technically speaking—we've done barely any "touristy" stuff since we arrived. But now we're heading to the Big Island and switching into vacation mode.

We land in Hilo, pick up our rental car, and set off across the island's volcanic interior. In the space of just a couple of hours, we cross from jungly, humid lowlands to a bare, moonlike lava flow landscape at an altitude of more than 6,700 feet. Here, we step out of the car to discover that the air is thin and cold, despite the blazing sun. Another hour of driving brings us across silvery, windswept grasslands, through a forest of flowering trees, and finally back down to sea level in Kona, a quaint and sunny coastal town that feels a world away from the urban jungle of Waikīkī. We have time for a swim before sunset, then over a dinner of pizza and cold beer we make our plan for the next day: we'll head to Kahalu'u Bay, just a few miles south of Kona, where I'll interview Cindi Punihaole, the head of the bay's education center and one of the people whom John De Fries, the head of the Hawai'i Tourism Authority, has told me I should speak to. While Cindi and I are talking, my husband and my mother, who's traveling with us, will snorkel and play on the beach with the kids.

We get to Kahalu'u just before nine the next morning. It's nearly low tide, and the black lava rocks that edge the small, palm-lined bay are warming quickly in the morning sun. The water here is a smooth lapis blue, and at this point in the day, it's still nearly free of tourists. Cindi—who's wearing a long-sleeved royal blue rash guard, with "REEFTEACH" in all caps across the chest—greets the five of us at the edge of a covered, open-sided space that serves as an information center and picnic spot for visitors. Cindi's long black hair is held back neatly with a clip, and I estimate she's probably a youthful fifty-five. (I later learn she's over seventy.) Three other people in REEFTEACH shirts man a couple of tables covered with informational posters and a handful of products for sale: bottles of mineral-based sunscreen, snorkel mask straps, reef guidebooks, photo prints of sea turtles. Within a few minutes, it becomes that clear that this space, which Cindi calls "the pavilion," is very much her stomping grounds.

"Come sit down, and we'll talk story," Cindi says, guiding me toward a picnic table in a quiet corner. She runs to find a tablecloth, throws it across the table, then pulls out a full breakfast spread: a bag of everything bagels, cream cheese, raspberry jam, a tub of fresh cherries, chilled cans of pineapple juice, all straight from her little blue cooler. This is for me and my family, Cindi tells me: she's already eaten.

*   *   *

Cindi grew up on the Big Island in the 1950s and '60s, without electricity or running water. She and her family lived farther inland, but they would come down to the bay to visit friends and family, and to swim, fish, and collect mollusks, which her father would sell in town. Cindi remembers the bay being impossibly full of life, and an important source of food for her community; it also attracted tourists, but not nearly so many as today.

Cindi moved to Oregon for college at the age of eighteen and ended up living on the mainland for thirty years. When she returned to Hawai'i in 1998 to care for her aging parents, she was shocked to discover that the bay was devastated. There was almost no life left, and it was easy to see why. Every year, before the pandemic, about 400,000 visitors swam in the four-acre Kahalu'u Bay, which is known as one of the best snorkeling spots on the Big Island. Visitors trampled on the fragile corals and squashed the young algae, a critical food for fish and turtles, while their sunscreen-soaked bodies drove the bay's oxybenzone levels up to more than a thousand parts per billion—two hundred and fifty times the "high risk" threshold for the chemical.

The bay got so busy, and the local species faced so many threats, that the group of residents who wrote the Big Island's Destination Management Action Plan, or DMAP, included Kahaluʻu Bay among the island's two dozen "tourist hot spots" in need of additional monitoring and protections. Cindi says that the DMAPs— the same plans that John De Fries described to me a few weeks earlier—are essential. Here on the Big Island, the DMAP aims to "rebuild, redefine and reset the direction of tourism"; it sets out specific goals as well as ways to measure progress toward them. There are no real enforcement mechanisms—if an indicator is missed, no one will be fired or forced to pay a fine—but Cindi says it's a start, and she's optimistic about the island's capacity to bounce back. She tells me that, within two months of Hawaiʻi's closure to visitors in 2020, the bay came roaring back to life, at a pace that astounded her. The rebound was so complete that Kahaluʻu was soon nearly as vibrant as Cindi remembered it from her youth. "I really believe that if we give Mother Nature a chance, she doesn't need a lot of time," Cindi says. "But we need to hear her, and listen to her needs, and continue this healing process."

Now, with tourism coming back, Cindi believes the key is to engage with tourists and educate them about the bay in a way that's easy and fun. It's not that people *want* to harm the reef, she says: they just don't know what not to do. So every day since 2006, REEFTEACH volunteers have been on hand in the pavilion to explain what kind of sunscreen visitors should and shouldn't use;

to rope off areas that need time to recover; and to point out the orange buoys that mark the beginning of the area where snorkelers should only float, and never stand, to prevent damage to the corals. Cindi loves the educational component of her work. It's wonderful, she says, because the visitors you train become part of your team: when they're out there snorkeling, they call out the people they see who are breaking the rules.

But Cindi is working on structural questions, too. She wants to build a "snorkel trail," a series of buoys that will mark out a path for visitors to follow and provide them with safe places to stand to catch their breath or clear the water from their masks. She's also working to build community support to close the bay for perhaps one day every week, to give the species a chance to breathe. A few months earlier, the marine conservation group Mission Blue named Kahalu'u Bay a "Hope Spot" for ocean conservation worldwide, and they named Cindi a "Hope Spot Champion," a fact that she manages never to mention in our two-hour conversation (I only know because I've read it online). But she does tell me that she's advising other small bays around the world on how they can follow Kahalu'u's lead.

*   *   *

About every fifteen minutes, our conversation at the picnic table is interrupted by someone who wants to speak to Cindi: to say thank you, to say hello, to say hello on behalf of a mutual friend. Most of these people are *haoles* like me: tourists in oversized swim trunks and dripping-wet rash guards; people with deep imprints of snorkel goggles around their faces and white swaths of sunscreen across their forearms. Cindi greets each of them with warmth and affection, and often by name. She seems delighted—and sometimes deeply touched—by these interactions.

As Cindi talks to her most recent visitor, I look down at the notes I've taken so far. It strikes me that the image Cindi paints of her childhood here among her Native Hawaiian community—the deep love for the land and ocean, the sense of community and collective effort—has almost nothing in common with the image that I got of Hawaiian culture at the "luau show" that I attended in a Waikīkī shopping mall the week before. I've also noticed Cindi uses the word "aloha" just about as much as our emcee did. But coming from her, the word—which translates literally as "breath of life," and which Native Hawaiians use to express selfless love, compassion, and mercy—seems to have a different meaning entirely.

Something makes me think of Kū'ike, and when Cindi finishes speaking to her guest, I tell her about him, and do my best to explain his view that tourism is a form of colonization, and that Hawai'i would be better off without its tourists. I ask Cindi how she would respond.

"Well, I can appreciate where he's coming from," she says, her tone thoughtful. "I think what we have done is gone overboard. It's not the community that got wealthy from it. It was the middlemen who were making all that money."

But this isn't the only way to do things, she says. Warming to the topic, Cindi starts talking about Palau, a Pacific archipelago where the president has forced an about-face in tourism: he put a stop to an onslaught of conferences and conventions and began requiring all guests to sign the "Palau pledge," in which they vow to "preserve and protect" the islands during their visit. Palau even amended its immigration laws to make signing the pledge, which is stamped into visitors' passports, a requirement for entry.

"We can do those things. It's not that we don't have the means to do it," Cindi says. "We have greedy people in power who don't want to change. They want that money in their pocket. They don't care about the reef."

Cindi's face remains calm, but her voice has taken on an intensity that surprises me. As she speaks, she pounds her palm on the picnic table with such force that my phone, which I've set out between us to record the conversation, jostles with each strike.

"We need to get rid of these people," she says, "and get people in positions of decision-making who are going to understand that *we have to have balance.*"

But Cindi also believes that Hawaiians need to shift their perspective on visitors. When she hears her fellow community members complaining about tourists, she likes to ask them if they ever go on vacation. "If you go to California or Vegas, you're a tourist, right? What's the difference? You want to go other places, and you expect to be able to enjoy them. It's the same as people coming here." She looks around at the tables manned by volunteers, the tourists browsing information displays, and the smooth blue bay beyond. "We should be able to work together. We should be able to respect each other, to love each other, to figure out together how to make it a better place. I know we can. I mean, I do it every day."

We're interrupted again, this time by a middle-aged couple in matching broad-brimmed sun hats. Cindi doesn't seem to recognize them at first, but they introduce themselves and her face lights up: "*Oh my God! The Goldbergs!*" she exclaims, jumping up from the picnic table with arms raised, and goes straight in for a hug. They chat for a few minutes, then Cindi turns back to me, apologetic. But I point out that she's already given me two hours of her time, in addition to breakfast, and I don't want to keep her. Cindi nods, but she isn't ready to let me go just yet.

As she starts talking again, I get the sense—as sometimes happens toward the end of an interview—that she's trying to sum up our long and meandering conversation, to find the through line that she wants me to take away. And it goes something like this: what they're doing there in Kahalu'u Bay is harnessing the power of tourism to *care for* Hawai'i, rather than exploit the place or wear it down. To do that, you have to respect the notion of carrying capacity, which sometimes means imposing hard limits. But you also have to engage with your visitors, educate them, and welcome them with a sense of respect—and *aloha*.

"That's what I want," Cindi says, wrapping up. "And that's what I want our children to learn."

* * *

The whole time I've been talking to Cindi, my husband, my mom, and the kids have been keeping themselves occupied. For the first half hour or so, they chatted with the volunteers and browsed the materials on display under the pavilion. Then they stripped down to their swimsuits, applied some of the reef-safe sunscreen available from free dispensers, and went for what turned out to be a ninety-minute swim.

Finished with the interview, I wander over and find my family sprawled on the sand. Our older daughter, Alice, who is eight that summer, is flipping through *A Snorkeler's Guide to Kahalu'u Bay*, a spiral-bound, laminated book that my mom just bought from the information stand. Wrapped in a towel and with her hair still dripping bay water, Alice points to the species she's already spotted: blue-eyed damselfish, yellow tang, blue-spined unicornfish, as well as dozens of humuhumunukunukuapua'a, the state fish of Hawai'i, which Alice is very proud to have learned to pronounce. But she hasn't seen a sea turtle yet. We decide to head out together to see if we can find one.

Goggles suctioned to my face, I ease into the knee-deep water, which is cold against my bare legs. A cloud has hidden the sun, and for a moment the bay looks inky and uninviting. But Alice is already several feet ahead of me, and I need to keep up. So I take a breath, plunge my head below the surface, and come face-to-face with two yellow tang, as bright as a pair of lemons against the black lava rock behind them. Walking my hands across the sand, I ease past the fish and out toward the deeper water, my scanning eyes catching flashes of blue and silver in the shadowy shallows. Something smacks me on the shoulder, and I jump: it's Alice, waving at me underwater. I find the sand with my feet, then lift my dripping face.

"Mama, do you see those big orange balls?" Alice points to the buoys ahead. "Once you pass them, you don't stand up anymore, okay? From there, you just float."

"That's right," I say, but Alice is already back underwater, her little feet kicking a gentle swirl as she glides away. I adjust the plastic mouthpiece between my teeth, then lower my head and follow her into the reef. Past the buoys, swimming with as much care as I can, I hover over bulbous corals spiked with spiny black sea urchins. The cloud passes and fat rays of sunlight pierce the surface, dancing in lacelike patterns on the scene below me. Tiny polka-dot fish dash in and out of the corals. A plump sea cucumber lolls in a sandy corner. A regal-looking striped fish hovers below my circling arms, parading its arching dorsal fin, as long and fine as a piece of thread. My senses are at once clipped and amplified: the taste of salt on the mouthpiece; the rush of my breath through the snorkel; the lap of water on my skin, which is no longer cold.

Alice touches my elbow when she sees it: a sea turtle, medium-sized, so maybe a juvenile, is hovering several yards away, just below the surface. We swim a little closer, keeping a good distance, and watch as half a dozen yellow tang start to nibble at the animal's smooth, mottled shell. The turtle raises its head and holds its flippers still. I realize I'm probably projecting, but it seems like this teenage reptile is basking in the fish's attention, and perhaps in ours as well. The turtle floats; we float. For a moment, time seems to pause. But then the turtle waves its flippers and eases away from us, into the blue. We watch until it disappears, then turn and head back to the shore.

Acknowledgments

Writing this book was a journey in every sense of the word. I had so much help along the way.

Enormous thanks to Veronica Goldstein, whose sharp intellect and steady nerves were essential to both the conception and realization of this book. Equally generous thanks to my editor, Rick Horgan, for his dedication to this book (and its author) and his astute guidance in getting the manuscript across the finish line. I am indebted to Sophie Guimaraes, Olivia Bernhard, Rob Sternitzky, Georgia Brainard, Laura Wise, Lauren Dooley, and the rest of the team at Scribner for their essential support in bringing this book into the world. And I am so grateful to have had the chance to work with Fid Thompson, my first reader and dogged fact-checker, whose enthusiasm and attention to detail have done much to improve the manuscript.

This book would not exist without the early and persistent support of Simon Akam, a good friend and fellow journalist who has encouraged me in my career for more than a decade. At the *New York Times*, Suzanne MacNeille has been a guiding light in my career for the last five years; I'm deeply grateful for her smart editing as well as for the many ways she's encouraged me to spread my wings. Many thanks also to Amy Virshup and the rest of the team on the Travel desk, who cover the world of travel and tourism with a refreshing mix of awe and scrutiny.

Thank you to everyone who spoke to me for the book, whether on or off the record; I'm humbled by your time and trust. The following people either made essential introductions or granted me extended—and often multiple—interviews: Rick Steves, Tony Wheeler, Mark Ellingham, Hilary Bradt, Pauline Frommer, Jude Brosnan, Joe Cummings, Daniel Houghton, Philippe von Borries, Nitya Chambers, Elizabeth Becker, Rafat Ali, Thomas Kohnstamm, Kevin Raub, Justin Francis, Alex Stein, Mahmoud Abu Eid, Susan Jarzembski Holmer, Peter Rømer Hansen, Jose Torres, Freya Higgins-Desbiolles, Gabriel Zuchtriegel, Mechtild Rössler, Dean MacCannell, Peter Jordan, Keith Jenkins, Gabby Beckford, Shivya Nath, Bobby, Donald Leadbetter, Sean Smith, Mar Santamaría Varas, Pablo Martínez, Janet Sanz, Alícia Puig Fernández, Daniel Guttentag, John De Fries, Ilihia Gionson, Kalani L. Kaʻanaʻanā, Mālia Sanders, Cindi Punihaole, Rae DeCoito, Kuhao Zane, Luka Kanakaʻole, Frank Haas, Jay Talwar, Delsa Moe, Kūʻike Kamakea-Ohelo, Kuʻuipo Kumukahi, Siliilagi Williams, Manisha Pande, Rupesh Kumar and the team at the Responsible Tourism Mission in Kerala, Akhil Kalidas, Benjamin Claret, Damien Girardier, Brad Carlson, Hillary Gerardi, Eric Fournier, Ludovic Ravanel, Emmanuel Salim, Jean-Marc Peillex, Steven Barrett, David Victor, Andreas Schäfer, Eliza Reid, Inga Hlín Pálsdóttir, Egill Bjarnason, Fanney Gunnarsdóttir, John Fitzpatrick, Mike Robinson, Michael Parkinson, Chris Brown, Claire McColgan, Wayne Colquhoun, Geerte Udo, Elena Simons, Stefanie Caton, Natalia

ACKNOWLEDGMENTS

Portnoy, Brenda, Lennard Roubos, Josse Koolen, Theodoor van Boven, Ionis Thompson, Peter Harrigan, and Fatimah Al Zimam.

I am grateful to Marisa Ryan, Jason Moore, Nadia Owusu, and Amy Duncan for being early and enthusiastic cheerleaders of this book, and to Scott Cooper, Mark Bauman, and Aziz Abu Sarah, who became friends and collaborators over the course of this book's gestation. I will be forever indebted to Andrew Billingsley and Angela Padilla for taking me in in a moment of need. Harold Goodwin offered essential encouragement, insights, and introductions at several points in the book's development. Matthieu Guillier and Anastasiia Savotina provided thoughtful and timely research support. Zeva Bellel guided the idea for this book through its earliest stages of gestation, and—alongside Servane Gaxotte, Céline Berlizon, Estelle Delmas, and Marion Hue—also gifted me with a wise and encouraging community as I wrote the manuscript. Kelly Kennedy and Gavin Kennedy were very generous with their daily schedules, as well as their comments on an early draft, while Jean Bowyer Brown and Vivian Brown provided essential introductions and support. Thank you to my fellow MEJDI travelers for inspiring me and welcoming me with open arms. Thank you to Irina Zodrow for believing in me and pushing me through moments of self-doubt. Thank you to Meredith Clements Waldon for being the dearest lifelong friend a woman could hope for.

I am deeply grateful to my parents, Bob and Susan McClanahan, who have always cheered my writing efforts and encouraged my wanderings, even when it scared them. And I am forever indebted to my grandfather, the late Bob Bain, for believing in my writing from the very beginning. I've never forgotten.

ACKNOWLEDGMENTS

And finally, thank you to the three people to whom I dedicate this book: to Oli, for embarking on an adventurous life with me and encouraging this book on every step of its journey. And to Alice and Nora, for giving me the gift of your curiosity, compassion, and fascination with the world. I love you so much.

Notes

Introduction

1 "The Federal Budget in 2019: An Infographic," Congressional Budget
   Office, April 15, 2020, https://www.cbo.gov/publication/56324.
2 Economic Impact Research Hub, World Travel and Tourism Council,
   https://wttc.org/research/economic-impact.
3 Ralf Buckley, "Tourism, Conservation and the Aichi Targets," *Parks* 18,
   no. 2 (December 2012): 12–19, https://citeseerx.ist.psu.edu/document
   ?repid=rep1&type=pdf&doi=691c1f25a8c27d866e055f1019755ac3ef
   846fef#page=12.
4 Manfred Lenzen et al., "The Carbon Footprint of Global Tourism," *Nature
   Climate Change* 8, no. 6 (June 2018): 522–28.
5 UNTWO Tourism Data Dashboard, UN World Tourism Organization,
   https://www.unwto.org/tourism-data/global-and-regional-tourism
   -performance.
6 "Glossary of Tourism Terms," UN World Tourism Organization, https://
   www.unwto.org/glossary-tourism-terms.

Chapter One **A Groove on the Map**

1 I gathered the pieces of the story of Lonely Planet from my two Zoom
   interviews with Tony Wheeler, conducted in February and March 2022;
   an interview that Tony and Maureen conducted with Guy Raz for the
   How I Built This podcast; interviews that Tony conducted with Rick
   Steves for the *Travel with Rick Steves* radio show and with Amanda

Kendle for *The Thoughtful Travel Podcast*; news stories about the Wheelers that were published in the *New York Times* and the *New York Times Magazine*; as well as the book that the Wheelers cowrote, *Unlikely Destinations: The Lonely Planet Story* (Hong Kong: Periplus Editions, 2007).

2 Wheeler and Wheeler, *Unlikely Destinations*, 15.

3 Laurie A. O'Neill, "A Famous Traveler Marks Anniversary with a Trip," *New York Times*, March 9, 1986.

4 From Tony's interview with Rick Steves for the *Travel with Rick Steves* radio show, November 25, 2007, https://soundcloud.com/rick-steves /tony-wheelers-lonely-planet.

5 Sune Bechmann Pedersen and Christian Noack, "Crossing the Iron Curtain: An Introduction," in *Tourism and Travel during the Cold War: Negotiating Tourist Experiences across the Iron Curtain* (New York: Routledge, 2019), https://library.oapen.org/bitstream/id/c44656ab-e470-4154-a89d -f50e4843b929/9780367192129_oaintroduction.pdf.

6 As cited in *Forbes*, using data from the US Department of State/US Census Bureau. "More Americans Than Ever Hold a Passport: Percentage of the U.S. Population Holding a Passport from 1989–2017," *Forbes*, 2018, https://blogs-images.forbes.com/niallmccarthy/files/2018/01/20180111 _Passports.jpg.

7 John F. Kennedy, "Statement Upon Signing Order Establishing the Peace Corps, March 1, 1961," John F. Kennedy Presidential Library & Museum, https://www.jfklibrary.org/archives/other-resources/john-f-kennedy -speeches/peace-corps-establishment-19610301.

8 Sara Wheeler, "The World with Its Trousers Down," *Guardian*, September 13, 2008.

9 Martha Gellhorn, *Travels with Myself and Another: A Memoir* (London: Allen Lane, 1978), 293.

10 This and other quotes are from Tony Wheeler, *Across Asia on the Cheap* (Sydney: Lonely Planet, 1973).

11 These and other quotes are from Wheeler and Wheeler, *Unlikely Destinations*, 39–40.

12 Ibid., 43.

13 Rolf Potts, "Travel Writer: Bill Dalton," Ralf Potts, February 1, 2003, https://rolfpotts.com/bill-dalton/.

14 Hilary Bradt, author Zoom interview, March 2022.

NOTES

15 Mark Ellingham, author Zoom interview, March 2022.

16 "'Notable Alumni," Let's Go, https://www.letsgo.com/alumni.

17 Serena Jampel, "Let's Go: Gone at 63," *Harvard Crimson*, April 13, 2023, https://www.thecrimson.com/article/2023/4/13/lets-go-travel-guide/.

18 Rick Steves, author Zoom interview, February 2023.

19 "Airline Deregulation: When Everything Changed," National Air and Space Museum, December 17, 2021, https://airandspace.si.edu/stories /editorial/airline-deregulation-when-everything-changed.

20 Joe Cummings, author Zoom interview, May 2022; see also Joe Cummings, "Plenty of Whiskey, Few Backpackers: The Wild Story behind Lonely Planet's First Thailand Guidebook," CNN Travel, updated April 23, 2020, https://edition.cnn.com/travel/article/joe-cummings-lonely -planet-thailand/index.html.

21 Pico Iyer, "The Smiling Lures of Thailand," *Time*, October 17, 1988, https:// time.com/vault/issue/1988-10-17/spread/90/.

22 *Sports Illustrated* 68, no. 7 (February 2, 2015), https://archive.org/details /sports-illustrated-1988-02-15-swimsuit-issue-b/mode/2up.

23 The 1960 figure is from James Elliott, "Government Management of Tourism—A Thai Case Study," *Tourism Management* 8, no. 3 (September 1987): 223–32. The other figures are from Nick Kontogeorgopoulos, Anuwat Churyen, and Varaphorn Duangsaeng, "Success Factors in Community-Based Tourism in Thailand: The Role of Luck, External Support, and Local Leadership," *Tourism Planning & Development* 11, no. 1 (November 2013): 106–24.

24 Kevin Raub, author Zoom interview, February 2023.

25 This line used to appear in a note on the author's (or more often authors') page of Lonely Planet guides, as documented in A. Alacovska, "Legitimacy, Self-Interpretation and Genre in Media Industries: A Paratextual Analysis of Travel Guidebook Publishing," *European Journal of Cultural Studies* 18 , no. 6 (2015): 601–19.

26 Nicholas Kristof, "Good Digs in Timbuktu," *New York Times*, February 23, 1986, https://www.nytimes.com/1986/02/23/travel/good-digs-in -timbuktu.html.

27 Philip Shenon, "The End of the World on 10 Tugriks a Day," *New York Times Magazine*, June 30, 1996, https://www.nytimes.com/1996/06/30 /magazine/the-end-of-the-world-on-10-tugriks-a-day.html.

28 Ibid.

29 The figure of 120 million is from Emily Brennan, "A Lonely Planet Founder Looks Back," *New York Times*, June 7, 2013, https://www.nytimes.com/2013/06/09/travel/a-lonely-planet-founder-looks-back.html.

30 David Sacks, "Paradise Enough," *New York Times*, March 16, 1997, https://www.nytimes.com/1997/03/16/books/paradise-enough.html.

31 Alex Garland, *The Beach* (London: Viking, 1996). The quote is from page 137 of the Kindle edition.

32 Austin Bush, "Thailand's Iconic Maya Beach Reopens with New Sustainability Efforts," Lonely Planet, January 6, 2022, https://www.lonelyplanet.com/news/maya-bay-thailand-sustainable-visitor-rules.

33 "21st Century Stationary Steam Engines in Thailand," International Steam Pages, 2006, https://www.internationalsteam.co.uk/mills/thaimill01.htm.

34 Jonathan Allen, "'Lonely Planet Effect' Sparks Omelette War in India," Reuters, April 5, 2007, https://www.reuters.com/article/us-india-omelette-idUSSP17542220070405.

35 "The Lonely Planet Effect and How to Avoid It," *Vagabond Journey*, December 6, 2011.

36 Katie Carlin, "Lonely Planet Co-Founder on the Country He Wishes He Ruined," *International Traveller*, February 25, 2020, https://www.internationaltraveller.com/middle-east/tony-wheeler-afghanistan/.

37 Thomas Kohnstamm, author Zoom interview, February 2023.

38 Thomas Kohnstamm, *Do Travel Writers Go to Hell?* (New York: Three Rivers Press, 2008). The quote is from page 1 of the Kindle version.

39 The original article, which was published in Australia's *Sunday Telegraph*, no longer appears online, but numerous outlets reported on and quoted from the *Telegraph*'s story, and these can still be found online. For example: Reuters, "Travel Writer Says He Made Up Parts of Books," April 14, 2008, https://www.reuters.com/article/us-plagiarism-idUSSYD21440120080414/, and Victoria Thieberger, "Lonely Planet Writer Faked It," News24, April 13, 2008, https://www.news24.com/news24/lonely-planet-writer-faked-it-20080413.

40 Thomas Kohnstamm, author Zoom interview, February 2023.

41 Kohnstamm, *Do Travel Writers Go to Hell?*, 2.

42 Harry McCracken, "Print Travel Books Are Dead, and There's No Good Replacement," *Time*, March 25, 2013, https://techland.time.com/2013/03/25/print-travel-books-are-dead-and-theres-no-good-replacement/.

43 Allie Jones, "The Death of the Travel Guide," *Atlantic*, July 22, 2013, https://www
.theatlantic.com/culture/archive/2013/07/are-travel-books-officially
-over/313056/.

44 Elena Moya, "BBC Buys Lonely Planet to Expand Online Content," Reuters, October 1, 2007, https://www.reuters.com/article/us-bbc-lonely
planet-idUSL0166342020071001.

45 The Wheelers told the story of the sale of Lonely Planet in an interview
to Guy Raz. "Lonely Planet: Maureen & Tony Wheeler," *How I Built This*
podcast, July 9, 2018, https://www.npr.org/2018/07/06/626649702
/lonely-planet-maureen-tony-wheeler.

46 Rafat Ali, "Exclusive: BBC Selling Lonely Planet to Kentucky Cigarette
Billionaire Brad Kelley," Skift, March 4, 2013, https://skift.com/2013/03
/04/bbc-selling-lonely-planet-to-kentucky-cigarette-billionaire-brad
-kelley/.

47 Pauline Frommer, author phone interview, February 2023.

48 Nitya Chambers and Philippe von Borries, author phone interview,
March 2023.

Chapter Two **Under the Influence**

1 Jonathan Raban, *For Love & Money: Writing, Reading, Travelling, 1969–1987*
(London: Collins Harvill, 1987). The quote cited is from page 331 of the
Kindle edition.

2 Kylie Cardell and Kate Douglas, "Visualising Lives: 'The Selfie' as Travel
Writing," *Studies in Travel Writing* 22, no. 1 (June 2018): 104–17.

3 Here is a list of the major sources that I drew from in writing this uber-
condensed history of travel's jump from analog to digital: Dennis Schaal,
"The Definitive Oral History of Online Travel," Skift, June 1, 2016, https://skift
.com/history-of-online-travel/; "Microsoft Expedia Travel Services Debuts
on the Web," press release, Microsoft, October 22, 1996, https://news
.microsoft.com/1996/10/22/microsoft-expedia-travel-services-debuts
-on-the-web/; "The History of Booking.com," Medium, May 24, 2019,
https://medium.com/keycafe/the-history-of-booking-com-cc213a735380;
"Our Story," Priceline, https://press.priceline.com/our-story/; Jeffrey
Bussgang, "The Secrets to TripAdvisor's Impressive Scale," *Harvard Business Review*, October 2, 2012; Greg Sterling, "Google Travel Search Takes

Flight with First ITA Travel Product," Search Engine Land, September 13, 2011; Jared Wein, "Google Travel Is Worth $100 Billion—Even More than Priceline," Skift, September 18, 2017.

4 Graeme Wood, "Travel Writing Is Dead," *Foreign Policy*, October 5, 2010, https://foreignpolicy.com/2010/10/05/travel-writing-is-dead/.

5 "Instagram Launches," Instagram, October 6, 2010, https://about.instagram .com/blog/announcements/instagram-launches.

6 Malcolm Jones, "Paul Theroux and the Death of Travel Writing," *Daily Beast*, April 24, 2017, https://www.thedailybeast.com/paul-theroux-and -the-death-of-travel-writing.

7 *Journeys, Granta* 138, Winter 2017, https://granta.com/products/granta -138-journeys/.

8 "The End of an Era: The Last Best American Travel Writing with Jason Wilson," *Travel Writing World* podcast, October 11, 2021, https://www .travelwritingworld.com/the-last-best-american-travel-writing/.=

9 "Instagram Demographic Statistics: How Many People Use Instagram in 2023?," Backlinko, August 23, 2023, https://backlinko.com/instagram -users; "Time Spent in Primary Activities and Percent of the Civilian Population Engaging in Each Activity, Averages per Day by Sex, 2022 Annual Averages," U.S. Bureau of Labor Statistics, last modified June 22, 2023, https://www.bls.gov/news.release/atus.t01.htm.

10 "Facebook Demographic Statistics: How Many People Use Facebook in 2023?," Backlinko, March 27, 2023, https://backlinko.com/facebook-users; "How Many People Use YouTube in 2023?," Backlinko, March 27, 2023, https://backlinko.com/youtube-users.

11 Justin Marozzi, "The Best Travel Writers of All Time," *Newsweek*, May 23, 2011, https://www.newsweek.com/best-travel-writers-all-time-67725.

12 Don George, "Top Ten Travel Books of the Century," Salon, May 19, 1999, https://www.salon.com/1999/05/19/best_5/.

13 Shivya Nath, author Zoom interview, May 2023.

14 Gabby Beckford, author phone interview, May 2023.

15 The Black Travel Alliance, "Board Member Feature—Gabby Beckford," https://blacktravelalliance.org/board-member-feature-gabby-beck ford/.

16 Fanney Gunnarsdóttir, author interview, April 2023.

17 Justin Bieber, "I'll Show You," music video, YouTube, https://www.you tube.com/watch?v=PfGaX8Gof2E.

18 Paige McClanahan, "Iceland Tourism Prepares for a Comeback," *New York Times*, updated October 18, 2020, https://www.nytimes.com/2020/10/13/travel/iceland-tourism-pandemic.html.

19 David Jolly, "$2.5 Billion Is Added to Bailout for Iceland," *New York Times*, November 20, 2008, https://www.nytimes.com/2008/11/21/business/worldbusiness/21icebank.html.

20 "Mitigating Ash Impacts: What We've Learned and Improved Since 2010," International Civil Aviation Organization, *ICAO Journal* 68, no. 1 (2013), https://www.icao.int/publications/journalsreports/2013/6801_en.pdf.

21 Resources for this section: Matt Springate, "Promote Iceland: Inspired by Iceland," Institute of Practitioners in Advertising, Silver, IPA Effectiveness Awards, 2011, https://adfx.ie/upload/files/1386593033_Promote_Iceland_Inspired_by_Iceland_2.pdf; Wayne M. Gore, "Tourism Promo Campaign Helped the Industry," Tourism Review News, December 27, 2010.

22 Leslie Koch, "The Value of Blogger Press Trips: Interview with Jordan Tourism Board's Managing Director," *BIIB Blog*, Bridge to Bhutan, May 18, 2011, https://bridgetobhutan.com/blog/2011/05/18/the-value-of-blogger-press-trips/#more-1144.

23 Keith Jenkins, author Zoom interview, May 2023.

24 "Influencer Marketing Market Size (2016–2023)," influencer marketing hub, Oberlo, https://www.oberlo.com/statistics/influencer-marketing-market-size.

25 "Influencing Travel: How to Turn Lookers into Bookers," Stackla, 2019, https://www.nosto.com/wp-content/uploads/2019/03/Travel-Ebook-Digital-US_FINAL.pdf.

26 Expedia Group Media Solutions, "Gen Z Travelers: More Open to Influence and Inspiration Than Other Generations," Business Wire, November 14, 2018, https://www.businesswire.com/news/home/20181114005361/en/Gen-Travelers-Open-Influence-Inspiration-Generations.

27 Donald Leadbetter, author Zoom interview, May 2023.

28 *Elle*, "Elle's 30 Places to Instagram in 2023," June 28, 2023, https://www.elle.com/culture/travel-food/a27561982/best-instagram-spots/.

29 Philip Schofield, "Holiday Destination Chosen Based on How 'Instagrammable' the Holiday Pics Will Be," Schofields Insurance, April 3, 2017, https://www.schofields.ltd.uk/blog/5123/two-fifths-of-millennials-choose-their-holiday-destination-based-on-how-instagrammable-the-holiday-pics-will-be/.

30 Philip Schofield, "The New Travelling Generation: Gen Zs Mark TikTok as Their Top Holiday Influencer," Schofields Insurance, February 3, 2023, https://www.schofields.ltd.uk/blog/6850/gen-z-travel-influence/.

31 Sally French, "This Is the Most Instagrammed Place in the World," *New York Post*, May 10, 2017, https://nypost.com/2017/05/10/this-is-the-most -instagrammed-place-in-the-world/.

32 Sean P. Smith, "Instagram Abroad: Performance, Consumption and Colonial Narrative in Tourism," *Postcolonial Studies* 21, no. 2 (April 2018): 1–20.

Chapter Three Tourism Comes to Power

1 Thomas L. Friedman, *The World Is Flat* (New York: Farrar, Straus and Giroux, 2005), 173–74.

2 Joseph S. Nye Jr., *Soft Power: The Means to Success in World Politics*, Kindle ed. (New York: PublicAffairs, 2004), 4.

3 Ibid., 17.

4 Elizabeth Becker, *Overbooked: The Exploding Business of Travel and Tourism* (2013; New York: Simon & Schuster, 2016), 1–2, 43–75, 87–121, 207–87.

5 Simon Parker, "The Leaving of Liverpool: Managed Decline and the Enduring Legacy of Thatcherism's Urban Policy," *British Politics and Policy* blog, London School of Economics and Political Science, January 17, 2019, https://blogs.lse.ac.uk/politicsandpolicy/the-leaving-of -liverpool/#Author.

6 My understanding of Liverpool's evolution and the development of its tourism industry was also informed by in-person interviews with Claire McColgan, director of culture for the Liverpool City Council, and Chris Brown, the former director of Marketing Liverpool; I conducted both interviews in person in Liverpool in June 2023. Phone interviews I conducted in June 2023 with Michael Parkinson of the University of Liverpool, heritage expert Wayne Colquhoun, and Mike Robinson of Nottingham Trent University have also informed my writing in this section.

7 Michael H. Parkinson, "Urban Regeneration and Development Corporations: Liverpool Style," *Local Economy* 3 (1988): 109–18; Mohamed Fageir, Nicole Porter, and Katharina Borsi, "Contested Grounds; the Regeneration of Liverpool Waterfront," *Planning Perspectives* 36, no. 3 (August 2020): 535–57.

8 Kenn Taylor, "Tate Liverpool—a Modern Glory of the North," *Guardian*, September 13, 2012, https://www.theguardian.com/uk/the-northerner /2012/sep/13/tate-liverpool-biennial; Dan Haygarth, "The 'Experiment' Which Helped Lift 'Exhausted' City out of Its Darkest Days," *Liverpool Echo*, September 17, 2023, https://www.liverpoolecho.co.uk/news/liverpool -news/experiment-helped-lift-exhausted-city-27726944.

9 Claire Frankel, "Liverpool Gets Tate Branch," *New York Times*, May 22, 1988, https://www.nytimes.com/1988/05/22/travel/liverpool-gets-tate -branch.html.

10 "Advisory Body Evaluation (ICOMOS): Liverpool—Maritime Mercantile City," UNESCO World Heritage Convention, June 28, 2004, https://whc .unesco.org/en/documents/151886.

11 "Why Liverpool Won," BBC, June 4, 2003, http://news.bbc.co.uk/2/hi /uk_news/2962008.stm.

12 "Tourism Figures Show Continued Upward Trend," Liverpool City Region, August 14, 2018, https://liverpoollep.org/news/tourism-figures -show-continued-upward-trend/; "Liverpool Tourism Figures Continue to Climb," Invest Liverpool, July 10, 2019, https://investliverpool.com /news/liverpool-tourism-figures-continue-to-climb/.

13 Decision: 44 COM 7A.34, Liverpool—Maritime Mercantile City (United Kingdom of Great Britain and Northern Ireland) (C 1150), UNESCO World Heritage Convention, 2021, https://whc.unesco.org/en/soc /4031/.

14 Ian Hughes, "Liverpool's Tourism Sector Continues to Bounce Back," Invest Liverpool, August 8, 2023, https://investliverpool.com/news /liverpools-tourism-sector-continues-to-bounce-back.

15 "The Guardian View on Liverpool: The Right City for Eurovision," *Guardian*, May 7, 2023, https://www.theguardian.com/commentisfree/2023 /may/07/the-guardian-view-on-liverpool-the-right-city-for-eurovision.

16 Brand Finance City Index 2023: "Top 100 Best City Brands," Brand Finance, 2023, https://brandfinance.com/wp-content/uploads/2023/05 /brand-finance-city-index-2023-Best-City-Brands-Table-4.pdf.

17 Maya Wolfe-Robinson, "Scale of Problems at Liverpool City Council Revealed in Commissioners Report," *Guardian*, November 25, 2021, https://www.theguardian.com/uk-news/2021/nov/25/scale-of-problems -at-liverpool-city-council-revealed-in-commissioners-report; Liam Thorp, "Operation Aloft: Evidence File Sent to Crown Prosecution

Service," *Liverpool Echo*, June 26, 2023, https://www.liverpoolecho.co.uk /news/liverpool-news/operation-aloft-evidence-file-sent-27201323.

18 "Vilnius Receives International Gold Award for 'G-Spot of Europe' Ad Campaign," Go Vilnius, November 6, 2019, https://www.govilnius.lt/media -news/vilnius-receives-international-gold-award-for-gspot-of-europe-.

19 "GDP (Current US$)—Iceland," World Bank, 2022, https://data.world-bank.org/indicator/NY.GDP.MKTP.CD?locations=IS; Vermont's GDP data, U.S. Bureau of Economic Analysis, https://apps.bea.gov/regional /histdata/releases/1110gsp/index.cfm.

20 The Icelandic Tourist Board visitor statistics are from "Foreign Visitor Arrivals by Air and Sea to Iceland, 1949–2022," Ferðamálastofa, https:// www.ferdamalastofa.is/static/files/ferdamalastofa/Frettamyndir/2023 /mai/foreign-visitors-to-iceland-1949-2022.xls.

21 Eliza Reid, *Secrets of the Sprakkar: Iceland's Extraordinary Women and How They Are Changing the World* (Naperville, IL: Sourcebooks, 2022), 13.

22 "UNWTO Appoints First Lady of Iceland as Special Ambassador for Tourism and the Sustainable Development Goals," UNWTO, December 11, 2017, https://www.unwto.org/archive/global/press-release/2017-12-11 /unwto-appoints-first-lady-iceland-special-ambassador-tourism -and-sustainabl.

23 Ragnar Tómas, "First Lady of Iceland Hired by Promote Iceland," *Iceland Review*, October 31, 2019, https://www.icelandreview.com/news/first -lady-of-iceland-hired-by-promote-iceland/#:~:text=Reid%20will%20 not%20be%20a%20full-time%20employee%20of,will%20be%20paid%20 approximately%20ISK%20500%2C000%20per%20month.

24 Paige McClanahan, "Iceland Is a Magnet for Tourists. Its First Lady Has Some Advice for Them," *New York Times*, June 1, 2023, https://www .nytimes.com/2023/06/01/travel/iceland-tourism-eliza-reid.html.

25 Egill Bjarnason, author Zoom interview, September 2023.

26 Egill Bjarnason, "Peaceful Iceland Amazed at Weapons in Pence Security Detail," Associated Press, September 5, 2019, https://apnews.com /general-news-2ea1edf65f184a259279e64ff2924f54.

27 Eva Moreda Rodríguez, "What Did Franco's Spain Do to Spanish Music?," JSTOR Daily, January 15, 2020, https://daily.jstor.org/what-did-francos -spain-do-to-spanish-music/.

28 Sandie Holguín, "The Complicated History of Flamenco in Spain," *Smithsonian*, October 24, 2019, https://www.smithsonianmag.com/

travel/complicated-history-flamenco-spain-180973398/; Yossi Bartal, "Flamenco's Repression and Resistance in Southern Spain," Truthout, December 14, 2014, https://truthout.org/articles/flamenco-under-attack/.

29 David Geary, "Incredible India in a Global Age: The Cultural Politics of Image Branding in Tourism," *Tourist Studies* 13, no. 1 (January 2013): 36–61.

30 Jose Torres, author Zoom interview, June 2023.

31 "Hawai'i Visitor Statistics Released for 2019," Hawai'i Tourism Authority, https://www.Hawai'itourismauthority.org/news/news-releases/2020/hawai-i-visitor-statistics-released-for-2019/.

32 "HTA Resident Sentiment Survey 2019 Highlights," Hawai'i Tourism Authority, https://www.hawaiitourismauthority.org/media/4268/resident-sentiment-board-presentation-02-27-20.pdf.

33 "Resident Sentiment Survey Fall 2021," Hawai'i Tourism Authority, https://www.hawaiitourismauthority.org/media/9834/dbedt-resident-sentiment-fall-2021-accessible-final-092122.pdf.

34 Allison Schaefers, "Hawaii Visitors and Convention Bureau Files Protest over Tourism Contract Award," *Honolulu Star-Advertiser*, June 22, 2022, https://www.staradvertiser.com/2022/06/22/hawaii-news/hvcb-files-protest-over-tourism-contract-award/.

35 Carlie Procell, "9 Charts That Show How Hawaii Tourism Is Changing," Honolulu Civil Beat, July 10, 2019, https://www.civilbeat.org/2019/07/9-charts-that-show-how-hawaii-tourism-is-changing/.

36 Jessica Terrell, "Will Hawaii Finally Be Able to Break Its Dependence on Tourism?," Honolulu Civil Beat, October 12, 2020, https://www.civilbeat.org/2020/10/will-hawaii-finally-be-able-to-break-its-dependence-on-tourism/.

37 My writing about tourism in Hawai'i is informed by James Mak, *Developing a Dream Destination: Tourism and Tourism Policy Planning in Hawai'i* (Honolulu: University of Hawai'i Press, 2008); Hōkūlani K. Aikau and Vernadette Vicuña Gonzalez, ed., *Detours: A Decolonial Guide to Hawai'i* (Durham, NC: Duke University Press, 2019).

38 R. W. Butler, "The Concept of a Tourist Area Life Cycle of Evolution: Implications for Management of Resources," *Canadian Geographer* 24, no. 1 (1980): 5–12, http://www.numptynerd.net/uploads/1/2/0/6/12061984/butler_model_1980.pdf.

NOTES

39 Paul Brewbaker, Frank Haas, and James Mak, "Charting a New Course for Hawai'i Tourism," UHERO Brief, February 14, 2019, https://uhero .hawaii.edu/wp-content/uploads/2019/08/ChartingANewCourseFor HawaiiTourism.pdf.

Chapter Four Tourists, Go Home

1 M. Martínez Euklidiadas, "Barcelona '92: The Impact of Hosting the Olympics in the Interest of Global Exposure," Tomorrow.City, December 13, 2022, https://tomorrow.city/a/olympics-economic-impact-of-host-cities.

2 "Pressure of Tourism: Introduction," Barcelona City Council, https:// coneixement-eu.bcn.cat/widget/atles-resiliencia/en_index_pressio _turistica.html.

3 Astrid Ortiz and Marga Pont Algueró, "Tourism, between Wealth and Residents' Complaints," *Barcelona Metròpolis*, July 19, 2019, https://www .barcelona.cat/metropolis/en/contents/tourism-between-wealth-and -residents-complaints.

4 Stephen Burgen, "'Tourists Go Home, Refugees Welcome': Why Barcelona Chose Migrants over Visitors," *Guardian*, June 25, 2018, https:// www.theguardian.com/cities/2018/jun/25/tourists-go-home-refugees -welcome-why-barcelona-chose-migrants-over-visitors.

5 Will Coldwell, "Wish You Weren't Here: How the Tourist Boom—and Selfies—Are Threatening Britain's Beauty Spots," *Guardian*, August 16, 2018, https://www.theguardian.com/travel/2018/aug/16/wish-you-werent -here-how-the-tourist-boom-and-selfies-are-threatening-britains -beauty-spots.

6 *Kerala Tourism Statistics 2019*, Government of Kerala, https:// www.keralatourism.org/tourismstatistics/tourist_statistics_2019 _book20210306071249.pdf.

7 *Fourteenth Five-Year Plan (2022–2027)*, Kerala State Planning Board, Government of Kerala, March 2022, https://spb.kerala.gov.in/sites/default /files/inline-files/Tourism_WG%20report.pdf.

8 Harold Goodwin, "RT in India," Responsible Tourism Partnership, November 3, 2022, https://responsibletourismpartnership.org/rt-in -india/.

9 Rupesh Kumar, Jenefer Bobbin, and Harold Goodwin, "Tourism Impacts in Kumarakom, Kerala," Responsible Tourism Partnership, 2015, https://

haroldgoodwin.info/Kerala/RTPWP2Tourism%20Impacts%20in%20 Kumarakom.pdf.

10 You can watch this scene from *The Brady Bunch* here: https://www.you tube.com/watch?v=T3LO4s16kkY.

11 Ada Colau, "Mass Tourism Can Kill a City—Just Ask Barcelona's Residents," *Guardian*, September 2, 2014, https://www.theguardian.com /commentisfree/2014/sep/02/mass-tourism-kill-city-barcelona.

12 Tobias Buck, "Barcelona Takes Steps to Curb Tourist Surge," *Financial Times*, January 27, 2017, https://www.ft.com/content/d12114b8-e487 -11e6-8405-9e5580d6e5fb.

13 Paige McClanahan, "Barcelona Takes on Airbnb," *New York Times*, September 22, 2021, https://www.nytimes.com/2021/09/22/travel/barcelona -airbnb.html.

14 Daniel Guttentag, author Zoom interview, February 2022.

15 Miquel-Àngel Garcia-López et al., "Do Short-Term Rental Platforms Affect Housing Markets? Evidence from Airbnb in Barcelona," *Journal of Urban Economics* 119 (September 2020): 103278.

16 Anne-Cécile Mermet, "Who Is Benefiting from Airbnb? Assessing the Redistributive Power of Peer-to-Peer Short-Term Rentals," *Professional Geographer* 73, no. 3 (2021): 553–66.

17 Alberto Amore, Cecilia de Bernardi, and Pavlos Arvanitis, "The Impacts of Airbnb in Athens, Lisbon and Milan: A Rent Gap Theory Perspective," *Current Issues in Tourism* 25, no. 4 (April 2020): 3329–42.

18 Dustin Robertson, Christopher Oliver, and Eric Nost, "Short-Term Rentals as Digitally-Mediated Tourism Gentrification: Impacts on Housing in New Orleans," *Tourism Geographies* 24, no. 3 (May 2022): 954–77.

19 Kyle Barron, Edward Kung, and Davide Perserpio, "The Effect of Home-Sharing on House Prices and Rents: Evidence from Airbnb," March 4, 2020, https://ssrn.com/abstract=3006832 or http://dx.doi.org/10.2139 /ssrn.3006832.

Chapter Five **The Last Chance Saloon**

1 Benjamin Claret, author interview, January 2023.

2 Mary Shelley, *Frankenstein or, The Modern Prometheus* (Project Gutenberg, 2012), ch. 10, https://www.gutenberg.org/files/41445/41445-h/41445 -h.htm.

3   Mark Twain, *A Tramp Abroad* (Project Gutenberg, 2004), ch. 46: https://www.gutenberg.org/cache/epub/119/pg119-images.html.

4   "Montenvers: Past, Present, and Future," Chamonix-Mont-Blanc, July 13, 2021, https://en.chamonix.com/infos-et-services/espace-pro-presse/le-montenvers-une-histoire-des-projets.

5   "Le Forum," Remontées-Mécaniques.net, https://www.remontees-mecaniques.net/forums/index.php?showtopic=38916; "Rénovation du site du Montenvers/Mer de Glace: un nouveau glaciorium et un restaurant panoramique," *Le Messager*, July 6, 2022, https://www.lemessager.fr/43443/article/2022-07-06/renovation-du-site-du-montenversmer-de-glace-un-nouveau-glaciorium-et-un.

6   Emmanuel Salim, "Glacier Tourism without Ice: Envisioning Future Adaptations in a Melting World," *Frontiers in Human Dynamics* 5 (March 2023), https://doi.org/10.3389/fhumd.2023.1137551.

7   "The Last Chance Saloon," Historical Marker Database, https://www.hmdb.org/m.asp?m=96531.

8   Damien Girardier, author interview, February 2024.

9   Salim, "Glacier Tourism without Ice."

10 Wang Shijin, Xie Jia, and Zhou Lanyue, "China's Glacier Tourism: Potential Evaluation and Spatial Planning," *Journal of Destination Marketing & Management* 18 (December 2020): 100506.

11 Harry Zekollari, Matthias Huss, and Daniel Farinotti, "Modelling the Future Evolution of Glaciers in the European Alps under the EURO-CORDEX RCM Ensemble," *Cryosphere Discussions* 13, no. 4 (April 2019): 1125–46.

12 David R. Rounce, "Global Glacier Change in the 21st Century: Every Increase in Temperature Matters," *Science* 379, no. 6627 (January 5, 2023), www.science.org/doi/10.1126/science.abo1324.

13 Joseph Romm, "Bolivia's 18,000-Year-Old Chacaltaya Glacier Is Gone," *Grist*, May 8, 2009, https://grist.org/article/another-one-bites-the-dust-literally-bolivias-18000-year-old-chacaltaya-gla/.

14 "Great Barrier Reef in Danger, UN World Heritage Committee Draft Report Finds," UN News, June 22, 2021, https://news.un.org/en/story/2021/06/1094512.

15 "U.N. Says Great Barrier Reef Is 'in Danger.' Australia Bitterly Disagrees," *New York Times*, June 22, 2021, https://www.nytimes.com/2021/06/22/world/australia/unesco-great-barrier-reef-danger.html; "Australia Welcomes Lifting of UNESCO Threat to List Great Barrier Reef as

World Heritage in Danger," Associated Press, August 1, 2023, https://apnews.com/article/australia-great-barrier-reef-world-heritage-7839b26be184945fd259f1098fa7c581.

16 "Great Barrier Reef," Tourism and Events Queensland, https://teq.queensland.com/au/en/industry/industry-resources/great-barrier-reef-resources.

17 Daniel Manzo et al., "Facing Dire Sea Level Rise Threat, Maldives Turns to Climate Change Solutions to Survive," ABC News, November 3, 2021, https://abcnews.go.com/International/facing-dire-sea-level-rise-threat-maldives-turns/story?id=80929487.

18 Franziska Wolf et al., "Influences of Climate Change on Tourism Development in Small Pacific Island States," *Sustainability* 13, no. 8 (April 2021): 4223.

19 Emmanuel Salim et al., "Visitors' Motivations to Engage in Glacier Tourism in the European Alps: Comparison of Six Sites in France, Switzerland, and Austria," *Journal of Sustainable Tourism* 31, no. 6 (January 2023): 1373–93; Emmanuel Salim and Ludovic Ravanel, "Last Chance to See the Ice: Visitor Motivation at Montenvers-Mer-de-Glace, French Alps," *Tourism Geographies* 25, no. 1 (October 2020): 72–94.

20 Jackie Dawson, Emma J. Stewart, and Daniel Scott, "The Carbon Cost of Polar Bear Viewing Tourism in Churchill, Canada," *Journal of Sustainable Tourism* 18, no. 3 (April 2010): 319–36.

21 Raynald Harvey Lemelin et al., "Last-Chance Tourism: The Boom, Doom, and Gloom of Visiting Vanishing Destinations," *Current Issues in Tourism* 13, no. 5 (August 2010): 477–93.

22 Ahmet Yarış et al., "Last Chance Before It's Gone: Doom Tourism on Hasankeyf," First International Congress on Future of Tourism, 2017.

23 Emmanuel Salim, Ludovic Ravanel, and Philip Deline, "Does Witnessing the Effects of Climate Change on Glacial Landscapes Increase Pro-Environmental Behaviour Intentions? An Empirical Study of a Last-Chance Destination," *Current Issues in Tourism* 26, no. 6 (March 2022): 922–40.

24 "Welcome to Antarctic Ambassadors," IAATO, https://iaato.org/antarctic-ambassadors/.

25 Mar Vila et al., "Contrasting Views on Antarctic Tourism: 'Last Chance Tourism' or 'Ambassadorship' in the Last of the Wild," *Journal of Cleaner Production* 111, pt. B (January 2016): 451–60.

26 Manfred Lenzen et al., "The Carbon Footprint of Global Tourism," *Nature Climate Change* 8, no. 6 (June 2018): 522–28.

27 Hong-bumm Kim, et al., "Do Expectations of Future Wealth Increase Outbound Tourism? Evidence from Korea," Tourism Management 33, no. 5 (October 2012): 1141–47.

28 International Energy Agency, "CO2 emissions in aviation in the Net Zero Scenario, 2000–2030," July 11, 2023, https://www.iea.org /data-and-statistics/charts/co2-emissions-in-aviation-in-the-net-zero -scenario-2000-2030.

29 "85% of Offsets Failed to Reduce Emissions, Says EU Study," European Federation for Transport and Environment, May 17, 2017, https://www .transportenvironment.org/discover/85-offsets-failed-reduce-emissions -says-eu-study.

30 David Victor, author Zoom interview, October 2022.

31 Elena Berton, "Flight Shaming Hits Air Travel as 'Greta Effect' Takes Off," Reuters, October 2, 2019, https://www.reuters.com/article/us-travel-flying -climate-idUSKBN1WH23G; "'Flight Shame' Could Halve Growth in Air Traffic," BBC, October 2, 2019, https://www.bbc.com/news/business -49890057.

32 Paige McClanahan, "Could Air Someday Power Your Flight? Airlines Are Betting on It," New York Times, January 19, 2023, https://www.nytimes .com/2023/01/19/travel/airlines-climate-change-fuel.html?searchResult Position=2.

33 "Clean Skies for Tomorrow: Sustainable Aviation Fuels as a Pathway to Net-Zero Aviation," Insight Report, World Economic Forum and McKinsey & Company, November 2020, https://www.mckinsey.com/~/media /mckinsey/industries/travel%20transport%20and%20logistics/our%20 insights/scaling%20sustainable%20aviation%20fuel%20today%20for%20 clean%20skies%20tomorrow/clean-skies-for-tomorrow.pdf.

34 Lahiru Ranasinghe of easyJet, author Zoom interview, November 2022.

35 Jennifer Korn, "Alice, the First All-Electric Passenger Airplane, Takes Flight," CNN, September 27, 2022, https://www.cnn.com/2022/09/27 /tech/eviation-alice-first-flight/index.html.

36 Stephen Dowling, "Norway's Plan for a Fleet of Electric Planes," BBC, August 22, 2018, https://www.bbc.com/future/article/20180814-norways -plan-for-a-fleet-of-electric-planes.

37 Chen Zhou et al., "Greater Committed Warming after Accounting for the Pattern Effect," Nature Climate Change 11, no. 2 (February 2021): 132–36.

NOTES

Chapter Six **Tourist Trap**

1 Geerte Udo, author phone interview, July 2023.
2 Graham Greene, *Lawless Roads* (New York: Open Road Integrated Media, 2018), 92 Kindle ed. (*Lawless Roads* was originally published in 1939 by Longmans, Green & Co).
3 Ibid., 35.
4 You can watch the trailer for the horror movie *Tourist Trap* on YouTube: https://www.youtube.com/watch?v=sDpxEdIxxg4.
5 Carlton Reid, "You Are Not Stuck in Traffic, You Are Traffic," *Forbes.com*, December 3, 2018, https://www.forbes.com/sites/carltonreid/2018/12/03/you-are-not-stuck-in-traffic-you-are-traffic/.
6 Greene, *Lawless Roads*, 196.
7 "APA Dictionary of Psychology," American Psychological Association, https://dictionary.apa.org/escapism.
8 Katie Francis, "Disney Still Dominates Global Theme Park Attendance with Universal Close Behind in 2022 TEA Index," WDW News Today, June 14, 2023, https://wdwnt.com/2023/06/disney-still-dominates-global-theme-park-attendance-with-universal-close-behind-in-2022-tea-index/.
9 Paige McClanahan, "'It's Like Coming Home to Family': Disneyland Paris Reopens," *New York Times*, updated July 2, 2021, https://www.nytimes.com/2021/06/23/travel/paris-disneyland-reopening.html.
10 "La sanctuarisation de la colline de Lascaux," La Grotte de Lascaux, https://archeologie.culture.gouv.fr/lascaux/fr/la-sanctuarisation-de-la-colline-de-lascaux.
11 "Visitez les répliques Lascaux II et III," La Grotte de Lascaux, https://archeologie.culture.gouv.fr/lascaux/fr/lascaux-ii-et-iii.
12 Paige McClanahan and Debra Kamin, "52 Places, Virtually," *New York Times*, updated July 27, 2020, https://www.nytimes.com/2020/04/14/travel/52-places-to-go-virtual-travel.html.
13 "How to Spend €1,000 in Amsterdam," I amsterdam, YouTube video, https://www.youtube.com/watch?v=D_Yj4V_WzQo.
14 "Tourism 2010: A New Record for Amsterdam," City of Amsterdam, Fact Sheet Number 5, ISSUU, October 30, 2012, https://issuu.com/ldaly/docs/tourism_2010_-_a_new_record_for_amsterdam.

15 Simon Kuper, "Tourists Are Back. Is It Time to Tell Them to Stay Away?," *Financial Times*, July 15, 2023, https://www.ft.com/content/334c8e70 -8434-439a-b181-f07c5495af4c.

16 You can watch one of the "Stay Away" videos here: https://vimeo .com/812406264.

17 Senay Boztas, "Change Starts Here: Amsterdam Mayor Pledges New City Style," DutchNews.nl, November 20, 2022, https://www.dutchnews.nl/2022/11 /change-starts-here-amsterdam-mayor-pledges-new-city-style/.

Chapter Seven **The New Tourist**

1 Agnes Callard, "The Case against Travel," *New Yorker*, June 24, 2023, https://www.newyorker.com/culture/the-weekend-essay/the-case -against-travel.

2 "Vision 2030: How Saudi Tourism Is Evolving," Saudi Tourism Authority, https://www.visitsaudi.com/en/understand/vision-2030--how-saudi -tourism-is-evolving.

3 "LGBT Rights in Saudi Arabia," Equaldex, https://www.equaldex.com /region/saudi-arabia.

4 "Tourist," *Oxford English Dictionary*, https://www.oed.com/dictionary /tourist_n?tab=factsheet#18108703.

5 "Tourism," *Oxford English Dictionary*, https://www.oed.com/dictionary /tourism_n?tab=factsheet&tl=true#18108580.

6 Orvar Löfgren, *On Holiday: A History of Vacationing* (Berkeley: University of California Press, 2002).

7 Sarah Stodola, *The Last Resort: A Chronicle of Paradise, Profit, and Peril at the Beach* (New York: Ecco, 2022), Kindle ed. 33.

8 "Sold by Subscription Only," *Known to Everyone—Liked by All: The Business of Being Mark Twain*, Cornell University, https://rmc.library.cornell.edu /twain/exhibition/subscription/index.html.

9 Fyodor Dostoevsky, *Winter Notes on Summer Impressions*, trans. Kyril FitzLyon (1863; London: Alma Classics Evergreens, 2017), Kindle ed. 35.

10 Sune Bechmann Pedersen, "A Passport to Peace? Modern Tourism and Internationalist Idealism," *European Review* 28, no. 3 (February 2020): 389–402.

11 Sune Bechmann Pedersen and Christian Noack, ed., *Tourism and Travel during the Cold War: Negotiating Tourist Experiences across the Iron Curtain*

(London: Routledge, 2019), https://library.oapen.org/bitstream/handle /20.500.12657/23620/9780367192129_oaintroduction.pdf?sequence=1.

12 Bechmann Pedersen, "A Passport to Peace?"

13 "Marketing Peace through Tourism: A 35 Year History of IIPT," International Institute for Peace through Tourism, https://peacetourism.org /marketing-peace-through-tourism/.

14 Nell Leiper, "The Framework of Tourism: Towards a Definition of Tourism, Tourist, and the Tourist Industry," *Annals of Tourism Research* 6, no. 4 (October–December 1979): 390–407.

15 Freya Higgins-Desbiolles, "More Than an 'Industry': The Forgotten Power of Tourism as a Social Force," *Tourism Management* 27, no. 6 (December 2006): 1192–1208.

16 You can read this essay, "What Is America?," from Gilbert Keith Chesterton's book *What I Saw in America*, here: http://www.online-literature .com/chesterton/what-i-saw-in-america/1/.

Index

INDEX

Blue Guides, 4
boarding passes, 67–68
Bolivia, 134–35
Bonaparte, Napoleon, 130
Booking.com, 43
Bookings.nl, 43
Bradt, George, 12–13, 34
Bradt, Hilary, 12–13, 33–35
Bradt Travel Guides, 12–13, 34–35
Brady Bunch, The, 113–14
Brévent, 131
Bruinsma, Geert-Jan, 43
Burj Khalifa, 167
Bush, George H. W., 85
Butler, Richard, 93–94
  Tourism Area Life Cycle Model
    of, 93–95, 106, 125

caganers, 102–4
Callard, Agnes, 187–90, 198, 205–6,
  209
Cambodia, 66, 70
  Angkor Wat, 37–41, 46, 47,
    62–63, 65, 66
*Cambridge Introduction to Travel
  Writing, The* (Youngs), 47
Canada, 137, 203
cannabis, 158, 181, 182
capitalism, 204–6
Capitals of Culture, 75–76, 79
carbon dioxide (CO2), xvi, 140–41,
  153
  jet fuel made from, 145–46
  net-zero emissions goal for,
    143, 146, 147
  offset projects and, 141–43
Carlson, Brad, 149–55

"Case Against Travel, The"
  (Callard), 187–90, 198,
  205–6, 209
Caton, Stefanie, 184–86, 187
Catskills, 199
Chacaltaya, 135
Chambers, Nitya, 35
Chamonix, 129–31, 151, 152, 155
Champs-Élysées, 162
Charles III (Prince Charles), 74
Chatwin, Bruce, 44
Chesterton, G. K., 206–7
China, 8, 134, 177
Chisholm Trail, 133–34
CIA, 5, 6
city brands, 77
Claret, Benjamin, 128–29, 131–33,
  155, 176
Claret, Georges, 129
climate change, 51, 52, 132, 134–48,
  153, 177, 189, 190
  aviation's impact on, 140–48
  carbon offsets and, 141–43
  contrails and, 147
  coral reefs and, 135–36
  glaciers and, *see* glaciers
  last-chance tourism and,
    136–39
  net-zero carbon emissions
    goal and, 143, 146, 147
  Paris Climate Accord and, 148
  rockfall and, 152
CNN, 20, 29, 136, 189
cognitive dissonance, 137–38
Colau, Ada, 122–23, 125
Cold War, 8, 80, 146, 202–3
Colombia, 27, 29, 79, 87

INDEX

INDEX

INDEX